THE STOICS

MAJOR THINKERS SERIES

General Editor

Amélie Oksenberg Rorty

1. John M. Rist (editor), *The Stoics*

THE STOICS

Edited by John M. Rist

UNIVERSITY OF CALIFORNIA PRESS
Berkeley   Los Angeles   London

University of California Press
Berkeley and Los Angeles, California

University of California Press, Ltd.
London, England

ISBN 0-520-03135-0
Library of Congress Catalog Card Number: 75-27932

Printed in the United States of America

1 2 3 4 5 6 7 8 9 0

Contents

v

Preface

Philosophers and logicians now take the Stoics, particularly
Chrysippus, seriously. This is not the place to explain the mechan-
ics of such a change from the view of most historians of philosophy only a few years ago. In compiling this collection of new
essays, I have attempted to secure papers that both sum up our
new knowledge about the Stoics and also break new ground. Most
of the main themes of Stoicism, in logic, ethics, physics, and philosophical psychology will be found here, at least in passing. Naturally some of the essays are bolder than others, and none of the
contributors should be held responsible for the views of his col-
leagues. But it is to be hoped that they will be of some philosophical interest and will help to confirm the revised attitude to the
Stoics and to spread the good news more widely. Although some
readers may wish to limit themselves to particular essays that deal
with topics in which they have a special interest, I hope that the
book can also be read as a whole, for although the collection does
not purport to provide a full-scale description of the Stoic system,
such a description, at least in its broad outlines, should become
apparent.

J. M. R.

Abbreviations

The following abbreviations are used to refer to philosophical and classical periodicals:

AGP   *Archiv für die Geschichte der Philosophie*
AJP   *American Journal of Philology*
AUMLA   *Journal of the Australasian Universities Modern Language and Literature Association*
BICS   *Bulletin of the Institute of Classical Studies of the University of London*
CQ   *Classical Quarterly*
DK   Die Fragmente der Vorsopratiker[9] ed. H. Diels and W. Kranz. Berlin, 1960
JHI   *Journal of the History of Ideas*
JHS   *Journal of Hellenic Studies*
PAS   *Proceedings of the Aristotelian Society*
PQ   *Philosophical Quarterly*
PR   *Philosophical Review*
SVF   *Stoicorum Veterum Fragmenta,* ed. H. von Armin. Reprint Stuttgart, 1964
TAPA   *Transactions of the American Philological Association*

1

An Introduction to Stoic Logic

Ian Mueller

In the first comprehensive history of western logic Prantl[1] described Stoic logic as "dull," "trivial," and "pedantic." Prantl's dismissal of Stoic logic was accepted by most interpreters of Stoicism
for three quarters of a century. However, since the publication of
Łukasiewicz's article, "On the History of the Logic of Propositions" in 1934,[2] Prantl's evaluation has been largely abandoned.
Bochenski's remark, "The development of formal logic in antiquity
reached its peak in the works of the thinkers belonging to the Me-
garic and Stoic Schools," exemplifies well the radical rehabilitation of the Stoics as logicians.[3] The cause of this rehabilitation is
not the discovery of new texts, but rather the twentieth-century
revolution in the subject of logic itself. Łukasiewicz and others,
working with a full understanding of modern logic, have succeeded in retrieving from the ancient texts a Stoic logical theory of
startling originality which rivals the achievement of Aristotle, the
founder of logic. The failure of Prantl and his successors to accomplish this retrieval stems not from their obtuseness or stupidity but
from the fact that the background scientific knowledge needed to
understand the Stoic achievement was not available to them.

A factor contributing to Prantl's low opinion of Stoic logic was
the character of the ancient texts themselves. There are no primary

1

sources for Stoic logic analogous to Aristotle's *Prior Analytics*, and the ancient secondary sources are brief and usually hostile in their treatment of the subject. In many cases Prantl's evaluations simply repeat or develop remarks in the sources themselves. The unsatisfactoriness of the sources (on this see Mates, *Stoic Logic* 8-10) makes any but a tentative reconstruction of Stoic logic impossible. Unless an indication is given to the contrary, what I describe will be the most certain features of the theory.

One of the uncertain features is chronology. The history of Stoicism proper covers five centuries during which the logical theory, like other doctrines of the school, underwent modification and development. In the case of logic we know of some disagreements within the school and some ideas that can be ascribed to individuals, but most of our sources refer simply to "the Stoics," as if there were a single, unambiguous Stoic logical theory. Commentators have tended to assign the major Stoic achievements in logic to Chrysippus (c. 280 B.C.-c. 206 B.C.), the third leader of the Stoa, of whom it was said, "If there were a dialectic among the gods, it would be none other than the Chrysippean one." (D.L. 7.180. At 7.198 Diogenes mentions that Chrysippus wrote 311 books on logical matters.) In general I shall not attempt to assign logical doctrines to specific persons, but simply speak of "Stoic logic." Occasionally, however, it will be necessary to refer to possible disagreements within the school.

From the modern point of view, the core of Stoic logic is the analysis of arguments. To understand this analysis it is helpful to compare and contrast it with its predecessor, Aristotelian syllogistic. Aristotle considers the following argument at *P.A.* 2.24. 69^{a}5-7:

I. Since then [war] against neighbors is bad, but [war by Athens] against Thebes is against neighbors, it is evident that war [by Athens] against Thebes is bad.

Leaving out of account here the difference between an argument and a complicated inferential sentence of a form such as 'Since this therefore that' or 'If this then that,'[4] we may restate this argument as

II. (i) [War] against neighbors is bad;
  (ii) [War by Athens] against Thebes is against neighbors;
  (iii) War [by Athens] against Thebes is bad.

The Stoics defined an argument as "a system consisting of premises and a conclusion" (D.L. 7.45). In II, (iii) is the conclusion, (i) and (ii) the premises. They used the word *syllogism* to apply to arguments that are valid, i.e., in which the conclusion follows from the premises, as it does in the case of II. Aristotle does not define argument but characterizes a syllogism in much the same way:

> A syllogism is speech in which some things are laid down and something different from them follows necessarily because they are what they are. [*P.A.* 1.1. 24^{b}18-20]

The fundamental problem of logic is the more precise specification of what a syllogism is, or, in modern terminology, what validity is. Aristotle is the founder of logic because he was the first person to see and state clearly that validity is formal or depends upon form. To indicate what is meant by the word *form* in this context I shall show how Aristotle would analyze II. First it is necessary to give a standardized formulation of the argument.

III. (i) All war against neighbors is bad;
  (ii) All war by Athens against Thebes is war against neighbors;
  (iii) All war by Athens against Thebes is bad.

In this formulation the argument contains only the words 'all' and 'is' and three "terms," 'war against neighbors,' 'bad,' and 'war by Athens against Thebes.' The form of the argument is shown if we substitute the letters 'B,' 'A,' 'C' respectively for these terms, yielding

IV. (i) All B is A;
  (ii) All C is B;
  (iii) All C is A,

or, in more Aristotelian terminology,

IV'. If A is predicated of all B and B of all C, necessarily A is predicated of all C [*P.A.* 1. 4. 25^{b}37-39].

To say that the original argument I is formally valid is to say (1) that it can be construed as having the form IV and (2) that any argument of form IV is valid. One can render (2) more informative by saying that there is no way of making a uniform substitution of terms for letters in IV so as to produce true premises and a false conclusion. Hence one knows that if the premises of an argument of the form IV are true, the conclusion must be true.

The preceding example illustrates the general procedure of analyzing arguments logically. Arguments are put into a standard form. A distinction is made between the logical expressions that are held constant (in the example, 'all' and 'is') and the nonlogical expressions that are subject to variation (in the example, the terms). A valid argument is one in which no grammatically appropriate uniform change in the nonlogical expressions yields true premises and a false conclusion. In the core of his logical theory, the doctrine of the so-called assertoric categorical syllogism, Aristotle considered arguments containing only three sentences and three terms, each occurring twice in two different sentences. He recognized only four logical expressions, 'all,' 'some,' 'is,' and 'is not,' and hence only four forms of sentence:

A. All A is B.
E. All A is not B. (i.e., No A is B.)
I. Some A is B.
O. Some A is not B. (i.e., Not all A is B.)

Roughly, Aristotle considers all possible argument forms within these restrictions. To show that a pair of premises do not yield a conclusion, Aristotle substitutes two sets of terms making the premises true, one yielding a true A conclusion and hence a false E or O conclusion, the other a true E conclusion and hence a false A or I conclusion. For example, he writes

If M is predicated of all N and of all O, there will not be a syllogism. Terms for 'All O are N:' [M:] entity; [N:] animal; [O:]

man. For 'No O are N:' [M:] entity; [N:] animal; [O:] number. [*P.A.* 1.5. 27ª18-20]. (Clearly by interchanging the assignments to 'N' and 'O' one gets terms for 'All N are O' and 'No N are O.')

The way in which Aristotle shows that an argument is valid is more complicated. He distinguishes between perfect syllogisms and imperfect ones (*P.A.* 1.1. 24ᵇ22-26). Perfect syllogisms are transparently valid, but imperfect ones, although valid, require argumentation to make their validity apparent. IV' gives the form of a perfect syllogism, as does

   V. If A is predicated of no B, but B of all C, necessarily A will belong to no C. [*P.A.* 1.4. 25ᵇ40-26ª2]

On the other hand,

   If M belongs to all N and to no O, then N will belong to no O [*P.A.* 1.5. 27ª9-10]

is imperfect. Aristotle establishes its validity as follows:

   For if M belongs to no O, O will belong to no M. But M belongs to all N. Therefore, O will belong to no N. . . . But since the negative converts, N will belong to no O.
   [*P.A.* 1.4. 27ª10-14]

Here Aristotle "converts" the premise 'M belongs to no O' into 'O belongs to no M.' This statement form with the other premise, 'M belongs to all N,' yields, according to V, 'O belongs to no N.' Conversion of the latter yields the desired conclusion.

   I shall not describe any further the procedures Aristotle uses to validate imperfect syllogisms. The point I wish to make now is that Aristotle nowhere precisely specifies the procedures he uses. Łukasiewicz argued[5] that, in justifications like the one just given, Aristotle makes use of logical principles he never acknowledges. In that particular justification Aristotle takes for granted

   VI. If A implies B, and C and B imply D, then C and A imply D;

VII. If C and A imply D, and D implies E, then C and A
    imply E.

Arguments corresponding to these inferential forms are the core of
Stoic logic, and they provide a way of making clear the most fundamental difference between Stoic and Aristotelian logic. For Aristotle, as we have seen, the variable elements of logic are terms like
'animal.' However, any attempt to substitute terms for the letters
in VI and VII produces, if not nonsense, very artificial results. The
natural substitutes for the letters are statements, and statements
are the variable expressions in Stoic logic. An example of a Stoic
syllogism is

> If sweat flows through the surface [of the skin], the
> skin has intelligible [i.e., real but invisible] pores;
> Sweat flows through the surface;
> Therefore, the skin has intelligible pores.
>   [Sextus Emp. *P.H.* 2. 140]

To show the form of this argument one could, as modern logicians
do, substitute letters uniformly for statements, getting

> If A, B;
> A;
> Therefore, B.

However, the Stoics used ordinal number words and expressed the
form of the above argument as

VIII. If the first, the second;
      The first;
      Therefore, the second. [Sextus Emp. *Adv. math.* 8. 227]

Before describing the way in which the Stoics dealt with such
arguments, it is necessary to make a clarification. In many modern
discussions of logic a distinction is made between statements
(declarative sentences) and propositions. Statements can be written down and seen or spoken and heard, whereas propositions are
not physical entities at all; they are what statements express. Two

different statements, possibly in different languages, may express the same proposition, and the same statement, e.g., "I am cold," may express different propositions on different occasions. The Stoics seem to have made a distinction quite analogous to the modern one,[6] as the following passage shows:

> The Stoics say that three things are linked to one another: what is signified, what signifies, and what exists. Of these, what signifies is the sound, e.g. the sound Dion; what is signified is the very thing which is suggested by the sound and which we apprehend to subsist with our thought (the barbarians do not understand although they hear the sound); and what exists is the external object, such as Dion himself. Of these things two are bodies, namely the sound and what exists, one is not a body, namely the thing signified, the *lekton*, which also is true or false. [*Adv. math.* 8.11-12]

In the continuation of this passage Sextus tells us that a proposition (*axiōma*) is what is true or false and elsewhere (P.H. 2.104) that a proposition is a kind of *lekton*. I have already pointed out that for the Stoics an argument is a system of propositions. Presumably at least some Stoics used the distinctions between what is signified, what signifies, and what exists in their account of logic. We do not know the details of the application of the distinctions nor which Stoics made them. Sextus delights in what he takes to be incoherences and inconsistencies in the doctrine of the *lekton* and, in particular, its general incompatibility with Stoic materialism. This latter incompatibility does in fact present a serious problem for any interpreter of Stoicism. However, accounts of the content of Stoic logic are really independent of accounts of the *lekton*. This point can perhaps be seen most clearly on the basis of a comparison with Aristotle, who apparently considered thoughts rather than propositions to be the prime bearers of truth and falsehood. Ammonius, commenting on Aristotle's enunciation of this doctrine in chapter one of *De Interpretatione*, expresses the contrast with the Stoics very clearly:

> First, Aristotle teaches us here what are signified primarily and secondarily by sounds, [primarily] thoughts and [secondarily], through these intermediaries, things, and [he teaches] that it is not necessary to imagine anything else between the thought and the thing, such as what those called Stoics think fit to name a *lekton*. [Ammonius, *In Arist. Anal. Pr.* 17.24-28. Positioning the *lekton* between the thought and the thing is perhaps Ammonius's own rendering of Stoic teaching.]

The Aristotelian and the Stoic interpretations of language are neutral with respect to different logical theories. One could interpret a propositional logic in the Aristotelian way or a term logic in the Stoic way. The tendency of recent philosophers is to reject the Aristotelian way as "psychologism." There is no evidence that the Stoics developed any particular arguments against the Aristotelian view; for all we know, they simply proposed an alternative. Thus it seems fair to say that in antiquity either way of interpreting logic was viable and neither way would have any particular effect on the development or application of logic. In the sequel I shall leave out of account the Stoic doctrine of the *lekton* and use words like "sentence," "statement," and "proposition" indifferently. The reader may think in terms of *lekta* if doing so seems useful or enlightening.

We have seen that the variable elements of Stoic logic are propositions. What are the logical constants? One is expressed by the word 'if,' as in 'If the first, the second.' The Stoics developed a precise technical terminology for referring to the forms of sentences. A sentence of this form was called a conditional, the first sentence in it its antecedent, the second its consequent. Two other Stoic logical constants are expressed by 'and' and 'or,' as in

> It is day and it is light.
> It is day or it is light.

Sentences of these two forms are called conjunctions and disjunctions respectively. Their component sentences are conjuncts and disjuncts. (In modern presentations of formal propositional logic it is customary to fix for each logical constant the number of propositions to which it can be applied. For example, 'and' will be said to join two propositions, and a proposition like

> It is day and it is light and it is cloudy

will be explained as the conjunction of two propositions,

> (1) It is day and it is light,
> (2) It is cloudy,

where (1) is itself a conjunction. Although many of the examples of conjunctions and disjunctions that occur in the ancient texts have only two components, there is no evidence that the Stoics adopted a similar practice and some that they did not. Probably they treated conjunctions and disjunctions of several propositions as being on a par with those of two (see Gellius, *Noctes Atticae* 16. 8).

The final important Stoic logical constant is one that when applied to a proposition produces its negation, that is, the proposition that is false if the original is true, and true if the original is false. In Greek as in English there are various linguistic mechanisms for negation. The Stoics introduced a drastic simplification, expressing all negations by placing the word "not" in front of the negated sentence. Thus

> Not it is day

expresses

> It is not day,

and

> Not it is day and it is night

expresses

> It isn't both day and night.

(It is customary in modern presentations of logic to use a device such as parentheses to show the "scope" of a logical constant. The last sentence might then be expressed by

> Not (it is day and it is night)

to distinguish it from the representation of

> It isn't day and it is night,

which would be

Not (it is day) and it is night.

The Stoics do not seem to have had any similar device. They relied on context to indicate the scope of a given logical connective.)

Although some Stoics added other logical constants (see Mates, *Stoic Logic*, 54-55), 'if,' 'and,' 'or,' and 'not' are the only ones that function in the fundamental part of Stoic logic. Aristotelian logic can also be said to have four logical constants, but there is an important difference in power between the two sets of constants. For the Aristotelian set permits only sentences containing two terms and two constants, but the Stoic set places no bounds on the potential complexity of a proposition. There is no reason to doubt that the Stoics recognized this fact, despite the lack of reference to it in surviving texts, and the absence of more complicated propositions than ones like 'If it is light and if it is day it is light, then it is day' (*Adv. math.* 8.421). According to Plutarch (*S.R.* 1047C-E), Chrysippus said, "The conjunctions made from ten propositions exceed one million." The mathematician Hipparchus, however, "demonstrated the monstrous error in the calculation, since the affirmation produces 103,049 conjunctions, negation 310,952." (No one has yet figured out a possible basis for these calculations.) Similarly, although Aristotle restricted attention to arguments containing two premises, it seems reasonable to suppose that the Stoics admitted the possibility of arbitrarily many premises, although the point is not made in the texts, and the most complicated surviving arguments have three premises.

What is certain is that for the Stoics every syllogism could be constructed out of basic syllogisms, of which there were, for Chrysippus, five forms:

A first infers from a conditional and its antecedent the consequent, e.g., 'If it is day it is light; it is day; therefore it is light.'

A second infers from a conditional and the opposite of its consequent the opposite of its antecedent, e.g. 'If it is day it is light; not it is light; therefore not it is day.'

A third infers from the negation of a conjunction and one of its conjuncts, the opposite of the remaining conjunct, e.g. 'Not it is day and it is night; it is day; therefore, not it is night.'

A fourth infers from a disjunction and one of its disjuncts the opposite of the remaining disjunct, e.g. 'Either it is day or it is night; it is day; therefore, not it is night.'

A fifth infers from a disjunction and the opposite of one of its disjuncts the remaining disjunct, e.g. 'Either it is day or it is night; not it is night; therefore it is day.' [*P.H.* 2. 157-158. Some later Stoics apparently added to these five basic syllogisms. See Mates, *Stoic Logic* 68. For difficulties in the precise formulation of the five basic syllogisms as argument forms like VIII, see Mueller, "The Completeness of Stoic Logic"[7]].

The argument forms described here are the analogues in the Chrysippean system of Aristotle's perfect syllogisms. Aristotle appears to have had a more or less psychological notion of perfection; for him the premises of a perfect syllogism by themselves make the conclusion evident whereas those of an imperfect syllogism require additions to make the conclusion evident (*P.A.* 1.1. 24^b22-26). The Stoic conception of the status of their basic syllogisms is more difficult to determine. They referred to them with the word *anapodeiktoi*, which is normally translated either 'undemonstrated' or 'undemonstrable.' According to Sextus Empiricus (*Adv. math.* 8. 223), Chrysippus used this word for the basic syllogisms to suggest that "they have no need of proof because that the inference is valid is in their case immediately evident." However, subsequently (228) Sextus divides undemonstrated arguments into simple and complex, identifying the simple ones with the five basic arguments, the complex ones with those constructed out of the simple ones. If, as seems likely, the distinction between simple and complex is due to Chrysippus, it is implausible to interpret Chrysippus's use of *anapodeiktos* psychologically. Syllogisms which are reduced to the basic syllogisms are undemonstrated because their validity is seen to depend upon the basic syllogisms, which have not themselves been demonstrated. If the validity of these syllogisms were immediately obvious, the complex syllogisms would in fact be demonstrated. Since for Chrysippus they are not demonstrated, he can not have been using *anapodeiktos* with psychological overtones. In calling his basic syllogisms *anapodeiktoi* he must have been claiming that they are unprovable or simply pointing out that he gives no proof for them. Since, however, Sextus characterizes the basic syllogisms as not needing proof, the first alternative seems more likely.

In chapters five to seven of the *Prior Analytics*, Aristotle reduces most of the possible assertoric categorical syllogisms to the perfect syllogisms. Although Cicero (*Topica* 57) tells us that almost the whole of Stoic dialectic consists in producing innumerable inferences from the basic syllogisms, only two complete Stoic analyses of complex syllogisms survive. Since the two are quite similar, it will suffice to reproduce Sextus's analysis of: If it is day then if it is day it is light; / It is day; / Therefore, it is light.

There is a dialectical theorem which is taught for the analysis of syllogisms, namely

> When we have premises implying some conclusion we have that conclusion potentially in the premises even if it is not asserted expressly.

Since then we have two premises, the conditional 'If it is day then if it is day it is light,' which begins with the simple proposition 'It is day' but ends with the complex conditional 'If it is day it is light,' and further the antecedent in this [main] conditional, 'It is day,' we infer from these by the first undemonstrable [syllogism] the consequent in that conditional, 'If it is day it is light.' This thing we have inferred we therefore have potentially in the argument although it is not expressly there; putting it with the premise 'It is day' of our argument, we will have [the proposition] 'It is light' inferred by the first undemonstrable [syllogism], which was the conclusion of our argument. Thus there come to be two first undemonstrable [syllogisms], one

> If it is day, then if it is day it is light;
> It is day;
> Therefore, if it is day it is light,

the other

> If it is day it is light;
> It is day;
> Therefore, it is light.   [*Adv. math.* 8. 231-233]

This passage makes clear the painstaking detail with which analysis was carried out by the Stoics. More importantly, Sextus's citation of the dialectical theorem suggests strongly that the Stoics, unlike Aristotle, made explicit the rules on which they based their analyses. (The tacitly used rules formulated as VI and VII above are in fact particular cases of the dialectical theorem.) Unfortunately our information about the Stoic rules is very obscure. It seems that a rule of analysis was called a *thema* rather than a theorem, as Sextus suggests. According to Diogenes Laertius (7. 78), "Syllogistic arguments are either undemonstrable or reducible to undemonstrable ones in accordance with one or more *themata*." Galen (*De plac.* 2. 3) refers to the analysis of some syllogisms through the first and second *themata* and of others through the third and fourth. Alexander (*In Arist. Anal. Pr.* 278. 6-14, 284. 10-17) also mentions second, third, and fourth *themata*, but he considers them to be pointless elaborations of a Peripatetic "synthetic theorem," allegedly discovered by Aristotle. This synthetic theorem is essentially equivalent to Sextus's dialectical theorem, and so is Alexander's formulation of the third *thema*:[8]

When from two [propositions] a third is inferred and one of the two is taken from external premises, then the same [conclusion] can be inferred from the other [proposition] and the external premises of the first. [278. 12-14]

Our final direct information about the Stoic *themata* comes from Apuleius, who quotes a first Stoic *constitutio* or *expositum* (apparently attempts to render the Greek *thema* into Latin):

If from two [propositions] a third is inferred, one of the two with the opposite of the conclusion implies the opposite of the other. [*De Int.* 191. 8-10]

Modern commentators have tended to assume that there were exactly four Stoic *themata*, although no ancient text really says this. In any case there is no direct evidence enabling us to formulate more than two nonequivalent *themata*. The important historical point is that some Stoic or Stoics specified explicit rules for the analysis of syllogisms and that this explicitness marks a logical advance over Aristotle, or at least a closer approximation to modern logical practice. Because we do not know all the *themata*, it is impossible to give a certain evaluation of the strength of the Stoic logical system. It is not even entirely clear what strength the Stoics claimed for their system. Sextus says that the undemonstrable arguments are "demonstrative" of the validity of other arguments (*P.H.* 2. 156) and that the other undemonstrable arguments can be "referred" to the five (*P.H.* 2. 157). He also says, "If the undemonstrable arguments are destroyed, all other arguments are thrown over, since the latter get the demonstration of their validity from the former" (*P.H.* 2. 194). According to Diogenes, "Every argument is constructed from (the five undemonstrable arguments); they are assumed in conclusive arguments, both syllogistic (i.e.,

Aristotelian) and hypothetical (i.e., Stoic) (D.L. 7. 79).

Thus the Stoics seem to have claimed that in some sense all valid arguments could be reduced to the undemonstrable arguments, using the *themata*. The question is, "In what sense?" The weakest way to construe the claim would probably be to render it as the assertion that all valid arguments of interest to the Stoics could be so reduced. Although such a construal would suffice to render Sextus's skeptical criticism of the Stoics intelligible, it seems unlikely that the Stoics would have contented themselves with such a weak claim, especially in the light of Aristotle's assertion (see especially *P.A.* 1. 23) that his syllogistic captured all deductive reasoning. A second construal of the Stoic claim turns it into one of "completeness" in the modern sense, i.e., into the claim that all valid arguments containing only 'not,' 'or,' 'and,' and 'if' as logical constants are reducible to the undemonstrable arguments. To evaluate this claim it is important to see how much would be presupposed in a satisfactory completeness argument. Here again the contrast with Aristotle is significant. In Aristotle's way of treating the assertoric categorical syllogism there are forty-eight possible pairs of premises, each corresponding to four possible conclusions. To show for each of these possible pairs either that no one of the possible conclusions follows by giving appropriate interpretations, or what the valid conclusions are by a reduction to the perfect syllogisms is to prove completeness. Aristotle does essentially this, although he never makes a completeness claim in the appropriate sense. His procedure presupposes no precise account of validity, so long as one is willing to accept the perfect syllogisms as valid, the reduction procedure as legitimate, and Aristotle's interpretational counterexamples as correct.

The situation changes in Stoic logic because of the infinity of possible arguments. No series of particular analyses and interpretations will suffice. One needs a general argument and, for this argument, a reasonably precise account of validity. There appears to have been some Stoic concern to give such an account, although no text connects this concern with the question of completeness. The accounts given all involve the inferential conditional corresponding to an argument, i.e., the conditional with the conjunction of the premises as antecedent and the conclusion as consequent. The correct procedure would be to give an informative definition of necessary or logical truth for a conditional and to describe an argument as valid when the corresponding inferential conditional is necessarily true. This procedure presupposes a distinction between the truth and the necessary truth of a conditional, a distinction that the Stoics do not seem to have made. For in Sextus Empiricus's reports of ancient discussions of the conditional the words 'true' and 'sound' are used interchangeably. The Stoic failure to make the distinction, which is by no means unique in the history of philosophy, can be readily understood in terms of examples. Most of the conditionals that we assert appear to express some kind of necessary connection between antecedent and consequent, e.g.,

> If it is day it is light,

or

> If sweat flows through the surface
> the skin has intelligible pores.

Such propositions, if true at all, seem necessarily true, unlike e.g., 'It is day and it is light' or 'Sweat flows through the surface or the skin has intelligible pores.' Three of the four known ancient accounts of the soundness of a conditional reflect this fact (*P.H.* 2. 110-112):

(1) Not having a true antecedent and a false consequent;
(2) Not having a consequent that is false at some time at which the antecedent is true;
(3) Having a consequent the opposite of which is incompatible with the antecedent;
(4) Having a consequent potentially contained in the antecedent.

Of these, only the first, which is due to Philo the Megarian, clearly severs the coincidence between necessary truth and truth for conditionals. For, according to it, conditionals such as 'If it is day I am conversing' are sound if I am conversing, but there is obviously no necessary connection between day and my conversing. (2) is due

to another Megarian, Diodorus, and ascribes to a sound conditional, truth in Philo's sense "for all time." It has been a matter of
scholarly debate whether truth for all time is analogous to logically necessary truth or to empirically necessary truth. (See Mates,
Stoic Logic 44-51). The same kind of difficulty would seem to
affect (3) and (4) in the absence of a precise account of incompatibility or of potential containment. The third view is traditionally
assigned to Chrysippus[9] on the basis of a passage that I shall discuss shortly. M. Kneale[10] suggests that the fourth view is Peripatetic, on indirect but plausible enough evidence. I shall not be discussing this view or the second one any further.

Although the first account of the soundness of a conditional has
an initial appearance of implausibility, it is in fact crucial in modern propositional logic, in which the truth of any compound sentence is made a function of the truth or falsity of its component
sentences. Similar truth-functional accounts are easily given for all
the Stoic logical constants:

> 'Not the first' is true if and only if the first is not true;
> 'The first and the second' is true if and only if the first is true
>   and the second is true;
> 'The first or the second' is true if and only if exactly one of the
>   first and the second is true.

(In modern logic it is customary to use "or" inclusively, and hence
to substitute "at least" for "exactly" in the truth conditions for disjunction. The fourth undemonstrable argument shows that disjunction is exclusive in the Stoic system.) Given these accounts,
one can define logical truth and hence validity. A proposition is
said to be logically true if and only if there is no way to assign
truth and falsity to its basic components and make the proposition
come out false. One easily establishes the validity of the five
undemonstrable arguments by showing that the corresponding
inferential conditionals are logically true. Becker[11] has shown that
all and only the valid propositional arguments can be analyzed
into the five undemonstrable arguments, using the first and third
themata, the following fourth *thema*,

> If two propositions imply a third, then the conjunction of the two imply the third,

plus some other assumptions that he considers trivial. I have discussed the details of Becker's completeness argument elsewhere ("The Completeness..."). Here I shall simply point out two significant facts about it. First, there is no justification, other than its useful role in Becker's completeness proof, for supposing the fourth *thema* to be what Becker says it is. Second, Becker's proof uses only the third undemonstrable argument and directly concerns only arguments using no constants except 'not' and 'and.' For the other constants Becker does not use the other undemonstrable arguments. Instead he invokes the well-known fact that the truth conditions for the other constants can be expressed in terms of 'not' and 'and.' For, given the truth-functional interpretations, 'If the first the second' is true if and only if 'Not (the first and not the second)' is; and 'The first or the second' is true if and only if 'If not (the first and not the second) then (not the first and the second)' is. However, if the Stoics recognized these equivalences and thought of them as definitions (Becker's term), it is hard to see why they would have taken any but the third undemonstrable argument as unanalyzable. It is perhaps not unfair to say that the steps that Becker has to go through to establish completeness suggest rather strongly that completeness in the modern sense was not a concern of the Stoics.

Before attempting to provide a more satisfactory interpretation of the claims made by the Stoics for the strength of their logical system, I would like to comment briefly on some other issues raised by Becker's argument. The first relates to the truth-functionality of the Stoic logical connectives. There are no ancient texts specifying the truth conditions for a negation, but this deficiency is perhaps explicable by reference to the simplicity and obviousness of the conditions. Sextus (*Adv. math.* 8. 125) attacks a Stoic truth-functional account of conjunction ("A conjunction is sound when it has everything in it true..., false when it has one thing false") on the seemingly frivolous ground that a conjunction with true and false conjuncts should be considered partly true and partly false. The texts for disjunction are much less clear. Although there are hints of a truth-functional conception, there is a tendency to invoke as truth conditions the incompatibility and exhaustiveness of the disjuncts. (See Galen, *Inst. Log.* 14. 5). As with the conditional, the murkiness is probably to be explained by reference to the examples used. The typical Stoic one is

> It is day or it is night,

in which one of the disjuncts must be true, and the truth of one guarantees the falsehood of the other.

The question of truth-functionality is closely connected with the question of interdefinability. On the latter subject Mates (*Stoic Logic* 55) writes, "One of the most interesting properties of the logical connectives is their definability in terms of one another. The discovery of this fact . . . must be dated at least as early as 250 B.C." The only evidence Mates cites for this claim is Chrysippus's hope that astrologers will substitute for the assertion

(1) If someone was born at the rising of the dogstar he will not die at sea

the assertion

(2) Not (Someone was born at the rising of the dogstar and he will die at sea). [Cicero, *De Fato* 15]

Despite syntactic appearances to the contrary, (1) is not a conditional nor (2) a negated conjunction. For the components 'He will not die at sea' and 'He will die at sea' are not independent sentences or abbreviations for independent sentences. Modern logic makes this fact clear by representing the 'he' in these components with a variable such as 'x.' The two sentences are then represented as

(1') For all x, if x was born at the rising of the dogstar x will not die at sea,
(2') Not (for some x, x was born at the rising of the dogstar and x will die at sea).

The equivalence between these two assertions depends not only on relations among the Stoic logical constants but also on those between the so-called quantifiers, 'for all x' and 'for some x.' Thus if Chrysippus thought he was suggesting the substitution of an equivalent within the framework of Stoic propositional logic, he was mistaken. More importantly, Chrysippus must have wanted to deny rather than assert the equivalence of (1) and (2). To understand why, it is necessary to look a little more closely at Cicero's presentation of Chrysippus's views. According to Cicero, Chrysippus wished to avoid the doctrine that astrological phenomena strictly determine a person's future. Arguments of the following kind seemed to Chrysippus to establish this doctrine:

If [the assertion] 'If someone was born at the rising of the dogstar he will not die at sea' is a true conditional, so is this one true: (i) 'If Fabius was born at the rising of the dogstar, Fabius will not die at sea.' Therefore, (ii) 'Fabius was born at the rising of the dogstar' and 'Fabius will die at sea' are incompatible.... Therefore, (iii) 'Fabius will die at sea' is in the genus of what is impossible. [*De Fato*,12]

Step (ii) of this argument is a clear application of the third account of the soundness of a conditional and is our strongest evidence that Chrysippus adopted this account. Step (iii) follows from (ii) and the unexpressed assumption that all true statements about the past are necessary. This assumption is brought out in Cicero's restatement of essentially the same argument:

If [the assertion] 'If you were born at the rising of the dogstar you will not die at sea' is a true conditional and if the antecedent in the conditional, 'You were born at the rising of the dogstar,' is necessary, (for everything true in the past is necessary, according to Chrysippus...)...then the consequent will also be necessary.
[*De Fato* 14]

This formulation of the argument leaves out step (ii), which makes explicit the necessity in a true conditional. Putting the two formulations together, we see the problem facing Chrysippus. He wished to accept the truth of the "laws" of the astrologers and the necessity of statements about the astrological conditions at the birth of living people, but deny the necessity for such people to fulfill the astrological laws. He could not reasonably do so, if he construed

the laws as conditionals or pseudo-conditionals, which are necessarily true, if true at all. He therefore suggested reformulating the
laws as negated (pseudo-)conjunctions to take away their necessity. This reformulation would hardly be effective if it were a matter of replacement with an equivalent. Moreover, if Chrysippus
worked with any but the Philonian notion of the conditional, the
reformulation could not be an equivalent unless 'not' and 'and'
were also interpreted nontruth-functionally. There is no evidence
to attribute such an interpretation to any Stoic. On the other
hand, if Chrysippus did work with the Philonian notion of the
conditional, the argument that perplexed him would never have
arisen, since the conditionals in question would be true but not
necessary. I conclude, then, that for Chrysippus 'not' and 'and'
were probably truth-functional, but a conditional was taken to be
true if its antecedent and the opposite of its consequent were
incompatible, in a not very precisely specified sense of 'incompatible.' We can not be sure about 'or,' but I suspect that a disjunction was taken to be true only if the disjuncts were mutually exclusive and exhaustive of the alternatives. Such a mixture of truth-
functional and nontruth-functional logical constants would make
progress on the question of their interdefinability difficult, if not
impossible.

   If the Stoics had made truth-functional accounts of the connectives fundamental, they could have developed a simple procedure,
analagous to Aristotle's, for establishing the invalidity of argument forms, namely, to assign truth values uniformly to ordinal
numbers in such a way as to make the premises of the form true
and the conclusion false. For example, to show the invalidity of

              If the first the second;
              The second;
              Therefore, the first,

one need only point out that if the first is false and the second true,
then, on the Philonian account of the conditional, the two premises are true and the conclusion false. (In fact, one could decide
whether any argument form is valid by considering all possible
assignments of truth values to the ordinal numbers in it.) There is
no evidence that the Stoics adopted any such procedure. Sextus's

principal discussions of invalidity (*P.H.* 2. 146-151; *Adv. math.* 8. 429-434) make it seem likely that they gave a verbal explanation of the invalidity of the argument form we are considering:

To concede the consequent is not in general to establish the antecedent. For the conditional does not assert that the antecedent follows from the consequent, but only that the consequent follows from the antecedent. [*P.H.* 2. 148]

If Sextus can be trusted, the Stoics did not treat invalidity systematically. Instead of a precise definition of invalidity or a uniform procedure for establishing it, they offered a somewhat confusing fourfold classification of invalid arguments:

(1) Arguments in which there is no connection between premises and conclusion (e.g., If it is day it is light; Wheat is being sold in the market; Therefore, Dion is walking);

(2) Arguments with unneeded premises (If it is day it is light; It is day; Dion is walking; Therefore, it is light);

(3) Arguments of a degenerate form (e.g., of the form just considered);

(4) Arguments with an omission in a premise (Wealth is good or wealth is bad; It is not bad; Therefore, it is good. A valid argument for this conclusion is said to run: Wealth is good or bad or indifferent; Wealth is neither good nor bad; Therefore, it is indifferent).

From a modern point of view, arguments of kind (2) are valid and so are arguments of kind (4), if we may judge from Sextus's example. The modern explanation of the invalidity of arguments of kind (1) is the same as the explanation for kind (3); it is possible to make the premises of the corresponding argument form true and the conclusion false. The fact that the Stoics classified (1) and (3) separately, that they gave descriptive explanations of invalidity rather than counterexamples, and that they mixed together cases of formal invalidity and cases of redundant or false premises suggests that they did not grasp as clearly as Aristotle the formal nature of invalidity.

This consideration of the Stoic conception of the logical constants and of invalidity only strengthens my contention that the Stoics were not concerned with completeness in the modern sense.

Diogenes' statement that all conclusive arguments are constructed from the five undemonstrable arguments suggests that the Stoics made an even broader claim of strength for their logical system, namely, that all valid arguments of any kind could be carried out within it. From one point of view this claim is absurd, since Stoic propositional logic is no more capable of handling arguments from Aristotle's term logic than term logic is capable of handling propositional arguments. However, the Peripatetics insisted on the universality of their master's logic and rejected Stoic logic as useless. In my article "Stoic and Peripatetic Logic"[12] I have argued that the Stoics may have made a similar claim to universality. For, in fact, every valid argument can be represented as a valid propositional argument by adding as a premise of the first argument its corresponding inferential conditional. Thus the Aristotelian syllogism,

> Phenomena appear to all;
> Signs do not appear to all;
> Therefore, phenomena are not signs,

can be reformulated briefly as

> If phenomena appear to all and signs do not appear
> to all, phenomena are not signs;
> The first;
> Therefore, the second.   [Adv. math. 8. 242]

Such a transformation is logically unassailable, but it places a greater burden on the person who would establish the conclusion 'Phenomena are not signs.' For with the second formulation the person must establish not only the premises of the first argument but also the added conditional. And this conditional cannot be considered logically true without admitting the independent validity of Aristotelian logical laws. Thus the reformulation might be considered a logical trick that standardizes the form of arguments but in an impractical way.

The charge of uselessness permeates the ancient literature on Stoic logic. Alexander is very concerned to defend Aristotelian logic as the tool (*organon*) of philosophy and science, a means for making unknown things known through known premises. For Sextus no logic is capable of serving these functions. The gist of both men's attack on Stoic logic is that with its arguments there is no way to establish the premises without first establishing the conclusion. The attack is usually made in terms of the first undemonstrable argument and depends upon the truth-functional interpretation of the conditional. Suppose one wishes to prove 'the second' by establishing 'the first' and 'If the first the second.' Then if 'the first' is established, the only way to establish 'if the first the second' is to establish 'the second,' i.e., to establish the conclusion one is trying to prove. Similar objections could be raised against the other undemonstrable arguments. In each case, when the second premise is taken as true, then the obvious truth-functional argument for the first premise requires establishing the truth of the conclusion. There is no way out of this situation, a fact that strongly suggests that Sextus's insistence on applying the truth-functional interpretation to the conditional represents an argumentative device rather than an accurate reflection of standard Stoic doctrine. If the first premise of an undemonstrable argument expresses a stronger than truth-functional connection between its component propositions, there is no reason why the first premise can not be established independently of the conclusion.

Of course, the position I have just ascribed to the Stoics means that philosophically a great deal of weight must be placed on the knowledge of necessary connections between propositions. Many of Sextus's arguments are directed against the possibility of such knowledge. To consider these arguments would take us outside the domain of logic and into epistemology. The point I wish to make is that the Stoics could have claimed universality for their propositional logic without subjecting themselves to attacks on grounds of uselessness. But to what use did the Stoics put their logic? It is tempting to suppose that the Stoics might have treated logic as a technical discipline developed for its own sake. The picture of Chrysippus analyzing innumerable arguments into the undemonstrable syllogisms lends color to this supposition, and the extraordinarily formalistic character of Stoic discussions of logical points makes it seem certain that to some extent logic was pursued for its own sake. But at least some Stoics thought of logic as more than a self-sufficient technical disipline.

[The Stoics] say that the study of syllogisms is extremely useful; for it shows what can be demonstrated and thereby adds much to the correctness of opinions.

Demonstration is an argument in which the less well grasped is inferred from the more well grasped.

Dialectic itself is necessary and a virtue embracing other virtues in species.
[D.L. 7. 45. 46]

Logic, then, had both an epistemological and a moral significance for the Stoics. Such a conception of logic can undoubtedly be given a very general interpretation. The study of argument is a form of mental training, and a well-trained mind is useful for learning about the world and for living well. But such an interpretation makes no special connection between the value of the study of argument and the particular kind of argument stressed by the Stoics. The interesting question is whether there are any significant connections between the details of Stoic logic and Stoic ethics and epistemology. Here I can make only a couple of brief suggestions.[13]

We have seen one example of such a connection in Chrysippus's treatment of astrological laws as negated (pseudo-)conjunctions. Chrysippus undoubtedly wished to defend a form of human freedom despite an apparent commitment to determinism. His purpose would seem to be partly moral, partly scientific or metaphysical. Another, perhaps more interesting example is provided by the Stoic doctrine of the sign (*P.H.* 2. 97-103). An indicative sign is a phenomenon that indicates something else not naturally apparent. A commemorative sign is a phenomenon invariably associated with another phenomenon and therefore commemorative of it. However, a sign is also described as "the antecedent proposition in a sound conditional which is revelatory of the consequent" (*P.H.* 2. 104). Mates (*Stoic Logic* 14-15) has described the difficulties involved in identifying signs and propositions of a certain kind. I shall here bypass those difficulties by treating such propositions as descriptive of signs. From this point of view the antecedent of the conditional,

> If sweat flows through the surface, the skin has intelligible pores,

describes an indicative sign. Commemorative signs involve generalizations from experience and so may have been expressed in the antecedents of pseudo-conditionals such as

> If someone was born at the rising of the dogstar, he will not die at sea.

The most important inferences from signs would be those based on the first undemonstrable syllogism. Questions about the viability of inferences from sign to thing indicated or commemorated would almost certainly end up as questions about the connection asserted to hold in the first premise, i.e., as questions of metaphysics or epistemology. One cannot expect logic to settle such questions, nor is there any reason to think the Stoics expected it to. The thrust of their logic was to provide a framework in which questions of inferential validity could be settled and questions that fall outside of logic, e.g., whether sweat implies the existence of pores, made precise. It seems fair to say that Stoic achievement in this area remained unparalleled until the time of Leibniz.

NOTES

1. C. Prantl, *Geschichte der Logik im Abendlande* (Leipzig, 1855) 408. I have generally given at most one ancient source for a doctrine. More information about sources can be found by consulting B. Mates, *Stoic Logic*[2] or M. Frede, *Die stoische Logik.*

2. Reprinted in J. Łukasiewicz, *Selected Works*, ed. L. Borkowski.

3. I. M. Bochenski, *Ancient Formal Logic* (Amsterdam, 1951) 77.

4. Łukasiewicz [*Aristotle's Syllogistic*[2] (Oxford, 1957) 1-3] insisted on the importance of the distinction between what I have called inferential sentences and arguments and made clear that Aristotle tended to work with the former, the Stoics with the latter. In the sequel I ignore this difference, which does not seem to have been felt by the ancients. More generally, my account of Aristotelian

logic has left out of account many details not relevant to the understanding of Stoic logic. For these details the reader should consult Łukasiewicz or G. Patzig, *Aristotle's Theory of the Syllogism*.

5. Łukasiewicz, *Aristotle's Syllogistik* 47-51.

6. The analogy between Stoic and modern accounts of the proposition should not be pressed too far. For the Stoics propositions can change their truth value and even cease to exist. See Frede, *Die stoische Lǫgik* 32-49.

7. To appear in the *Notre Dame Journal of Formal Logic*.

8. Sextus's dialectical theorem tells us that if we have premises $P_1, \ldots, P_n$ which imply $Q_1, \ldots, Q_m$, then if $P_1, \ldots, P_n, Q_1, \ldots, Q_m$ imply the conclusion R, $P_1, \ldots, P_n$ alone imply R. Alexander's third *thema* says that if $P_1, \ldots, P_{n-1}$ imply Q_1, and Q_1 and P_n imply R, then $P_1, \ldots, P_n$ alone imply R. The only logical difference between the theorem and Alexander's *thema* is the restriction at the beginning of the statement of the *thema* to an inference from two premises. Simplicius (237. 2-4) gives an even more restrictive version of the third *thema*. According to him, it amounts to the assertion that if P_1, P_2 imply Q_1, and Q_1, P_3 imply R, then P_1, P_2, P_3 alone imply R. Probably the restrictions in our two statements of the third *thema* are reflections of Aristotle's concentration on arguments with only two premises. In my discussion I ignore such restrictions.

9. See J. B. Gould, *The Philosophy of Chrysippus*, 74-82.

10. W. and M. Kneale, *The Development of Logic*, 129.

11. O. Becker, *Zwei Untersuchungen zur antiken Logik*.

12. *AGP* 51 (1969) 173-187.

13. There has not been much work done on the Stoic use of their logic. The best treatment of the subject is probably still V. Brochard, "La Logique des Stoiciens," *Etudes de Philosophie ancienne et de philosophie moderne* (1912) 220-251.

2

Principles of Stoic Grammar*

Michael Frede

I

H. von Arnim did not make a systematic effort to include testimonies on matters of grammatical doctrine in his *Stoicorum Veterum Fragmenta*. So for this part of Stoic doctrine one still has to
rely on R. Schmidt's *Stoicorum Grammatica* which appeared in
1839. In this monograph Schmidt quotes and discusses many of
the important texts. Since then, however, our general knowledge
of ancient grammatical thought has grown considerably, and
much has also been written on the Stoic contributions to the subject; one may mention here the work of Lersch, Steinthal, Pohlenz,
Dahlmann and, in particular, that of Barwick. Also most of the
relevant texts are now available in critical editions.

After all this work we should now be in a position to write a
monograph on Stoic grammar which would be much more com-

---

*This paper is dedicated to Jürgen Mau on his sixtieth birthday. The reader may
find it useful to consult the excellent survey of ancient Greek grammar by Jan Pinborg
in *Current Trends in Linguistics*, vol. 13, *Historiography of Linguistics* (The Hague,
1975), "Classical Antiquity: Greece," 69-126. Some questions only raised briefly in the
present paper are discussed at length in "Some Remarks on the Origins of Traditional
Grammar" in R. Butts and J. Hintikka ed., *Logic, Methodology, and Philosophy of
Science* (Dordrecht, 1976) 609-637.

plete and, in points of detail, more adequate and accurate than Schmidt's opusculum. It seems, however, that certain general questions have not yet been clarified sufficiently, and that this neglect has often vitiated the treatment of matters of detail. We still, for example, do not really know whether the Stoics had the notion of a discipline that somehow corresponds to something we could call grammar or why they had such an interest in grammatical questions or on what principles and with what methods they tried to resolve grammatical questions. It is to these general problems rather than to the details of Stoic grammatical doctrine that I would like to turn. In particular I want to discuss the question of whether there is such a subject as Stoic grammar for us to be concerned with. (For these purposes I will use "grammar" in a very generous and vague sense for any discipline that tries to set forth rules for a language as a whole such that purported sentences that satisfy these rules qualify as sentences of the language.)

The reader of the following pages may wonder why one should insist on a rather tedious treatment of this question. Historians of grammar have usually proceeded as if their subject had a continuous history starting in the fifth century B.C., with the Sophists. But even if one is willing to credit Sophists like Protagoras and Prodicus, and later philosophers like Plato and Aristotle, with a theory of language, i. 's obvious that their theories were not grammatical theories: they were not interested in finding out how a particular language, Greek, actually works in such detail as to be in a position even to attempt to start formulating the canons for correct Greek. Hence to treat them as part of one continuous tradition along with the later grammarians is to invite neglect of important questions. We may, for example, assume that those who actually started grammar had certain notions concerning the nature of language, and that these and other philosophical views influenced the way they set up their subject and thus also its later development. We may also assume that they had certain reasons for starting this enterprise and that these reasons influenced the way they went about it and hence, indirectly, the outlines of later grammar. For reasons of this sort it is important that we should have a better notion of the actual origins of the grammatical tradition.

Now our question concerning the Stoics is important, since it has been claimed that it was the Stoics themselves who first formulated traditional grammar. To substantiate this claim it will not be sufficient to show that traditional grammar is influenced in many respects by Stoic notions. For such a state of affairs would be completely compatible with the assumption that the Stoics still formed part of the earlier philosophical tradition, though they contributed more to this tradition than their predecessors, but that grammar itself only began among the classical scholars of Alexandria, who exploited the available philosophical tradition and the Stoic contributions to it. To substantiate the claim that grammar originated with the philosophers we have to show that it formed a definite part of Stoic philosophy (the evidence seems to rule out the other schools of philosophy as plausible candidates). But the origin of traditional grammar is not the concern of this paper. Even if grammar originated with the Alexandrians, it would be important to know whether in matters of language the Stoics still formed part of the earlier philosophical tradition or whether they were already engaged in doing grammar. For the evidence on the Stoic theory of language is so fragmentary that the context of the fragments and testimonies makes an enormous difference to their interpretation and evaluation.

II

The answer to the question whether there is such a subject as Stoic grammar is far from obvious for the following reasons. At least since the first century B.C. we find, besides rhetoric and dialectic, grammar as a third discipline supposed to deal with speech; hence later the "trivium" of the "artes sermocinales." But the Stoics in their division of philosophy only seem to recognize two disciplines dealing with speech (*legein*): they distinguish rhetoric and dialectic as the two parts of logic. And though these two parts are further divided, none of the subdivisions corresponds to grammar either. Later Stoics, of course, could not fail to realize that there were grammarians pursuing a particular discipline. And since there is no doubt that some Stoics had considerable interest in grammatical questions, one might think that they simply joined the grammarians in their own pursuits, either for ulterior philosophical reasons or merely out of interest in the subject itself. So we would have Stoic grammar in the sense that there were Stoics who also happened to be engaged in grammatical studies.

This is, in fact, a view one might obtain from a superficial reading of Seneca's letters. In *Epistle* 88 Seneca considers the liberal studies or arts, among which he includes grammar (88.3). But he wonders whether they are genuinely liberal, that is, whether they really help to make us virtuous and hence truly free, as philosophy supposedly does (88.2). And hence, later in the letter (88.42), he criticizes philosophers for losing themselves in such petty matters as the distinction of syllables and the properties of conjunctions and prepositions, matters that have no proper place in philosophy; philosophers, Seneca says, should not try to compete with the grammarians. Yet though Seneca here takes the view that such grammatical studies are external to philosophy, his language both here and elsewhere (e.g., *Ep.* 48.11) shows that the philosophers criticized think that it is very much their business as philosophers to discuss such questions. And there is ample evidence that in this they just followed a well-established tradition. In the case of the Stoics we have only to look at the catalog of Chrysippus's writings (D.L. 7.189-202) or at the two surveys of Stoic logic given in Diogenes Laertius (7.41-48 and 7.49-83). There we see how Chrysippus and his students dealt under the heading of "dialectic" with almost all the important topics that we find covered in treatises of grammar some centuries later. So it is clear, at least for the orthodox Stoic philosophers, that engaging in grammatical studies is an integral part of philosophy. And hence we may assert that to talk of Stoic grammar is more than to talk of grammatical studies that just happen to catch the interest of particular Stoic philosophers.

But this still leaves open the question whether the Stoics regarded all these grammatical studies as being part of one project covered by the notion of a discipline which more or less corresponds to the traditional notion of grammar. And it seems as if the answer to this question would have to be negative. The Stoics distinguished two parts of dialectic, one dealing with what is (or could be) said or meant or signified (the so-called *lekton*), the other with the way the human voice is articulated to say, express, mean, signify things (cf., e.g., D.L. 7.43; 62). Now many of the distinctions we would regard as grammatical are made in the part of dialectic concerning things said (*lekta*) rather than, as we would expect, in the part concerning expressions, whereas other grammatical points are made in fact where we would expect them, in the section dealing with expressions. Our knowledge of the Stoic doctrine of the *genera verbi*, for example, is largely derived from Diogenes Laertius 7.64. There Diogenes discusses various kinds of predicates, that is, incomplete *lekta* of a kind, which correspond to verbs, but which are explicitly distinguished from verbs as the corresponding *lekta* (D.L. 7.58). We can see that this distinction between *lekta* and the corresponding expressions is to be taken seriously, and that one has to keep in mind that many of the apparently grammatical distinctions are introduced as they apply to *lekta* rather than to expressions, from the fact that as an example of what would correspond to active verbs we are given *"dialegesthai"* (D.L. 7.58). The same point has to be kept in mind, though it has tended to be overlooked by historians of grammar, in connection with the two pieces of Stoic doctrine which are generally regarded as their main contribution to grammar: their doctrine of the cases of the noun and their verbal tense system.

As opposed to Aristotle's cases of the noun, which are nounforms in the oblique cases, inflected from the form in the nominative (cf. *De. Int.*, 16a 32 ff.), there is in Stoicism no immediate connection between cases and inflection. For inflection characterizes words, whereas Stoic cases are not words or features thereof; rather they seem to be what corresponds to the different forms of a noun on the level of what is signified or meant. This is strongly suggested by the fact that in the account of Stoic dialectic in Diogenes Laertius cases are introduced in the section concerning *lekta* and their parts (7.64-65; 70), and, moreover, by the position of the treatise "On the five cases, in one book" in Chrysippus's list of writings (D.L. 7.192). This in turn suggests that for the Stoics cases are the qualities that are said by Diogenes Laertius (7.58) to be signified by proper names and common, or rather appellative, nouns. (That qualities of material objects are held to be corporeal by the Stoics is perfectly compatible with their belonging to the level of what is signified and their being parts of *lekta*; there is no reason why material objects or corporeal entities should not be constituents of incorporeal *lekta*, e.g. states-of-affairs. Clement of Alexandria [*Strom.* 8, 9, p. 97, 6-7] operates on the assumption that a case is incorporeal, but this is due to the fact that he is not a Stoic and hence naturally thinks of properties as something incorporeal.) The qualities signified by nouns, including proper names, have to be distinguished from the external objects that have the qualities signified and which hence are called *tynchanonta*.[1]

Correspondingly the cases, being the qualities characterizing the external objects, are also called *teukta* (Simpl., *In cat.*, 209, 13). They are called "cases" because they fall (cadere, *piptein*) under a concept (Stob., *Ecl.* I, p. 137, 1 W.). It is not the concepts themselves which are constituents of the *lekta* signified by sentences but only their cases. For according to the Stoics, concepts or ideas are figments without real subsistence,[2] they are at best quasi-subsistent.[3] *Lekta* on the other hand, and hence their constituents, are something quite real in the way, for example, facts are. Though the Stoics refuse to call them "beings," since they are incorporeal, they grant *lekta* the status of "somethings," whereas concepts or ideas are denied even that status. Hence cases rather than the corresponding concepts are constituents of *lekta*. Now cases enter the constitution of *lekta* in various ways, depending on how they are related to, or constructed with, the other constituents of the *lekton*. Corresponding to these ways we get the analogue of the distinction between the traditional cases of the noun. But in order to understand the Stoic doctrine of cases, it is important not to overlook the fact that the Stoic distinction of cases does not primarily apply to nouns, but to their counterparts, to the constituents of what is signified, rather than to the constituents of what has signification. If one overlooks this crucial difference one will not, for example, be able to understand how the Stoics could insist that a nominative case is a case strictly speaking, and as much so as any other case (cf. e.g., Ammon, *In de int.* 42, 30 ff.). But what is of importance for our argument in this paper is that a Stoic doctrine which historians of grammar regard as an important part of Stoic grammar is not dealt with in the part of dialectic concerned with expressions, where we would expect to find it, and where in fact other matters of grammar like the parts of speech are treated.

The same, it seems, may be said with reference to the other piece of Stoic doctrine to which historians of grammar attach particular importance, the Stoic verbal tense system. The Stoics, like Aristotle before and the grammarians afterward, distinguish between past, present, and future. But whereas the grammarians tend to

neglect aspect and to regard imperfect, perfect, aorist, and pluperfect as primarily differing in their temporal distance from the
present (the aorist leaving it open whether something is near or far
away in the past), the Stoics emphasize the importance of aspect in
the tense-system, in particular whether an action is complete or incomplete (hence the terms "perfect" and "imperfect"). And so they
call the present "present imperfect," the perfect "present perfect,"
the imperfect "past imperfect," and the pluperfect "past perfect"
(cf., e.g., *Schol. in Dion. Th.* 250, 26 ff.). In this connection Pohlenz and others have suggested that Zeno and Chrysippus, because
of their Phoenician background, would be particularly sensitive to
the difference in aspect of the various tenses. And in general it
seems to be assumed that the Stoics came to make this classification according to aspect because of careful observation of the use
of differently tensed verbs.

Another explanation, though, seems to be much more plausible.
Aristotle had tried to distinguish two kinds of activities (in a suit-
ably wide sense of the word); those which have their end in themselves, which are complete or perfect at any time at which they can
be said to take place, and those which are incomplete. As one test
for this distinction he used the following: to see something is complete because at any time at which one can be said to see something one can also be said to have seen it; on the other hand, to
build something is incomplete because at no time at which one can
be said to be building a house can one be said to have built the
house; to build something is not to have built it, but rather to have
not built it. It would be clear from this test that there is no essential
connection between the Greek perfect tense as such and the past;
hence the test would draw attention to the importance of aspect in
the tense-system. Since the test occurs in various crucial contexts
in Aristotle, the Stoics cannot but have been familiar with it and
have recognized its significance.

More to the point, however, is the distinction between perfect
and imperfect propositions in an argument reported by Sextus
Empiricus (*Adv. Math.* 10.85 ff.). Diodorus Cronus maintains
that there is no motion; it is never true to say of something that it
moves or that it is moving or that it is in motion; all one can say of
something is that it did move or that it has moved. Against this the
critics (who use Stoic terminology) argue that such a claim

wrongly presupposes that perfect propositions could be true without the corresponding so-called "imperfect" propositions being true also: that is, "A has moved" cannot be true unless "A moves" or "A is moving" is true also (*Adv. Math.* 10.92). It seems clear that the argument is not stated precisely. For it cannot be claimed that for "A has moved" to be true now it must be true now that A moves or is moving. The claim rather must be that for "A has moved" to be true it must be true at some time that A moves or is moving, and hence, that there is motion. Diodorus tries to counter this argument in various ways which, in turn, are answered by his opponents. For example, he points out that it may be true that Helena had or had had three husbands without its ever being true that she has three husbands. But we are only concerned with this argument to the extent that it sheds light on the distinction between perfect and imperfect propositions. Translators and commentators tend to suggest that the distinction is one made in terms of the tense of the verb. But though the "imperfect" propositions are all specified by means of present-tensed verbs, in the case of the "perfect" propositions both the perfect (10.92, 101) and the aorist (10.92, 97, 98, 101, 102) are used indiscriminately. Moreover, though the Aristotelian test may not suffice to make the distinction Aristotle wants to make, it does show that it would be a mistake to assume that the present tense necessarily marks imperfection. Hence the distinction does not seem to be in terms of tense, but rather between propositions whose truth presupposes that the activity referred to is complete or completed, and propositions whose truth does not require such completion.

So what we have is a logical rather than a grammatical distinction in Diodorus and also, as it seems from the terminology, in the Stoics, to discuss a philosophical problem. Now the terms used in this discussion to distinguish the two kinds of propositions are basically the terms used by the Stoics to characterize the aspects. *Paratatikon* is the term used by the Stoics both in this discussion and later to mark imperfectness. The agreement is all the more remarkable since the use of the term in non-Stoic grammarians will be restricted to verbs in the imperfect tense, whereas in this discussion it is used for propositions expressed by means of verbs in the present tense, just as the Stoics used it for both present tensed and imperfect tensed verbs. The term for perfect propositions in this discussion is *syntelestikon*, an expression not extant in this sense in any other source and put to quite different purposes by Epicurus, whereas the Stoics use the term *syntelikon*. But the correspondence is close enough, in fact so close as to suggest that the distinction of aspects which is characteristic of the Stoic verbal tense system is derived from, and secondary to, a corresponding distinction of propositions, which for the Stoics will be a distinction of *lekta* rather than of expressions.

That the Stoics were in fact interested in such a distinction can be seen from two titles in the section of Chrysippus's catalog which concerns *lekta*: "On things said according to tenses, in two books" and "On perfect propositions, in two books" (D.L. 7.190), and moreover from the fact that Chrysippus in his *Logical Investigations* (SVF 2.96 ff.), repeatedly speaks of present, past, and future predicates, which he regards as incomplete *lekta* and not as expressions. So there seems to be an analogue of the whole verbal tense system on the level of the *lekton*. And of this analogue there is, as we have seen, good reason to believe that, with regard to the distinction of aspect, it was prior to the verbal tense system. In fact, whereas we have at least some evidence of the analogue for the time of Chrysippus and Diogenes of Babylon, it is quite unclear when the verbal tense system itself was introduced. Hence for the Old Stoa the situation in the case of the tense system is rather similar to what we found with regard to the cases of the noun: there is evidence for a piece of doctrine of obvious grammatical relevance, which is therefore often treated by historians of grammar as a piece of grammatical doctrine. Insufficient attention is paid to the fact that it is a fragment of a theory concerned with *lekta* and their parts, rather than with sentences and their constituents.

So the position seems to be as follows: the evidence for many of the grammatical distinctions attributed to the Stoics comes from the part of dialectic concerned with *lekta*. If we proceeded as if the distinctions on the level of *lekta* were grammatical distinctions, it would be clear that there is no such subject as Stoic grammar in any interesting sense; for its reconstruction would be patched up from pieces taken out of context from the two quite different parts of Stoic dialectic. So if there is to be Stoic grammar in a sufficiently strong sense, it has to have its systematical place in one of the two parts of dialectic. It lies in the nature of the subject that this can hardly be the part concerned with *lekta* and their parts. And even if it were, we should expect to find within that part of dialectic some division between grammatical and other questions, for example, logical questions. But there is no trace of such a division in this part of dialectic, and a glance at the way these quasi-grammatical categories come to be introduced in this part of dialectic shows why it would be misguided to expect these apparently grammatical notions to form part of a subtheory of their own. What the Stoics in this part of dialectic are concerned with is an investigation of the kinds of things that could be said (and hence thought). This investigation is to supply us with criteria by means of which we can decide what we should say and what we should avoid saying: in the simplest case, that of propositions, criteria for truth to help us avoid saying what is false. Such an investigation of course, involves the classification, characterization, and analysis of *lekta*. And for this we need a fairly complex conceptual framework. It appears that the seemingly grammatical categories that we find in this part of dialectic come in naturally as part of this conceptual framework. We will, for example, pay special attention to tensed propositions and their relations to one another in order to be able to deal with Diodorus's Master Argument or The Sea-Battle Tomorrow; hence the distinction of tenses will come in. We have seen above how an analogue to the distinction of aspects would be introduced. Similarly for logical reasons, we will be interested in various kinds of negations and hence will distinguish between various kinds of negatives (cf. D.L. 7.69, 70, 190). Both the distinction of various kinds of simple propositions and that of various kinds of predicates seems for the Stoics to involve the notion of case and the distinction between oblique and direct cases (D.L. 7.64-65, 70). The distinction between kinds of atomic propositions involves in addition the notions of a demonstrative and an indefinite particle (D.L. 7.70). The *genera verbi*, or rather their analogues, are introduced to distinguish kinds of predicates (D.L. 7.64). The notion of a conjunction and its various kinds is needed to characterize molecular propositions and their kinds (D.L. 7.71-73). One could extend this list, but the examples given should suffice to show that these quasi-grammatical distinctions in this part of dialectic form an integral part of the machinery by means of which the Stoics try to do logic.

So Stoic grammar would seem to have to be a part of the theory of expressions. But if we take this position and try to reconstruct a Stoic system of grammar just from evidence concerning the Stoic theory of expressions, our subject again seems to be in danger of disappearing for lack of substance: for to get a sufficiently substantial system of grammar we have to have many distinctions of the kind for which we only can get evidence from the Stoic theory of *lekta*. And this lack of evidence from the theory of expressions casts doubt on the very existence of the subject as a part of the theory of expressions. We could try to evade this difficulty by assuming that the Stoic theory of expressions will have counterparts for those parts of the theory of *lekta* which are of obvious grammatical relevance. But that would be to beg the question. For we are only justified in postulating such counterparts if we are justified in believing that a system of grammar formed part of the Stoic theory of expressions. But this is exactly what is in question.

What reason, then, do we have for attributing to the Stoics a system of grammar as part of the theory of expressions? Very little, it would seem. For if we look at the relevant part of Diocles Magnes' account of Stoic dialectic in Diogenes Laertius (7.55 ff.), the most comprehensive ancient report of the matter, it is apparent that grammar cannot be identified with the whole part of dialectic which deals with expressions. After all, it is supposed to deal also with such matters as definition, concepts, genera, species, and divisions of various kinds (D.L. 7.60-62). It could be argued on the basis of Diogenes Laertius 7.44 that these topics do not really belong to the theory of expressions, but found a place there because they had to go somewhere; but then there are still such topics as poetics (D.L. 7.60) and ambiguity (ibid., 62), or even meter and music (ibid., 44) which have to be dealt with under this head. So it seems that we cannot identify grammar with this whole part of dialectic. But neither is grammar set off in any way as a separate part within this part of dialectic. It is true that the first paragraphs of Diocles' account (D.L. 7.55-59) cover grammatical topics, but it is difficult to see how the treatment of these topics would amount to a grammar. And, what is more, the paragraph on the virtues and vices of speech (D.L. 7.59), which follows sections on, roughly, phonology and the parts of speech, seems to presuppose a point of view according to which the grammaticality of an expression (its Hellenism, as it is called) is just one, though perhaps the most important, of the features that are constitutive of good style. Thus the comparatively detailed account of Diocles in Diogenes Laertius gives us very much the impression that grammar is not a special part of the theory of expressions or, for that matter, of Stoic logic. And the short survey of Stoic logic at Diogenes Laertius 7.44 reinforces this impression: if grammar had been regarded as a separate subject, it would have been natural to refer to it as one of the items dealt with under the appropriate heading.

Hence it seems to be a problem whether there is such a subject as Stoic grammar in the sense of a separate discipline pursued systematically, as opposed to a collection of grammatical remarks made in the pursuit of various other enterprises. In spite of these difficulties I will, in what follows, try to argue that there is such a Stoic discipline as grammar or, at least, that what the Stoics are doing in the first part of the theory of expressions comes sufficiently close to such a separate discipline.

III

To start with, it seems that there is evidence that the Stoics had the notion of such a discipline before grammar had become an established subject of its own. We have already had occasion to refer to a section in Diocles' account of Stoic dialectic on the virtues and vices of speech (D.L. 7.59). This doctrine of virtues and vices of speech goes back at least to the third book of the *Rhetoric*, in which Aristotle deals with diction or good style. He recognizes (1404b 1-2) one virtue of diction or speech (*lexis*): clarity (*saphē einai*). Theophrastus apparently tried to elaborate this and distinguished four virtues of diction. Good speech for him is (I) pure, proper Greek, (II) clear, (III) fitting, and (IV) ornate (cf. Cicero, *Orator* 79). The Stoics in turn adopted the doctrine from Theophrastus and incorporated it into their dialectic. For the virtues of speech attributed to them in Diogenes Laertius (7.59) turn out to be those of Theophrastus in exactly that order, except that between the second and the third virtue the Stoics added another, conciseness, a virtue they cherished so much that Cicero could say of Cleanthes' and Chrysippus's treatises on rhetoric that they provided ideal instruction for one desiring to fall silent (*De fin.* 4.3.7).

Of these virtues obviously the most important is the first, Hellenism. Aristotle already had said (*Rhet.* 3, 5 [1407a 19-20]) that Hellenism is the principle of diction. What one says may not be concise, need not be particularly elegant, could be less than crystal clear, and might not be completely appropriate, but it at least has to be proper Greek. The relative importance of this virtue was generally stressed. Dionysius of Halicarnassus, for example, says that the other virtues are of no use if they are not accompanied by this primary virtue (*Ad Pompeium* 3). In our text the prominence of this virtue is indicated not only by its first place on the list of virtues but also by the fact that the only vices of speech explicitly mentioned in Diogenes Laertius (7.59) are those associated with the virtue of Hellenism: barbarism and solecism.

According to the account in Diogenes (7.59) Hellenism or pure Greek is defined as a way of speaking which is in accordance with the technical, and not some (random or) arbitrary usage. It is not very clear what this definition amounts to, but it does not seem to be the following: "Not any usage which is in accordance with the usage of some Greek-speaking community is acceptable; it has to be the technical usage." It rather seems that "arbitrary" here characterizes the kind of usage rejected and that "and not some arbitrary" is supposed to clarify by contrast what is meant by "technical."

What, then, may the Stoics have in mind when they talk of a random or arbitrary usage? Since we are talking about usage, that is, a specifiable way of speaking and hence a way of speaking covered by some set of rules, they cannot have in mind that the rejected usage is random or arbitrary in that it lacks a set of rules or principles which govern it. Its arbitrariness must rather consist in some arbitrariness of its rules. By contrast the technical usage must be characterized by the fact that its rules are subject to certain constraints or principles; because of these constraints they are nonarbitrary. If one looks around for the kind of principle the Stoics may have in mind, one comes across a whole number of passages in which it is said that pure Greek (or Latin) is constituted or determined or defined by factors like etymology, reason, analogy, age, usage, nature. Quintilian, for example, says of good Latin that it is determined by reason, age, authority, and usage (*Inst.* 1.6.1). Leaving aside the details it seems to be fairly clear how these principles are supposed to be used. If we employ a word or a phrase or a construction that is not immediately recognizable as part of common or educated Roman usage, we may appeal to reason, age, or authority for support; we may, for example, point out that it is already to be found in Ennius or that it is accepted by Cicero. But if our usage cannot be justified by reference to one of these principles and if we still insist on speaking in this way, our usage will be arbitrary even if a whole group adopts it. That the ancient grammarians in general have in mind principles of this kind when they try to distinguish the pure language from some other (arbitrary) form of the language (say the Greek used by the Egyptians) seems to be clear from the way Sextus Empiricus criticizes them. In *Adversus Mathematicos* (11.176-247) he considers the question whether, as the grammarians maintain, there is an art of Hellenism, that is, whether there is a theory that supplies us with canons for the distinction. And he apparently believes he has shown that there is no such discipline by showing that the two principles of analogy and etymology cannot be accepted as criteria for Hellenism. Hence it is plausible to assume that when the Stoics talk of a technical usage, as opposed to some arbitrary one, they have in mind a way of speaking which is governed by a set of principles of the kind we have mentioned, as opposed to a way of speaking which cannot be justified with references to such principles.

If this is what the Stoics have in mind when they speak of the technical usage, we may still wonder why they use the term "technical" rather than some adjective like "proper," "correct," "natural," "rational," or "common," all of which would have been appropriate and in accord with their doctrine. It may be the case that "technical" is used here to indicate that the proper usage is not acquired, as Sextus tries to argue, merely by experience and observation (*empeiria, paratērēsis, Adv. Math.* 1.177); and it is not a matter of scientific knowledge either. That such epistemological questions concerning the status of grammatical knowledge were widely treated in Hellenistic times one can see, for example, from the discussion in Sextus, (*Adv. Math.* 1.60-89) and from the Scholia on Dionysius Thrax (cf. p. 6, 31 ff.; 118, 19 ff.). Sometimes, in fact, scholars tried to divide philology (of which philologists then took grammar to be a part) according to the supposed epistemo-

logical status of its divisions. Of this kind is the division suggested
by Tauriscus, a pupil of the Stoic Crates, into a rational (*logikon*),
an empirical (*tribikon*), and a "historical" (*historikon*) part (Sext.
Emp., *Adv. Math.* 1.248). It would take some effort to specify
exactly what Tauriscus meant by these terms, but if one looks at
the terminology used to describe empirical medicine, or at the language of Sextus Empiricus, it is obvious that the terms used by
Tauriscus are taken from epistemology. The same is true, just to
mention one other example, of the division of "grammatica" into
"methodice" and "historice" to be found in Quintilian (1.9.1). The
Stoics can hardly have failed to take a position on this matter.
Hence it is natural to assume that, in the definition of Hellenism,
"technical" is chosen to mark the Stoic attitude.

But if the Stoics thought of proper usage as being technical in
this way, it is difficult to believe that they did not entertain the
notion of a *technē*, a discipline or art, which would set forth the
principles and canons by means of which we could judge whether
some usage is proper; and this all the more so since the educated
general public of the time regarded a pure Greek language, to be
shared by all who wanted to use Greek, as highly desirable. In
fact, in view of such a desire, it is difficult to believe that no effort
was made by the Stoics to work out such a discipline. That some
scholars engaged in such an enterprise can be seen from the way
Sextus deals with the question "Whether there is an art of Hellenism?" (*Adv. Math.* 1.176 ff.) and from what remains of such treatises as Varro's *De Lingua Latina*.

That this enterprise, which ultimately led to the art of grammar,
was originally regarded as an extension of the theory of the virtues
of speech in a doctrine of style or diction, is suggested by the following: one can still see from the third book of Cicero's *De Oratore* (10. 28, 13, 48 f.) that a division of labor was envisaged
according to which it fell to the grammarian to teach pure and
clear Latin (or Greek), whereas the teacher of style or rhetoric
would concern himself with the other, higher virtues of speech.
Quintilian, too, presupposes such a division of tasks between the
grammarian and the rhetorician. He distinguishes (*Inst.* 1.5.1)
three virtues of speech, of which the first, correctness, corresponds
to Hellenism (or Latinity). And this virtue—as opposed to the
others—is dealt with by the first part of grammar. Now, by "the

first part of grammar" he means, as the context shows (cf. 1. 4. 2 and I.9. 11), what we would call "grammar," as opposed to philology (or the rest of philology), which makes up Quintilian's second part of grammar. Since it would be understood that it is not philology that deals with the other virtues of speech, it would be clear that these were to be handled by the rhetoricians. Of relevance here may also be the corresponding distinction between *loqui* and *dicere* as falling within the province of the dialectician and the rhetorician respectively (cf. Cic., *Orat.* 32.113).

Once we are willing to entertain the assumption that the Stoics had the notion of a discipline at least in its aims sufficiently like grammar, a notion moreover which led to the development of grammar, we may also be willing to reconsider the question whether Diocles' account of Stoic dialectic does not after all provide evidence for the existence of such a Stoic discipline. It seems clear that if the subject is to be found anywhere it has to be found in the part of dialectic concerned with expressions. Now the main reasons that seemed to tell against this possibility were two: (1) though the topics discussed in Diogenes Laertius 7.55-58 could be dealt with in a treatise of grammar, it is difficult to see how a treatment on just these topics could amount to a grammar; and (2) wherever we might consider drawing the line in Diogenes' account between a survey of grammar and a survey of something else, there seems to be no natural point of division; certainly no such point is indicated explicitly—which is strange if grammar was regarded as a distinct part of dialectic.

Perhaps these difficulties can be overcome. As to the first, we are fortunately able to point out that this is a problem that arises for the historian of ancient grammar in any case. For the contents of the majority of ancient grammatical treatises correspond very closely to the topics dealt with in Diogenes Laertius 7.55-59: they contain some general introductory remarks and basic definitions along the lines of 7.55-56, have a section on phonology corresponding to chapters 56-57, then mainly deal with the parts of speech, and finally, may have a section on the virtues and vices of speech. Sometimes treatises on grammar would only deal with the parts of speech. Hence the first difficulty does not arise just for those who want to attribute a system of grammar to the Stoics. Hence the apparent incompleteness of Diogenes Laertius 7.55 ff. as a survey of grammar should not be counted as evidence against assuming a Stoic discipline of grammar. Although it calls for an explanation, such an explanation is also called for by other texts.

Nevertheless, to disperse possible doubts on this score, we may proceed further. As a first step we distinguish between the elements of grammar and scholarly grammar. The topics discussed in Diogenes Laertius 7.55 ff., in the ancient grammatical treatises of the type referred to above, and in such surveys of grammar as we find in Sextus and Quintilian's first book, correspond to the elements of grammar rather than to a full-fledged scholarly grammar. Such a distinction is suggested, for example, by Quintilian (*Inst.* I.4-7). Quintilian there goes through the topics in grammar which a boy should have covered before he can profitably proceed to the study of rhetoric. That the topics mentioned are not supposed to exhaust the subject of grammar is clear from the fact that Quintilian insists that boys should also learn to inflect nouns and verbs before they pass on to more advanced grammatical subjects. There is a suggestion that some schoolmasters pass over the matter (I.4.22). In general we have to keep in mind that the introductory grammatical treatises cover the material to be taught to children at about the age of twelve. So what is in question is certainly not the scope of *scholarly* grammar, but the elements of grammar with which the young student would be confronted upon entering secondary school. If this distinction is granted we may say that, once grammar was an established subject represented in the curriculum, the topics discussed in Diogenes Laertius 7.55 ff. might be referred to as the elements of grammar. When, for example, Seneca complains (*Ep.* 48.11) that the philosophers, having promised heaven, descend to the elements of the grammarians, we may safely assume that it is the part of dialectic corresponding to Diogenes 7.55 ff. which he is thinking of.[4] Now clearly the Stoics were not interested in outlining an elementary grammar course for children. But if we could explain that the account in Diogenes Laertius was supposed to represent no more than the elements of grammar, we would be in a better position to explain the apparent incompleteness of the account as a survey of grammar as a whole.

Our second step is to see how what we have called the elements of grammar could be thought of as elements of grammar, how a treatment of them might serve as an introduction to grammar not just for children but even at a rather advanced level. It is easy enough to see how the material referred to in Diogenes Laertius 7, paragraphs 55, 56, and the first part of 57, could serve as an introduction at any level. This explanation, though, puts the main burden of representing grammar on to the section concerning the parts of speech; too much of a burden, it would seem. But a look at ancient treatises of grammar, such as Priscian's *Institutiones* or the remains of Apollonius's special treatises on the various parts of speech, shows that at least the ancients thought that most of the material covered in grammar *could* be organized around the various parts of speech. Even syntax could be covered this way to a considerable extent, as one can see from the organization of Apollonius's Syntax. In fact, Apollonius's treatises on pronouns and adverbs both contain sections on the syntax of these parts of speech. We do not at this point have to discuss what the Stoics themselves dealt with under the parts of speech. For our present argument it is sufficient to see that even a treatment of the parts of speech could be, and was, regarded as an introduction to grammar even at a rather advanced level. Thus the apparent incompleteness of the survey in Diogenes is by itself no evidence that the Stoics did not recognize grammar as a distinct part of dialectic.

Now it might be objected that if Diogenes Laertius 7.55 ff. was not supposed to represent Stoic grammar as a whole, but only the elements of grammar, one might expect at least a comment to that effect. This objection brings us to our second difficulty: not only is no part of the account in Diogenes marked off as covering grammar (or, for that matter, the elements of grammar) but one cannot even see where such a cut could be made.

The explanation may be as follows: the items that later were treated as the elements of grammar were originally not introduced as such. They were there, at the position in this part of dialectic which they still occupy in Diocles' account, not as the elements of grammar, but as part of a theory of diction or style (*lexis*). The account in Diogenes might be thought of as representing a stage in which grammar has grown from a negligible part of such a theory of diction to a full-blown and complex discipline, which, however, at least formally, was still regarded as part of the theory of diction. Hence the treatment of the virtues and vices of speech—and among the virtues of speech the treatment of Hellenism—is not set off from the discussion of the other virtues as the subject matter of a distinct discipline.

What, then, is the evidence for saying that the elements of grammar originally formed part of a theory of diction and that even later the Stoics still considered grammar as embedded in such a theory?

According to Alexander (*In Top.* 1.10 ff.) the Stoics regarded dialectic as the discipline that tells us how to speak well (*eu legein*); and to speak well, Alexander says, they make a matter of saying what is true and saying what is fitting. Saying what is true is the concern of that part of Stoic dialectic which deals with what is signified. Hence it contains an epistemology (D.L. 7.43, 42, 45),[5] a doctrine of truth-conditions for the various kinds of propositions (D.L. 7.73-74), a theory of arguments, in particular syllogisms (D.L. 7.76 ff., 45),[6] and a treatment of fallacies (D.L. 7.82, 44). But it would be imprecise to say that this part of dialectic is exclusively concerned with truth. For among things signified or said the Stoics not only distinguish propositions but also commands, questions, wishes, oaths, and the like (cf., e.g., D.L. 7.66 ff.). So it would be more precise to say that this part of dialectic is concerned quite generally with what it is that should be said, though of course, it would mainly deal with truth and falsehood. This raises the question whether it was this very point that Alexander had in mind when he explained that Stoic dialectic is also concerned with saying what is fitting. But this is very improbable. For by the time of Alexander it seems to have been completely forgotten that Stoic dialectic was conceived by Chrysippus as also dealing with such topics as the logic of commands or the logic of questions. What then does Alexander have in mind? The most plausible assumption seems to be that he wants to point out that for the Stoics to speak well amounted to two things: that it is the right or true thing that is said, and that what is said is said the proper way. This in turn would suggest that the two main parts of dialectic (cf. D.L. 7.43) corresponded to the double function of dialectic: the theory of what is signified or said tells us what it is that we should or could say; the theory of expressions tells us how it is to be said.

More light may be shed on this by a further passage of Diogenes. Unfortunately the remarks he makes at 7.83 about the general aims of Stoic dialectic are too short; and in addition the text seems to have suffered considerably. But the passage still shows that the dialectician tries to provide us with criteria for what one should say. From the end of the paragraph we may infer that knowledge of what one should or should not say involves a two-fold competence. For the dialectician will know both what things are and what they should be called. Presumably this can be generalized so that the dialectician's expertise amounts to both knowledge of what it is that should be said and knowledge of how it should be said. If this is regarded as the characteristic competence of the dialectician, then it is natural to regard the two main parts of Stoic dialectic as corresponding to this twofold competence: the theory of *lekta* tells us what it is that should be said, whereas the theory of expressions will tell us how we should say it.

Traditionally dialectic had been concerned with truth. But where would one turn to if one tried to develop a theory of how one should express oneself as a second part of dialectic? It seems that the theory of diction would be a natural source to draw on. Rhetoric was familiar with the contrast between knowing what to say and knowing how to say it; it was exactly this contrast that Aristotle used to introduce the theory of diction in the third book of the *Rhetoric* (1403b14 ff.) as being concerned with the way in which we should speak.

The theory of diction seems also to have become a repository for much earlier Greek speculation on language; one associates grammar in the fifth and fourth centuries B.C. very much with philosophical debates concerning the nature and origin of language, in particular the correctness of names. There is no doubt that as a result of these debates there existed in the fourth century a considerable body of linguistic notions and assumptions. What is in doubt is what happened to this body of knowledge when the Early Academy and the Stoa started to divide philosophy into sections and subsections. They attempted to make the division on principles which gave them confidence that somehow all that there is to be known by philosophers could find its place in the schema. There was a natural tendency to make the cuts follow the boundaries of the established disciplines that had to be incorporated. But this meant that for subjects which had not yet been safely established, there was a tendency to pursue them just to the extent to which they fitted into the program of study suggested by the division of philosophy, and with that program in view. One of the subjects discriminated against in this way would be language in general and the Greek language in particular. For even with an author as late as Aristotle, whose works do contain numerous short remarks on the topic, there is no suggestion that there is a place in philosophy where language would be dealt with systematically and on its own. It is significant that by far the most grammatical text in the Aristotelian corpus is the passage on diction in the *Poetics*. Hence there is no reason to expect that philosophers like Xenocrates and the first Stoics would try to provide a separate place for the study of Greek in their classification of philosophy. So we should not be surprised to find that the tradition of philosophical speculation about language, when channeled through this classificatory scheme, should come up in a subordinate place like the theory of diction. That this place is not necessarily entirely inappropriate, however, can be seen from the fact that of the five points Aristotle mentions as particularly important for Hellenism (the principle, as he says, of diction) the first concerns conjunctions (*Rhet.* 1407a20 ff.), the fourth grammatical gender (1407b6 ff.), and the fifth grammatical number (1407b9 f.). How the philosophical tradition is integrated at this point can be seen, for example, from the references to Protagoras in the *Rhetoric* (1407b6) and the *Poetics* (19.1456b15 ff.).

In any case it is clear that the Stoics turned to the theory of diction. The account in Diogenes (7.55-59) can be read as a report of a theory which culminates in a doctrine of the virtues and vices of speech. It certainly has to be read as a report of a theory in which the virtues and vices of speech play an important role. But, as we have seen, the doctrine of the virtues and vices of speech was regarded as a central part of the theory of diction. What is more, we have already seen that in their doctrine of the virtues and vices of speech the Stoics depend heavily on Theophrastus's theory of diction. So at least for this important part of their theory they must have turned to the theory of diction.

Our survey in Diogenes also shares another important topic with Theophrastus's *On diction;* a large part of Diocles' account is taken up by the section on the parts of speech, and this seems also to have been one of the main topics in Theophrastus's treatise. For it is generally agreed that a list of topics that Simplicius (*In cat.* 10,

23 ff.) says are discussed by Theophrastus in *On the elements of speech* represents the contents of one part of Theophrastus's *On diction;* and in this list the parts of speech figure very prominently. At all events it seems clear both that the parts of speech would be discussed in theories of diction and why this was so.

A certain Theodectes is said to have distinguished just three parts of speech: nouns, verbs, and conjunctions (Dion. Hal., *De comp. verb.*, 2.8; Quint. 1.4.18). Whence could this information ultimately be derived if not from Theodectes' remarks on diction in one of his rhetorical writings? Moreover, when Diocles reports (D.L. 7.57) that the Stoic Antipater suggested the adverb as a sixth part of speech, he gives as the title of Antipater's treatise *On diction and things said.* It is also fairly clear why the parts of speech would be mentioned in a theory of diction or style. Dionysius of Halicarnassus tells us in the second chapter of his treatise on composition that composition is a certain arrangement of the parts of speech, and then goes on to give a short account of how the number of parts of speech was increased after Aristotle. We may also notice that the four parts of speech that, it is generally assumed, were already distinguished by Zeno and Cleanthes, namely noun, verb, conjunction, and article (supposing that Chrysippus introduced the distinction between proper name and common noun as separate parts of speech), are exactly those on which we find remarks in theories of diction in the fourth century B.C.[7] In any case it is clear at least for Theophrastus that another important topic of the Stoic theory, the parts of speech, had been the topic of systematic discussion within the theory of diction.

Many of our texts, especially the chapters on diction from Aristotle's *Poetics,* also show that *most* of the topics dealt with in this part of dialectic, certainly those covered in Diogenes Laertius 7.55-59, were also regarded as falling within the province of the theory of diction.[8]

So it turns out that the topics of this part of dialectic can be regarded as topics of the theory of diction; and it is also clear that at least for some of them the Stoics turned to the theory of diction. But on the other hand it is also clear that their treatment of these topics does not amount to a theory of style of the kind we find in Aristotle, Demetrius, or Dionysius of Halicarnassus. Too many of the standard topics of such a theory are missing. Hence the claim that this part of Stoic dialectic was conceived of as some kind of theory of diction needs further qualification and explanation.

To start with, it is obvious that in this part of dialectic the Stoics are not interested in a *rhetorical* theory of style. For the theory whose original purpose we are trying to grasp more clearly is pursued as part of dialectic rather than rhetoric. The rhetorical theory of style is concerned with the composition of artful speeches or, when we come to the age of the book, with the kind of "Kunstprosa" we find, for example, in Thucydides. Dialectic, on the other hand, is concerned with language, or at least educated language, in general. (If it was sometimes said that dialectic was concerned with dialectical discussion, this was an anachronistic attempt to preserve the traditional contrast between dialectic and rhetoric; the actual scope of Stoic dialectic gives no indication of such a restriction.) So the material covered by the original rhetorical theory of diction will be divided into two parts, one part that deals in a general way with any (educated) use of language, and which will become the part of dialectic with which we are concerned as, so to speak, a general theory of diction; and another part that deals with the specifically rhetorical use of language, and which will remain a part of rhetoric.

This distinction between a general theory of diction and a specifically rhetorical doctrine of style was to have an enormous effect on the general part of the original theory of diction. The primary concern of the original theory was rhetorical or stylistic; hence linguistic or grammatical matters would only come in incidentally and would not be developed systematically. Once a systematic division was made between a general theory of diction and a specifically rhetorical part, the grammatical questions, which philosophers had in any case taken particular interest in, had to be treated more systematically.

This division of labor also had another advantage. A theory of diction was needed not just for artful prose but also for poetry. Hence diction was dealt with in two places, in rhetoric and in poetics (cf. Arist., *Poetics* 19, 1456b8-18; *Rhet.* 1404a28-39). Aristotle tries to justify this by saying that poetical diction and rhetorical diction are two quite different matters (1404a24-29); hence each should be the subject of a different study. But even given two such theories there would still be the problem of whether the general part of the theory of diction, which is neither tied to rhetoric nor to poetics, should be dealt with not only in rhetoric but also in poetics, as in fact happens in Aristotle (*Poet.* 20-21). For the Stoics this problem does not arise. They have one general theory of diction which is then immediately followed by "poetics" (D.L. 7.60; cf. 44), and which will be presupposed by rhetoric.

The whole matter might be much clearer if we knew more about Theophrastus's theory of diction. For already Theophrastus may have, in practice, made the distinction between a general and a specific theory of diction by treating of language quite generally in the first part of *On diction*. The matter would also be much clearer if we knew more about Xenocrates' treatment of dialectic. Zeno had been a student of Xenocrates (D.L. 7.2; Eus., *P.E.* 13.5, 11), and the Stoics seem to have followed Xenocrates in the relevant part of the division of philosophy. Like him they divided philosophy into logic, physics, and ethics (Sext. Emp., *Adv. Math.* 7.16), and they followed him in the division of logic into rhetoric and dialectic as well as in the definition of rhetoric (*Adv. Math.* 2.6-7). Like the Stoics Xenocrates made one part of dialectic deal with voice (*phōnē*, Porph., *In Harm. Ptol.*, 193 W., frg. 10 Heinze), and like the Stoics he dealt with both prose and verse under this heading (*ibid.*). Now, on the authority of Aristoxenus, Xenocrates is reported to have been rightly criticized for including the discussion of voice in dialectic. This may suggest that Xenocrates' procedure was a novelty. In that case it would be particularly significant that the Stoics followed Xenocrates. And hence for our problem it would be important to know what role Xenocrates attributed to the treatment of voice within the system of dialectic. The catalog of Xenocrates' writings lists two *Studies on Diction*, in 15 and 16 books respectively, immediately after a treatise on dialectic in 14 books. But this will hardly suffice as evidence that Xenocrates regarded the part of dialectic in question as a theory of diction.

So there is some reason to believe that the first part of the Stoic doctrine of expression, the part corresponding to D.L. 7.55-59, was originally conceived of as a general theory of diction or style. We have also seen that, given such a division between a general theory on the one hand and specific rhetorical and poetical theories on the other, questions concerning language in general could now be dealt with in a more systematic way. But it is still the case that a theory of diction or style, however general, is not a grammar. So some further explanation is still necessary.

It may be relevant that one could take two positions with reference to the theory of diction. One could take the attitude that the grammatical part of it was trivial and negligible, because anybody with a decent upbringing would know Greek anyway. What he might still lack in this regard was much too subtle to be acquired through a "discipline"; for that he had to read good authors and to associate with the right people; experience of the right kind rather than doctrine was needed. Hence the important, difficult, and really technical part of the theory would be the one concerned with the finer virtues of speech which would give it elegance and effectiveness. Not that excellence in these virtues could be achieved just by reading treatises, but that there is an enormous amount of technical knowledge which can be acquired in this way. This is the attitude that we still find in Cicero's *De oratore* (cf., e.g., 3.37 ff., 151). But if one did not follow Cicero in his praise of rich style and preferred instead a very plain language, as the Stoics did, the treatment of the other virtues of speech would lose much of its urgency.

Moreover, though the higher virtues of speech would be regarded as being relevant to language in general, it would commonly be granted that they were the particular concern of the rhetorician. We saw above how a division of labor was envisaged according to which it was the grammarian who was responsible for Hellenism, whereas the rhetorician dealt with the higher virtues. Even if he did not agree in theory that the higher virtues quite generally fell into the province of rhetoric (as a Stoic obviously did not), in practice a representative of the general theory of diction will have concentrated on what was indisputably his own area. The general and, in a way, justified concern for Hellenism, a common dialect of pure Greek (*koinē, kathareuein*), would considerably increase the relative importance of the primary virtue of speech. But quite apart from this general interest in Hellenism, it was never called in doubt—rather it was often stressed by authors on style like Dionysius of Halicarnassus—that there is no excellence of style unless the requirements of Hellenism have been met. So if one believed that Hellenism admitted of the kind of systematic treatment on the basis of which canons of correct usage could be established, it was only natural that one would devote most of one's energy to this primary virtue of speech.

The Stoics may also have been impressed by the idea that it was in ordinary rather than in highly refined language in which reason articulated itself, and that hence a study of ordinary language was philosophically much more relevant. It should also be kept in mind that the questions concerning language in which philosophers had traditionally taken an interest would now be classified as problems concerning Hellenism. Their systematic treatment seems to have gathered such momentum that it vastly outgrew investigation into the higher virtues of speech. For all these reasons one should not be surprised that a treatment of what was originally conceived of as a general theory of diction would later turn out to be little more than a treatment of Hellenism, that is, a grammar of some sort.

If there is any truth in this account, we have also removed our second difficulty, that grammar in Diocles' account is not marked off as a distinct part of dialectic; indeed that it could not be so marked off because no radical distinction is made among the virtues of speech between grammatical correctness and the higher virtues of diction. The explanation would be that grammar has grown out of a general theory of diction from which the specifically rhetorical elements have been removed and in which so much emphasis is placed on the primary virtue of speech that the remaining general theory of diction amounts basically to the elements of grammar. This is the subject matter of Diogenes Laertius 7.55-59; and to this are appended certain other subjects that, given the division of Stoic philosophy, would naturally go there, as we explained in the case of poetics, or which would not find a suitable place elsewhere, like definition, genus, and species. Grammar originally would not be marked off, because in the time of Chrysippus and Diogenes of Babylon, on whom Diocles seems mainly to draw, grammar had not yet been established as a discipline of its own, let alone as one distinguished from dialectic. Later the Stoics would feel no particular need to mark it off, since it would be clear that it basically corresponds to what is covered in Diogenes 7.55-59. That this, in addition to grammar, also included at least a short treatment of the higher virtues of speech does not seem to have been regarded as a disadvantage. For even much later we find treatises that profess to be treatises on grammar but which still at least touch on the other virtues of speech (or the corresponding vices).[9] Some treatises, at least in a very rudimentary form, even cover the topics of definition, genus, and species.[10] Charisius's treatise, in fact, also covers such topics as the tropes.

In any case, grammar only came to be a subject of its own, independent of dialectic, by being lifted out of this context and being put into a new one: it was made the first, introductory part of philology, sometimes also called "the technical part" (cf. Sext. Emp., *Adv. Math.* 1.91). And since philology was called "grammar," our subject acquired the labels "grammar" or "art of grammar." It is for this trivial reason that the Stoics at the time of Chrysippus or Diogenes of Babylon were not in a position to say something like "this part of dialectic starts with grammar, and then deals with . . ." Grammar only came to have its name when and because it was put in a different context. Some Stoics who also taught philology like Crates and his followers would, of course, also teach grammar in the new context (cf. Sext. Emp., *Adv. Math.* 1.79 and 248). In fact they may be responsible for the introduction of the technical part of philology as a discipline, and in this way for the establishment of grammar as a discipline distinguished from both dialectic and rhetoric. But there was no need for the Stoics in general to lift grammar out of its original context. For though the Stoics had a great interest in the classical authors, and hence in the philology needed to deal with them, philology, after all, was not a part of philosophy. In fact, there would have been systematic reasons for leaving grammar in its place. The notion of Hellenism was normative, and hence grammar would naturally go with the doctrine of the other virtues of speech. More important, there was, as we will see, a systematic connection between grammar and the theory of *lekta* which would be obscured by separating grammar from dialectic. Finally, one might argue that such a radical separation of logic and grammar proves to be disastrous, at least for grammar.

It turns out, then, that the facts which at first sight seemed to tell against the existence of Stoic grammar also fit a plausible picture according to which grammar was already a fairly well defined and rather developed part of Stoic doctrine. So we seem to have reached the following point in our argument: (1) the evidence considered does not rule out the possibility that the Stoics recognized grammar as a philosophical subject; (2) the Stoics seem to have the notion of such a subject as grammar; (3) there is a clearly distinct part of Stoic dialectic, a general theory of diction, which we could identify with their grammar; (4) it is very tempting to identify this part of dialectic with Stoic grammar, since in its contents it seems to correspond to the elements of grammar; and (5), as nobody will deny, the Stoics do deal with a great number of grammatical questions: they contribute to the terminology and conceptual framework of grammar; they have an influence on grammatical doctrine from Dionysius Thrax onward; and they are even in antiquity regarded as being particularly concerned with language.[11]

But all this is still compatible with the assumption that the Stoics failed to pursue grammar systematically as a distinct subject within dialectic. Hence the existence of Stoic grammar in this sense is still an open question. In what follows I will try to provide some positive evidence for this assumption by trying to reconstruct the basic structure of Stoic grammar, so that it may become clearer whether their grammatical studies amount to systematic grammar or not.

There is reason to believe that the Stoics divided the subject into two parts, one concerned with individual words taken in isolation, the other with the assembling of words into sentences. This is what one would expect if it were true that grammar developed out of the theory of diction. For the theory of diction has two primary parts, the first concerned with individual words, particularly the choice of words, the second with the assembling of these words (cf., e.g., Cic., *De. orat.* 3.149). This seems to be a natural way of bringing order into the material of the grammarian, and it is in fact followed by later grammarians like Priscian, who first deals with the parts of speech and then their organization into sentences. It is referred to as a principle of organization in Quintilian (1.29.2); it is used in treatises that are agreed to be heavily influenced by Stoic doctrine, like Varro's *De lingua latina* and Augustine's *Dialectica*. When Seneca characterizes logic in the Stoic sense, he says "It goes into the properties of words, into their combination, and into arguments to ensure that falsehoods do not creep in in place of truth" (*Ep.* 89.9). A comparison with *Ep.* 88.42 suggests that Seneca, when he talks of the properties of words, is thinking of the characterization of words as the different parts of speech. Thus he seems to characterize dialectic by referring to what he regards as the main topics of its two parts: the theory of argument representing the part concerning *lekta*, grammar representing the part concerning expressions; and grammar, it would seem, is referred to under its two main topics, the doctrine of the parts of speech and the theory of their combination. Furthermore, the two vices that are associated with the virtue of Hellenism, barbarism and solecism, come to be distinguished accordingly: mistakes about individual words are barbarisms; violations of the rules of composition are solecisms.

Let us first consider composition. It seems appropriate to start with this for two reasons. First of all there does not seem to be anything in Diocles' account to correspond to it. And this throws doubt on our suggestion about the basic organization of Stoic grammar. Secondly, as one can infer from the definition of solecism in Diogenes Laertius (7.59), composition in grammar amounts to syntax. But partly because syntax seems to be missing in Diocles' account, this subject is often thought to be of much later origin.

There are two considerations that may help to explain the apparent lack of a syntax. To start with, we may argue that the omission of syntax in Diocles' account is simply due to the fact that syntax did not belong to the elements of grammar. And there is independent evidence for this; for syntax is covered neither in Sextus's discussion of grammar in *Adversus Mathematicos*, book I, nor is it dealt with in Quintilian or in many of the Roman introductions to grammar. But then, of course, the question arises why syntax, given its importance, is not counted amoung the elements of grammar. A number of factors may have come together to bring this about. If, for example, it should be the case that the elements of grammar are topics of the theory of diction reconstituted as the elements of grammar, we should not expect syntax to be among them. For syntax, though touched on (cf. Cic., *De orat.* 3.40), does not seem to have been dealt with systematically in the theory of diction. Or, as we have seen earlier, syntax could be dealt with to some extent under the different parts of speech; and this may have been thought to be sufficient for an introduction. There is one further factor, however, which deserves to be treated in more detail.

We noted earlier that in the theory of *lekta* the Stoics were also concerned with the *analysis* of *lekta*. In fact they seem to have distinguished various kinds of elements of *lekta* and to have investigated how these are put together to form various kinds of complete *lekta* corresponding to complete thoughts and sentences. Cases are one kind of element (D.L. 7.64, 70), predicates of a certain sort another kind (cf., e.g., D.L. 7.58, 64, 70), and there are still others, such as various kinds of particles (D.L. 7.67, 70) and conjunctives (*ibid.* 71 f.). These elements are thought to enter compounds according to certain laws of composition. The term regularly used for their composition is *syntattein*, the verb from which "syntax" is derived as the corresponding noun (cf. D.L. 7.58, 59, 64 four times, 72 twice). This syntax of *lekta* seems to have been the object of systematic study. For among the titles of Chrysippus's writings we find *On the syntax of the things said*, in four books, and *On the syntax and the elements of the things said, to Philippus*, in three books (D.L. 7.193). Since the things said are *lekta* (cf. D.L. 7.57), we have here two treatises on the syntax of *lekta* (and, incidentally, confirmation for the assumption that the Stoics worked with the notion of elements of *lekta*). That there was such a topic as the syntax of *lekta* we can also see from the fact that Plutarch refers to it in these very terms (*Adv. Colot.*, 1119F).

Now if one has such a syntax of *lekta* and if one thinks that there is a very close correspondence between the parts or elements of speech and the elements of *lekta*, one may think that to construct a syntactically acceptable sentence was basically a matter of putting together elements of speech in such a way that the corresponding elements of *lekta* form a *lekton* which satisfies the laws of the syntax of *lekta*. It seems that the Stoics adopted a version of this view, and that even Apollonius Dyscolus still wrote his *Syntax* on some assumption of this sort (cf. *De synt* I.2. p. 2, 10 ff., replacing "intelligibles" by "elements of *lekta*"). We will deal with the correspondence between the elements of *lekta* and the elements of speech when we come to the latter; for the moment I will suppose that the Stoics assumed such a correspondence. That they approached syntax in this way is suggested by the following facts: if we inspect the relevant section of the catalog of Chrysippus's writings (D.L. 7.192-193), we notice that the two treatises concerning the syntax of *lekta* mentioned above are preceded and followed by treatises dealing with the parts of speech. This suggests a systematic connection between the syntax of *lekta* and the parts of speech. Moreover, the first in this group of four treatises is not just on the parts of speech, but on the elements of speech and the things said, that is, it seems to compare and correlate the parts of speech and the elements of *lekta*. Similarly the third treatise is not just on the syntax of *lekta*, but on the syntax and the elements of things said. This suggests a systematic connection between parts of speech, elements of *lekta*, and the syntax of *lekta*, which could be accounted for if we assume that the Stoics took the approach to syntax mentioned above.

Moreover, it should be noticed that the series of four writings just referred to is listed in the catalog under the heading "Logical topics concerning expressions and the corresponding *logos*," that is, they are not listed in the part of the catalog which covers the theory of *lekta*. There would be a justification for putting treatises dealing with the syntax of *lekta* among treatises dealing with expressions and the sentences they constitute if the syntax of *lekta* was also supposed indirectly to serve the suggested function of a syntax for sentences. Similarly it may be pointed out that when Plutarch mentions (*Adv. Colot.* 1119 F) three topics in the theory of language, "syntax of *lekta*" is preceded by "sounds of some kind or other" and followed by "usage of words."

The most important passage, however, for our purposes is one from Dionysius's *On Composition* (4.32). Dionysius explains that for his treatise on composition he turned to two writings of Chrysippus, both entitled *On the syntax of the parts of speech*, but found them of no use for his purposes. For they dealt with dialectical matters, "the composition of true and false, possible and impossible propositions, propositions which are contingent and change their truth-value, ambiguous ones and others of such a kind." It is clear, both from the title and the reference to ambiguity, that in these treatises Chrysippus was also dealing with sentences and their composition. But though we may suspect that Dionysius selects examples of what was dealt with in these treatises in a rather one-sided way, to make his point that they were useless for composition as he was interested in it, the examples themselves make it clear that Chrysippus here too must have dealt with various kinds of *lekta*, and, what is more, with kinds of *lekta* in which the logician would be interested but which would be of no particular concern to the grammarian. An explanation for this, again, would be that the Stoics do syntax of expressions by recourse to the dialectician's syntax of *lekta* via the parts of speech and the elements of *lekta*. That the syntax of *lekta* would be determined very much by logical interests would help to explain why Dionysius, who is interested in style, would not find Stoic treatises on the composition of expressions particularly useful.

That the Stoics thought that by putting together parts of speech in the appropriate way we construct, as it were, the intended corresponding *lekton*, can also be seen from the characterization of the various kinds of molecular propositions in Diogenes Laertius 7.71 ff. These propositions are *lekta* and hence not expressions. Nevertheless they are characterized in terms of kinds of conjunctions which are supposed to be characteristic for the various kinds of proposition in question. But the text makes it clear that these conjunctions are thought of as expressions and hence not as constituents of the propositions to be characterized. If then Chrysippus and Diogenes are said to claim that the implicative proposition is formed by means of the implicative conjunction "if," their assumption must be that it is by putting parts of speech together in an appropriate way that we get the intended *lekton*, formed by parts corresponding to the parts of speech. So, if an account along these lines is acceptable, we have another explanation of why syntax was not counted among the elements of grammar. On the one hand it relied so much on the syntax of *lekta* that, given the knowledge of this syntax and the correspondence between parts of speech and elements of *lekta*, one was supposed to know the basic facts of the syntax of expressions anyway; on the other hand the syntax of *lekta* carried one far into the details of Stoic logic in a narrow sense—which would be inappropriate at least for elementary instruction in grammar.

But from what has been said it also should be clear that the Stoics did deal with syntax systematically: they not only had a syntax of *lekta;* they also had a syntax of expressions or parts of speech, that is, a syntax in the strict sense, though it was closely tied to the syntax of *lekta.* Hence there should be no doubt on this score that the Stoics, even in the days of Chrysippus and Diogenes of Babylon, systematically pursued grammatical studies.

IV

Having dealt briefly with composition or syntax, let us turn to the part of grammar which deals with words taken in isolation. From what has been said, it is fairly clear that an important, if not the most important, topic here is the parts of speech. But if the suggested program of grammar is taken seriously, this part of grammar has to do more than deal with questions that we associate with the doctrine of the parts of speech; it has, after all, to supply us with criteria as to what is to count as a proper Greek word. The Stoics certainly try to provide us with such criteria, for example, when they give us a definition of barbarism (D.L. 7.59).

It is in this context that authors like Sextus and Quintilian discuss such factors as etymology and analogy as criteria for Hellenism. Hence the question arises how discussion of these questions was related to the discussion of the parts of speech. No light is thrown on this by Diocles' account, and it is unclear how the question is to be answered. Since later the parts of speech and the criteria for Hellenism were discussed separately (cf. Sext. Emp., *Adv. Math.* 1), we will proceed on the assumption that to qualify as words all expressions have to fall under one of the parts of speech, and hence have to meet the conditions for belonging to the part of speech that is relevant to them. But in addition they have to satisfy certain further requirements in order not to be disqualified as barbaric. Our difficulty may be connected with the fact that in later antiquity, besides the treatises on the art of grammar, there was a separate class of treatises *On Latinity* (or *On Hellenism*) which are introductions dealing with the nature and origin of language and the criteria for Hellenism (or Latinity), and then proceeding to discuss the choice of words, their inflection, and sometimes also their orthography (cf. Barwick, *Remmius Palaemon* 228 f.).

The doctrine of the parts of speech was regarded by the Stoics as highly important from the start. When Epictetus characterizes the genuine philosopher and asks which theorems he is after, he answers, "Those which Zeno talks of, to know the elements of speech, what each of them is like, and how they fit together, and what is along those lines" (*Disc.* 4.8.12). This passage seems to indicate that Zeno already had an interest in the parts of speech, in fact even at least a rudimentary interest in their syntax. But beyond this, the remark taken in its context suggests a motive for this interest which we have not touched upon so far. For Epictetus begins his characterization by saying that the true philosopher deals with reason and that it is his end to possess right reason. Now the word rendered by "reason" here, and above, in "elements of speech," by "speech," is the very same word, logos. And it also seems that Epictetus means to use the same word throughout the characterization of the true philosopher. Hence some authors have doubted whether Epictetus is talking here of anything as trivial as the parts of speech. But this seems to be guaranteed by the fact that "parts of speech" and "elements of speech" are such firmly established technical terms that it would be highly misleading for Epictetus to use them in any but their usual technical meaning, unless the context fully determined a different sense—which it does not in our case. Hence we might be inclined to see in this apparent move from one sense of logos to another a piece of cheap rhetoric. But that, too, must be ruled out. For we find almost the same characterization, involving the same apparent equivocation, in a papyrus-text (Herc. 1020 = SVF 2.131) attributed to Chrysippus. According to this text "philosophy, whether it is the care for, or the knowledge of, right reason, is the discipline concerned with reason (logos). For if we are completely familiar with the parts of speech (logos) and their syntax, we will make use of it (i.e., the logos) in an expert way. By logos I mean the one that by nature belongs to all rational beings."

What is the supposed connection between the rightness of reason and the parts of speech and their syntax which would make such language understandable? There are various possibilities. According to the Stoics the discipline that is primarily responsible for the correctness of reason is dialectic. But for Zeno the main function of dialectic was avoiding and dissolving fallacies (cf. Plut., S.R. 1034E; D.L. 7.25; Stob., Ecl. II, 22, 13 ff. W.). Now we can see from Aristotle's Sophistical Refutations, especially from the section on fallacies in diction, from Galen's treatise on such fallacies (SVF 2.153), and from various fallacies in which the Stoics took a particular interest (cf., e.g., D.L. 82; Simpl., In cat. 105, 13 ff.) that a distinction of parts of speech and a consideration of their construction was regarded as useful or even necessary for the analysis of fallacies. So Zeno may have seen the relevance of the parts of speech and their composition to the correctness of reason in their relevance to the analysis of fallacies. But the way Epictetus and Chrysippus speak suggests some "deeper" connection.

Reason is articulated in thought. Now the articulation of thought in which we are interested when we are interested in the correctness of reason is the articulation of its content. But thought, in this sense of the content of thought, according to Stoic doctrine, is a *lekton*. Hence we are interested in the articulation of *lekta*. We can see the way in which knowledge of the articulation of *lekta* is essential for the correctness of reason by looking at Diocles' account of Stoic logic. According to this arguments, and in particular syllogisms, are *lekta* (D.L. 7.63, 76). And one can easily see also how in a very literal sense the articulation of the argument is decisive for the question whether we have a valid syllogism or not. What, then, does this have to do with the parts of speech and their syntax? The articulation of thought is described in terms of the elements of *lekta* and their syntax. Given the supposed close correspondence between the elements of *lekta* and their syntax and the parts of speech and their syntax, it is clear how an investigation into the parts of speech and their syntax is relevant to an investigation of the articulation of thought, and hence to correct reason; how in fact it could be regarded as an investigation of the elements of thought and their syntax. But, though this may be part of what Chrysippus had in mind, we may doubt whether it was a concern of Zeno's. For it is not clear that Zeno was already thinking in terms of *lekta* and their constitutive elements as opposed to sentences and their constituents, the parts of speech. Furthermore, Zeno does not seem to have been concerned with the elaboration of a positive theory of inference as an aid to correct reason.

There is yet another possibility, though admittedly a rather speculative and obscure one, by which we may explain the relevance of the doctrine of the parts of speech and their syntax to the correctness of reason. It may have been assumed that ordinary language, at least in its basic structure, is a reflection of the rationality and common sense of human beings. And it may have been assumed that this rationality is reflected in particular by the kinds of units from which speech is composed and by the laws of its composition. Hence one might hope that an investigation of the parts of speech and their syntax would reveal aspects of rationality to the extent that a linguistic community had achieved it. In any case the two passages referred to can be taken as evidence that right from the start the Stoics had a strong interest in the parts of speech, because of their relevance to the correctness of reason.

This interpretation again suggests that the Stoics, at least from Chrysippus on, relied on a very strong correspondence between the elements of *lekta* and the parts of speech. We should now examine this assumption more closely. In the *Quaestiones Platonicae* Plutarch devotes an entire essay to the question whether there are only two parts of speech, nouns and verbs, as a passage in Plato's *Sophist* (262 C) might suggest, or whether there are, in addition, all sorts of other parts of speech, as the Stoics claimed. Plutarch himself concludes that there are only two parts or elements of speech (1011E), and he refers to others who take the same view (1010B). Later this position will be shared by authors like Ammonius (*In de int.* 12, 20 ff.; cf. 11, 1 ff.), who goes so far as to attribute to Aristotle himself the view that conjunctions, articles, prepositions, and the like are not properly speaking parts of speech, (ibid. 12, 24; 14, 19 f.).[12] Ammonius suggests that we should distinguish between parts of speech and parts of diction (*lexeōs*, cf. 12.30 f.) and regard the other so-called parts of speech as parts of diction. By chance we know that this distinction had already been made by Theophrastus, and that already in his day it had been a matter of some discussion (Simpl., *In cat.* 10.24 ff.). It may be for this reason that some authors preferred the expression "elements of diction," instead of "elements" or "parts of speech" (cf. Dion. Hal., *De comp. verb.* 2.7-8). If, then, the Stoics insist on calling all parts "parts of speech," we may suspect that they are trying to make a point, especially since Theophrastus is supposed to have made this distinction in his treatise on diction—which we have seen that the Stoics followed in other respects.

Unfortunately our rather late sources are not very clear as to the grounds on which the distinction had been suggested; they also do not seem to have a clear notion of how the various parts of speech had been treated in Theophrastus's day. Simplicius (*In cat.*, 10.25 ff.), presumably following Porphyry, talks as if Theophrastus had dealt with the question "whether noun and verb are parts of speech or whether there are also articles and conjunctions and other kinds." Here the "and other kinds" is not to be taken as evidence that Theophrastus recognized other parts of speech or diction than the four explicitly mentioned. It seems certain that Theophrastus did not distinguish more than these four parts, and Simplicius did not find more than these specified in his source; but he still would want to add the phrase "and other kinds," since to him the list of four parts of speech would look curiously incomplete. Similarly we find Plutarch and Ammonius trying to explain why adverbs and participles are not properly speaking parts of speech. But their discussion, as a report of the views of the ancients, is highly misleading, since in Theophrastus's day participles and adverbs were still classified as nouns or verbs, and so for "the ancients" would be parts of speech in the strict sense.

Hence the question really is why Theophrastus and others wanted to maintain that conjunctions and articles (in the larger old sense of the terms) are just parts of diction, whereas the Stoics insisted that they, too, like nouns and verbs, are parts of speech. Given this clarification, it is tempting to assume that the distinction has something to do with the Peripatetic tenet that only nouns and verbs have signification, that is, are the kinds of expressions that have corresponding items in ontology, and that the notion of these items is evoked by the particular term (cf. Aristotle, *De int.* 16a3 ff.; 16b20-21). (It may be noted that on this count adverbs and participles would not be just parts of diction.) Now it is still Plutarch's first move to argue that, as opposed to nouns and verbs, the other parts of speech do not signify (1009D). Ammonius similarly says of these parts of speech that they do not signify (*In de int.* 12, 13-15). But of what relevance is this for the distinction between parts of speech and parts of diction? The idea may have been that in the case of a statement, for example, we have to distinguish between what is claimed, that is, what would make the statement a true statement, and the way we happen to make this claim, that is, how we express it (cf. Ammon., *In de int.* 13,9 ff.). Now for the Peripatetics truths would be configurations of the ontological items signified by what they call nouns and verbs. These truths would be represented canonically in the language for which syllogistic is developed in the *Analytics* or in the simpler language of the *Categories*. This very simple language only contains nouns, verbs, and a negation-sign; in the more complex form it may contain, in addition, quantifiers. But, as one can see from the *De interpretatione*, it does not contain sentence-connectives, the paradigms of conjunctions. The *De interpretatione*, of course, does refer to conjunctions (cf. 17a9; 17a16; cf. also 18a18 ff.), but only, it seems, to point out that propositions formed by means of them are not strictly speaking one or simple. It then neglects them completely for the rest of the treatise. This might lead to the idea that conjunctions and articles owe their existence just to our way of speaking about things and dealing with facts; there is nothing in the basic facts themselves which corresponds to them. Hence they are just parts of diction, whereas nouns and verbs are also parts of speech.

If this was Theophrastus's point, we can easily see why the Stoics would disagree. As far as conjunctions are concerned, the Stoics maintained that there are real connections between states of affairs in the nature of things, implication, disjunction, incompatibility, which are reflected in language by the different conjunctions, especially those crucial in logic. When Apollonius Dyscolus (*De coni.* 247, 22 ff.) reports that most authors agree that expletive conjunctions do not have signification, we may assume that the minority includes Stoics, who even in the case of expletive conjunctions want to maintain that there is signification. Apollonius does in fact tell us in another passage (*De coni.* 214, 4-6) that Posidonius in his treatise on conjunctions argued against those who maintain that conjunctions do not signify but only tie expressions together.

As far as articles are concerned, let us consider "This (pointing to Socrates) runs," to use a simple example (at this time the class of articles would include pronouns). According to our interpretation, for Theophrastus and his party the state of affairs relevant to this statement would be that Socrates runs; its canonical expression would be "Socrates runs." It is for reasons of style, convenience, ignorance of Socrates, his kind, or his name, and the like, that instead we might say "this runs." The *logos*, what is claimed, is the same; just the expressions differ. Again the Stoics would disagree. For them there are many important logical differences between "This runs" and "Socrates runs"; hence they assume that there are two different *lekta* corresponding to the two sentences (cf. Sext. Emp., *Adv. Math.* 8.97-98). So for the Stoics both conjunctions and articles will be parts of speech, since they have their counterpart in what would make the statement come out true and do not owe their existence merely to our way of speaking about the world.

If this is why the Stoics insisted that all words can be classified as parts of speech, then the very term "part of speech," as opposed to "part of diction," is meant to suggest that there is a correspondence between the parts of speech and the elements constitutive of *lekta*. It is because of this supposed correspondence that even conjunctions and articles can claim to be parts of speech. It is tempting to think that the Stoics not only assumed that something on the level of the *lekta* corresponded to the parts of speech but that the different parts of speech corresponded to the different elements of *lekta* kind by kind. Even Apollonius Dyscolus in one passage (*De pron.* 67.5-7) claims that the parts of speech should be distinguished according to what they signify, implying not only that all parts of speech have signification but also that each of them has a kind of signification peculiar to itself. The most important text in this connection is the part of Diocles' account in which we are given the definitions of the various parts of speech (D.L. 7.58). There the first three parts of speech are indeed distinguished by the different kinds of elements of *lekta* they signify; an appellative noun signifies a common quality, a proper name an individuating quality, a verb a certain kind of predicate.

So far, then, the assumption seems to be confirmed. It derives further confirmation from the fact that the Stoics, following Chrysippus, distinguished between appellative and proper names as two parts of speech, a distinction not accepted by Aristarchus, by Dionysius Thrax in the *Technē* (cf. though *Schol. in D.Th.* p. 160, 26-28 H.), and by later traditional grammar. For though differences in the inflectional pattern were claimed as evidence for the distinction, the main reason for it was clearly the difference between common and proper qualities.

Difficulties with the assumption that the parts of speech can be distinguished with reference to the kind of element of *lekta* to which they correspond arise with the fourth part of speech, the conjunction; it is defined syntactically and by its morphology. This complication seems to be owing to the following: the class of conjunctions is supposed to include both the conjunctions proper and the prepositions (cf. Apoll. Dysc., *De coni.* 214, 7-8). And it is difficult to see how one could specify one kind of signification for both conjunctions and prepositions. It is, of course, possible that in the representation of the form of *lekta* both conjunctions and prepositions could be represented by the same operator with a characteristic function in the syntax of *lekta*. And hence it would still be true that even to conjunctions in the broad Stoic sense there corresponds one kind of element of *lekta*. But unity of this kind would be due to the function of elements of this kind in the syntax, not to a common denominator in the signification of conjunctions. Since the Stoic Chaeremon was willing to speak of conjunctions in the case of expletive conjunctions, though they could not be regarded as sentence-connectives (cf. Apoll. Dysc., *De coni.* 248.1 ff.), it may also be the case that some Stoics were willing to admit that at least some conjunctions do not have signification. Hence such conjunctions would not be covered by a definition in terms of a supposed characteristic signification of conjunctions. But they would be covered by a definition of the kind given in Diocles' account.

Much more difficult to deal with are the so-called articles that include both our articles and pronouns (cf. Apoll. Dysc., *De pron.* 5.13). Part of the difficulty is that so far we do not have a clear view of how the Stoics treated articles, except that we know that they tried to construe the definite article as an indefinite pronoun. For reasons analogous to those in the case of conjunctions, we can understand why this class of articles cannot be characterized by what they signify in the way proper names, for example, can. But in their case it is even difficult to see how one could give plausibility to the claim that on the level of *lekta* there is one kind of element which corresponds to all articles. Hence it does not seem plausible to assume that the Stoics maintained a strict kind by kind correspondence between parts of speech and elements of *lekta*. But in this case the question arises how the parts of speech were identified, if not with reference to the kind of thing they signify. There cannot have been a clear answer to this question, for the parts of speech tended to proliferate, a proliferation associated with the Stoics in particular (cf. Quint., 1.4.19; Dion. Hal., 2.8-9; D.L. 7.57). As late as the second century A.D. Apollonius Dyscolus devoted a monograph to the problem of the division of the parts of speech, which unfortunately is not extant.[13] As it is we have very little evidence concerning the principles used by the Stoics to determine what is to count as a part of speech.[14]

In any case it is clear that the Stoics had a strong interest in the parts of speech. They wrote special treatises on the subject long before the grammarians, and they even devoted monographs to individual parts of speech, as we can see from Posidonius's *On conjunctions* (Apoll. Dysc., *De coni.* 214.4). The next question, then, is what they dealt with under the parts of speech. Since this was a matter of debate, we may assume that they would discuss the division of the parts of speech. Under each part they would presumably discuss the appropriate definition of this part of speech. Given that they insisted that all the parts of speech have signification, they would have to discuss the signification characteristics of the part of speech in question. In the case of conjunctions and articles this would immediately lead to a distinction of various kinds of conjunctions and articles. We can see in Dionysius Thrax how the conjunctions proper are classified, obviously under Stoic influence, according to their signification (p. 87, 1 ff); the Stoic influence is apparent from the logical terminology.

Another topic that would be raised under the relevant parts of speech are the so-called accidents or secondary grammatical categories like gender, number, case, tense. Barwick (*Remmius Palaemon* 97 f., 107 f.) has argued that the very term "accident" in this use is of Stoic origin. This may very well be so, but the explanation given for the use of the term seems to be doubtful: supposedly the accidents are accidental in the Aristotelian sense; it is not essential for a word to appear with particular accidents; a noun remains the same noun whether it appears in the singular or the plural, the dative or the nominative.[15] The fact that Greek grammarians standardly use the term "consequents" (*parepomena*) instead of "accidents" suggests that, to use Aristotelian terminology again, these accidents in one respect are thought of as being rather like per se accidents in the way oddness and evenness are per se accidents of number; just as natural numbers come as odd or even, so a noun necessarily comes in one of the cases, in one of the *numeri*, in one of the genders, and so forth. The word (the *genikon onoma*), to occur in a concrete context, has to take on a determination in each of the relevant secondary categories; a noun, for example, would have to take on determinations with reference to number, case, gender, and whatever other accidents of nouns one may want to distinguish. Which particular accidents the Stoics distinguished under the various parts of speech is so far unclear. Similarly one would wish to know whether and to what extent the Stoics discussed syntax under the parts of speech, or inflection.

But in any case it seems to be fairly clear that, even given the doctrine of the parts of speech, more needed to be said about the grammatically adequate choice of words. To avoid barbarisms, that is, mistakes about individual words rather than their composition, more had to be taken into account than what had been laid down in the doctrine of the parts of speech. There is no guarantee that a word that satisfies the conditions specified under the relevant part of speech is not, nevertheless, a barbarism as defined in D. L. 7.59. A barbarism is the use of an expression "against the usage of those Greeks who have a good reputation." This definition seems to suggest that "Hellenism," beyond the doctrine of the parts of speech and syntax, is not a technical matter, to be covered by rules and theorems, but rather a matter of long familiarity with good authors. From this, one gets some kind of feeling for the proper choice of words and phrases.

On the other hand there is evidence that the Stoics were more ambitious than this and had some sympathy for those grammarians who thought that even this aspect of the choice of words could be captured by rules of art. It is well known that the Stoics were the main proponents of the study of etymology. We also know that etymology was regarded as one of the most promising tools to test the "Hellenicity" of an expression (cf. Sext. Emp., *Adv. Math.* 1.241 ff.). To understand how the Stoics could use etymology as a criterion for the "Hellenicity" of a word, one has to know something about the Stoic doctrine of the origin of language, another dark matter, complicated by the fact that important testimonies concerning the subject (like Ptolemaeus' *De criterio*, p. 7, 18 ff. Lammert) present positions whose origin is not easily identified.

In the old controversy whether names are significant by nature or by convention the Stoics took the view that the relation between names and what they signify is natural (cf. Origen, *Contra Celsum* 1.24. p. 74.13K). That immediately raised the objection that, if this were so, we should expect all human beings to use basically the same language. But the Stoics clarified their thesis by saying, it seems, that names are not formed by nature; they are not, for example, fully determined by the nature of human beings and the nature of things; rather they are formed by human imposition, which may differ from group to group, and hence would produce different languages. Nevertheless names are natural because they have been imposed in such a way that they naturally reflect the nature of things by somehow imitating them.[16] To bring such an imposition about it took wise men who had grasped the nature of things and who knew how best to impose names (cf. Philo, *De opif. mundi* 148; *Quaest. in Genes.* 1.20). And being wise they would arrange this imposition in the most reasonable way possible. If the same things in different cases, for example, Socrates in the dative and Socrates in the accusative, had different names, say "Sophroniscus" and "Philoxenus," or if related things like Athens and the Athenians, justice and the just, running and the runner, did not have systematically related names, we would not be able to remember the correct names of things and hence would never learn the language (Varro, *De lin. lat.* 8.5). Varro mentions Cosconius who had said that if there were one thousand primitive words, there could be five hundred thousand words or word-forms by derivation (*De lin lat.* 6.36; cf. 37); and he goes on to explain that one could easily have as many as five million different forms if one took prefixes into account (6.38). Hence the wise man puts down a certain number of basic, primitive names, and then has everything systematically related to what is named by the primitive words named by systematically related names. The original imposition of names is at first accepted by the whole community. For at this early, incorrupt stage of society its members are at least reasonable enough to recognize the superiority of the wise who, for this reason, will also be kings.[17] This would seem to answer the Epicurean objection as to how the mysterious name-giver could be supposed to make his fellow human beings adopt his names.[18]

Given such a picture of the origin of our languages, it is apparent how one could try to establish the Hellenicity of a word: it is necessary to show that it is one of the original impositions of the wise responsible for the origin of Greek, or that it is systematically derived from one of the original impositions. And in this way etymology, which is the doctrine of the original impositions and the derivatives from them, could be thought to serve as a criterion for the Hellenicity of a word. A word derived from a Latin or Persian primitive will be disqualified unless some special justification is given why it should be accepted after all. Now the fact that a word somehow can be traced to a Greek primitive word only shows that it is somehow Greek rather than barbarian. But the mere existence of some historical causal link between a word and a Greek primitive surely does not qualify an expression as a proper Greek word. The derivation of nonprimitives from primitives has to follow certain rules.

We noted above that the name-givers proceeded economically: they envisaged two kinds of derivation, inflection (*klisis*) and derivation in a narrow sense (*paragōgē*). Inflection we have, for example, in the case of declension or conjugation; derivation we have in cases like "Romulus"-"Rome," "Rome"-"Roman," or "justice"-"just." It would be difficult, though very important, to make the distinction precise; important, for example, because the question what is to count as one word will depend on where we draw the line between inflection and derivation. In addition to these two kinds of derivation, we shall also have to have assumptions about the phonetic changes words may undergo in their history, if we are to have any chance of retracing the derivation of a word to its origin (cf. Varro, *De lin lat.* 5.6; Aug., *Princ. dial. c.* 1321A).

Derivation in the narrow sense seems to have been guided by two sets of principles, one covering the relation in meaning between terms in the derivational chain, the other covering the phonetic relations. The first set of principles seems to conform to Stoic notions about the associations of ideas and the formation of concepts. It is assumed that, if a word A is used for x, then it is natural and reasonable that a derivative of A should be used for something similar to x or something in the vicinity of x or something contrary to x. How exactly derivatives of patronyms and the like were fitted into this scheme is unclear. The principles governing the phonetic changes in the chain similarly seem to have been rather loose and mechanical. The changes allowed include the dropping of letters, the acquisition of letters, and the change of letters (Varro, *De lin. lat.* 6.2).

If the principles of word-derivation in the narrow sense are so loose as to lead to absurd derivations and to expose Stoic etymology to ridicule, inflection was so obviously guided by more stringent principles that any work on inflection could not fail to be more successful than Stoic etymology. The declension of nouns, for example, shows a striking amount of regularity. This basic regularity was generally accepted, but its precise nature, status, and explanation were a matter of some dispute. The participants in this dispute are called "analogists" and "anomalists" depending on whether they stress the regularity, or even demand the elimination of anomalies, or whether they stress the anomalies and resist their elimination in texts and in speech.

Presumably the most important testimony concerning this debate comes from Varro's *De lingua latina* (9.1). According to Varro, the Stoic Crates takes the position of an anomalist and, relying for this on Chrysippus, argues against Aristarchus who had defended analogy. But, Varro says, Crates seems to have misunderstood both Chrysippus and Aristarchus: Chrysippus and Aristarchus are talking about different things when they discuss anomaly and analogy and hence are not really in disagreement. Aristarchus maintains that similar words should have a similar declension to the extent that usage permits this (Varro, *De lin. lat.* 9.1). And he tries to single out the relevant features with reference to which one could decide whether two nouns have the kind of similarity that would make us expect that they have the same declension. The features he suggests as relevant are six: gender, case, word-ending, number of syllables, accent, and figure (i.e., whether a word is simple or composite) (Charis. p. 149, 26 ff. Barwick). Obviously this set of features will not be sufficient if one tries to formulate a set of rules in terms of such features which will completely cover Greek declension; in fact no such nontrivial set will do. But later grammarians introduced more and more features to capture the analogy in declension. The point that needs to be emphasized in connection with Aristarchus is that he did not maintain that there could be a complete set of rules or canons in terms of such features. His claim that declension is governed by analogy is severely restricted by the qualification "to the extent that usage permits this." But this qualification tended to be overlooked later. In Gellius's report of the controversy, for example, Aristarchus's position is described as if the Alexandrian had defended the unqualified thesis. And it is clear from the extensive criticism by Sextus (*Adv. Math.* 1.176 ff.; cf. 1.97-99) that there was a faction among the grammarians who were tempted to "reform" ordinary language by regularizing its patterns of inflection against established usage.

Chrysippus, on the other hand, says Varro, maintained that language is anomalous because similar things are referred to by dissimilar names and similar names refer to things quite unlike each other. The anomaly Chrysippus had in mind seems to be of the following kind: "immortal" is formed by means of a privative prefix as if immortality were a privation (Simpl., *In cat.* 396, 5, ff., esp. 396, 19 ff.), Athens has a name in the plural though it is just one place (Sext. Emp., *Adv. Math.* 1.154), words do not have their natural gender, and so on. Chrysippus devoted a special treatise to such anomalies (D.L. 7.192). This insistence by Chrysippus on anomaly has tended to be misunderstood, as if Chrysippus thought that language is utterly irregular and irrational.

Varro suggests (*De lin. lat.* 91) that the positions of Chrysippus and Aristarchus are perfectly compatible, and that hence Crates misunderstood them; and this is certainly true if we just go by Varro's characterization of their positions. But we may wonder whether Crates could have been so entirely wrong on the matter. As the later history of work on declension shows, Aristarchus was not just overoptimistic when he thought that six features would be sufficient to formulate canons of declension, and that the odd exception could be written off as being due to usage. Chrysippus seems to have taken a much dimmer view of the possibility of bringing order into the system of declensions. For according to Varro (*De lin. lat.* 10.59) he said that only sometimes it is possible to reconstruct the nominative from an oblique case or an oblique case from the nominative. This difference in attitude could make a great difference in the establishment of texts, where one constantly has to decide whether one is facing another anomaly or a corruption.

Moreover, the reason why the positions of Chrysippus and Aristarchus appear to be quite compatible is that Chrysippus is concerned with the anomaly between meaning and word-form, whereas Aristarchus is concerned with the analogy between word-forms in inflection. But the very fact that Aristophanes of Byzantium and Aristarchus try to establish classes of nouns with analogous declension, without reference to the meaning of the nouns, may invite criticism by the Stoics. The Stoics may have argued that in a rationally constructed language the different declensions should have a semantic function; that hence the classes of analogous nouns should be set up with a view to some such function; and that, if this did not turn out to be feasible, this just showed the amount of anomaly pervading the declension system, anomaly exactly of the kind Chrysippus had talked about when he pointed out that the correspondence between inflection or word-form and meaning often breaks down. That the Stoics may have argued in this way can be seen from the fact that they tried to show that proper names and common nouns differ in declension; that is, the difference between individuating and common qualities is supposed to be reflected by the declension of the names that stand for these qualities (*Schol. in D. Th.* 214.19 ff., 356.27 ff.; Charis., 80.1 ff. Barwick). In fact, Varro himself tells us (*De lin. lat.* 10.68) that Aristophanes had written on analogy in declension exactly in the sense in which Chrysippus stressed anomaly. And Aristarchus, too, on the basis of analogy in this sense, argued for the accent *pterýgos* rather than *ptérygos* in Homer B 316 and Ψ 875. Hence Crates may have had good reason, after all, to see a conflict between the Alexandrian and Stoic positions on this matter. But even if he was mistaken, it does not seem to make much sense to deny that he managed to start a lively controversy. For otherwise it is difficult to understand why the relative claims of analogy and usage should be given such attention in Sextus, Quintilian, and Varro.

That Stoic etymology did not find general acceptance, and that the debate concerning analogy and anomaly did not come to a decisive conclusion meant, of course, that attempts along these lines to establish criteria for the "Hellenicity" of words did not result in a generally recognized *technē*. Given the lack of satisfactory criteria, the Stoics seem to have taken a conservative attitude toward ordinary language, which would be reinforced by their notion of style. Hence the notion underlying their definition of barbarism in Diocles (D.L. 7.59) may be more representative of their position than it first seemed: in the choice of words and their forms we have to follow the usage of good authors.

V

We are left with the doctrine of the parts of speech and a syntax as the two parts of Stoic grammar sufficiently elaborated and established. These two more or less amount to a grammar. They correspond to what was done later in antiquity under the title of "grammar," which, in turn, corresponds to traditional grammar. There is good reason to believe that the Stoics had a notion of grammar and that they came to pursue the study of the parts of speech and syntax as parts of this discipline. Hence there seems to be a fairly straightforward and strong sense in which we may speak of Stoic grammar. It is a discipline pursued by the Stoics as part of their philosophy; partly for historical, but also for systematic reasons, it is so much embedded in their dialectic that we had considerable difficulties finding it and isolating it from its context. In its details it is very much influenced by philosophical views concerning meaning, reference, the origin and rationality of language, metaphysical views concerning facts, states of affairs, qualities, and individuals, and finally by Stoic logic in a narrow sense. Hence there is such a subject as Stoic grammar, and it would deserve a treatment that incorporates the material uncovered since Schmidt's monograph appeared almost 140 years ago. But such a treatment should not approach the topic as if it were from the outside; it should reconstruct a Stoic notion of grammar as a part of Stoic philosophy and follow its natural articulation; and it should do more justice to the connections between Stoic grammar and other parts of their philosophy. The effort is worthwhile, especially since there is reason to believe that traditional grammar has its origin in Stoic grammar. Many of the real or apparent incongruities of traditional grammar should appear in a different light once we have a better understanding of the philosophical background.

NOTES

1. Cf. Sextus Empiricus, *Adv. math.* 8.12, 13, 75; Plut., *Adv. Col.* 1119 f.; Philo, *Leg. All.* 2.15; Philop., *In an. pr.* 243, 2 ff.; Ammon., *In an. pr.* 68, 5 ff.;

Alex., *In soph. el.* 20, 29 ff. and Stob., *Ecl.*, 1.137, 6W.; Simpl., *In cat.* 209, 13; Clem., *Strom.*, 8.9 p. 97, 6-7.

2. Stob., *Ecl.* 1. 137, 4 W.

3. Stob., *Ecl.* 1. 136, 21 ff. W.; cf. D.L. 7.60; *Orig.*, *In Joh.* 2, 13, 93; cf. also Simpl., *In cat.* 105, 8 ff.; Syr., *In met.* 106, 7 ff.

4. Cf. also the *elementa loquendi* in Cic., *Ac. pr.* 24. 92.

5. Though, for a different arrangement, cf. D.L. 7.41, 49 and 55.

6. On the whole matter cf. Sext. Emp., *P.H.* 2. 194, 247; Ammon., *In an. pr.* 9, 27.

7. Cf., e.g., Arist. *Rhet.*, 1404b5; 1407a20 ff.; the whole of *Rhet. ad Alex.* 25; *Poet.* 20; for the *Technē* of Isocrates (?) cf. Syrianus, *In Hermog.* 1, 28, 6 ff. Rabe = Radermacher, *Artium Scriptores* B 24. 22.

8. As noted above, the remark in D.L. 7.44 that according to some Stoics definition and division do not belong to this part of dialectic (cf. also D.L. 7.41) would justify the suggestion that the sections in D.L. 7. 60-62 on definition, concepts, genus, species, division, and partition were not regarded as forming part of the core of the theory of expressions. One may have doubts concerning poetry— on which see D.L. 7.44 and 60. These doubts are easily removed since for this section on poetry Diocles refers to a treatise by Posidonius entitled *Introduction to Diction;* but more on this below.

9. Cf. K. Barwick, *Remmius Palaemon* 95 ff.

10. Charisius, p. 192, 20-193, 2 Barwick; Diomedes p. 326, 30-35; p. 420, 24 ff.

11. Dion. Hal., *De comp. verb.* 4, 31; Apollonius Dyscolus, *De coni.* 213, 8 ff.

12. The basis for this in Aristotle is presumably chap. 20 of the *Poetics*. There (1456b20 f.) the parts of speech occur in a list of parts of diction, and both conjunctions and articles are said to lack signification (1456b38 f.; 1457a6 f.).

13. For the testimonies and fragments cf. *Grammatici Graeci*, vol. 2. 3, ed. Schneider-Uhlig.

14. Cf. Schol. in D. Th. 214, 19 ff.; 356, 27 ff.; Charis, p. 80, 1 ff. Barwick; Apoll. Dysc., *De pron.* 5. 20 ff.; *De coni.* 214, 17 ff:; 248. 1 ff.

15. Barwick, *Probleme der stoischen Sprachlehre und Rhetorik* 48; A.C. Lloyd, "Grammar and Metaphysics in the Stoa," 59, in A. A. Long, *Problems in Stoicism.*

16. *Orig.*, *Contra Celsum* 1.24; Ammon., *In de int.* 35. 1 ff.; 30, 23 ff.; Aug., *Princ. dial. c.* 1319A ff.; cf. Procl., *In Crat.* 8. 1 ff., 8. 7 ff.; Dion. Hal., *De comp. verb.* p. 62, 9-12; Varro, *De lin. lat.* 6.3; Philo, *Quaest. in Genes.* 1.20; Diogenes of Oenoanda, fr. 10, c. 3, 9 ff. Chilton.

17. Cf. Varro, *De lin. lat.* 5. 8, 9; Philo, *De opif. mundi* 148; *Quaest in Genes.* 1. 20.

18. Diog. Oen., fr. 10, c. IV f.; if we take this passage, as suggested, to be a criticism of the Stoic view, it seems that in 4. line 11 we should restore *basilees* with Heberdey and Kalinka.

3

The Stoic Theory of Meaning

Andreas Graeser

Whether or not the Stoics conceived of any "science" correspond-ing in scope and methods to formal semantics in the sense described, for example, by J. Moravcsik[1] seems hard to determine. Evidence regarding this issue is scanty, particularly in view of the fact that some of the isolated testimonies relating to the Stoic theory of meaning are extremely difficult to assess and still require a good deal of extensive analysis. From the meager reports con-cerning the bare essentials of this theory as incorporated into later manuals and elsewhere, it would appear, however, that in the course of their school's history the Stoics developed a fairly de-tailed semantic theory. It is a theory of meaning that has invited comparison with modern theories and obviously stood it well. In fact, it is generally agreed that the Stoic account of semantics is superior to and more sophisticated than the more influential one offered by Aristotle in the *De Interpretatione* (16a3-18).[2] It is also considered to figure among the very few definitely modern-minded contributions to the systematic study of philosophical problems carried out by ancient Greek thinkers.

Semantics in general, according to Stoic philosophers, seems to be an integral part of what they called "Logic" or "Dialectic" re-spectively, that is, the study of the utterance and the study of the utterance as meaningful. It is integral inasmuch as the Stoic conception of logic is one that depends again on their theory of meaning. In the analysis of meaning three components seem to have been distinguished. The components or aspects under consideration are: first, the sign (*sēmainon*, i.e., that which signifies) which is a phoneme or grapheme; second, the significate (*sēmainomenon*, i.e., that which is signified) which is expressed by the sound and which we apprehend as it arises in our mind; and third, the external object referred to.

It is this semantic triad, as reported by the skeptic philosopher Sextus Empiricus (*Adv. math.* 8. 11-13) which has been considered in terms of reference to modern theories such as the ones proposed by G. Frege ("sign"-"sense"-"reference") and R. Carnap ("designator"-"intension"-"extension").[3]

Like the modern theoreticians the Stoics meant these concepts to apply to whole sentences as well as to their parts, and since according to its classification in a respective category each linguistic sign is, in Stoic theory, indicative of a meaning which is said to subsist with our thought, they held that there are entities as intensions for, or rather various types of significates corresponding to, the various kinds of expression. Now with regard to the level of expression, that is, significant speech that indicates the "thing thought" (*to nooumenon pragma*), the Stoics were accustomed to recognize at least four "elements" or "parts" that are, in fact, classifications of words of which it seems proper to speak in terms of syntactic categories. They were labeled as *proper name* or *common name* respectively, *verb, connective particle* (including prepositions), and *demonstrative pronoun* (including definite articles). These syntactic categories seem to have semantic counterparts. That is to say, the much discussed terms *subject, qualification, disposition*, and *relation*[4] are probably meant to serve as classifications of the basic types of meaning signified by linguistic expressions according to their classification in different syntactic categories. Thus a sign belonging to the class of significant expressions referred to by "proper name" (*onoma*) signifies a meaning that conveys what some Stoics seem to have called "individual quality," such as Socrates, whereas a sign belonging to the class of words called "common name" (*prosēgoria*) is indicative of meaning that conveys what was thought of as "common quality," such as horse, man, and the like. Let us next consider *verb:* the Greek technical term is *rhēma,* which even before Plato had been taken to denote a sign that indicates any affection of the subject named or anything that characterizes it. A *rhēma* in Stoic theory signifies a predicate (*katēgorēma*). It is by no means sure, however, whether or not the Stoics managed to take into account predicative expressions consisting of an adjective (or noun) and the copula. In any case, from the semantic point of view the verb undoubtedly belongs with the category called disposition. We know that the Stoics liked to explain states of affairs referred to by a sentence expressing a proposition such as "Socrates is running" in terms of reference to the subject's soul being in certain disposition. And there is good reason to suppose that their attributing a disposition to something individually qualified has to be related to their view of the external world as a moving continuum.[5]

While it is not difficult to see that the categories called *qualification* and *disposition* respectively were meant to serve as classifications of the basic types of meanings carried by any expression belonging to the respective categories called *name* and *verb,* less evidence is available in the case of the categories called *subject* and *relation.* Without entering into the discussion of the intricate theory of articles and pronouns, we may call attention to the fact that within the range of what they called "definite articles" the Stoics recognized a subclass the members of which apparently approximate B. Russell's notion of "logically proper name." In fact, as the truth of a singular proposition, such as the one expressed by "Socrates is running," depends on the truth of a corresponding "definite proposition" in which the subject referred to is indicated by a demonstrative pronoun, it seems sound to infer that the definite article corresponds to the category called *subject.* As for the category called *relation,* one may feel tempted to make use of what the Stoics called *syndesmoi.* Yet "connective particles" (including prepositions) cannot be presumed to carry meanings of their own. In fact, Aristotle is said to have maintained that connective particles have syncategorematic meanings only, and therein express a relation that actual carriers of meaning have to one another. However, the Stoics might well have held a different opinion. We do not know for sure. On the whole it would make more sense to allow for the possibility that the Stoics, when think-

ing of *relation,* had in mind meanings such as the ones signified by
transitive verbs or expressions for two-place-predicates.

The Stoic theory of syntax and semantics clearly suggests a correspondence between linguistic expressions as carriers of meaning
and the meanings themselves signified by them. But how do these
meanings relate to reality? Inasmuch as the meaningful language
always implies a connection between word and reality, and as the
meanings themselves signified by words apparently were conceived of as thoughts that mind naturally tends to impose on
reality,[6] and as the Stoics may have believed that the true proposition has a structure corresponding to a similar structure in the
object described,[7] one may be tempted to assume that features of
description were therefore features of nature.[8] This is particularly
true since the Stoics shared Heraclitus's belief that *Logos* was part
of nature; they also claimed that language was "by nature." Unlike
Aristotle, however, whose categories were partly about language
and partly about reality, but basically about "things-that-are"
(*onta*), the Stoics conceived the total sum of existence in terms of a
moving continuum and thus were not likely to conceive of the
denotations of meaningful expressions as natural classes of extralinguistic entities. They were not likely to commit themselves to
the position that physical existents belong to one appropriate category only. That is to say, in referring to things as being particulars
of such-and-such kind, we must be aware that we are approaching
reality through predicates and propositions and that we are talking about segments of the total universe, and that it is our mind
that divides and articulates reality, arriving at logical constituents
even where the physical components are inseparable.[9] Hence it is
by meaningful language which always implies a connection between word and reality that we articulate reality. To talk about
something as being in a certain disposition need not prevent us
from talking about it in terms of reference to something individually qualified.[10] Accordingly, the categories that serve as classifications of the basic types of meanings signified by expressions
according to their classification in different syntactic categories
may be called general reference classes.[11]

We may conclude then that according to its classification in a
respective category, each linguistic sign is, in Stoic theory, indicative of a meaning which is said to subsist with our thought and

taken to reveal something about the manner in which the outside object is being given. While the linguistic sign and the external object were both held to be corporeal, the thing that is signified is supposedly incorporeal, and thus not capable of acting or being acted upon.

There arise, as a matter of course, quite a few problems concerning the exact status of what the Stoics understood by "things meant" or "things which are signified." For the time being we may settle with the notion that all things signified (*sēmainomena*), be it the meanings carried by isolated expressions such as nouns and verbs, or the meanings expressed in well-formed sentences, were thought of as incorporeal entities alike. These linguistic contents somehow happen to exist, although it is quite obvious that they were not held to be "real existents" in the sense in which physical bodies were said to "exist." For to exist is, according to Stoic ontology, to be capable of prompting a rational presentation, one that can be articulated in speech. And to be capable of prompting such a rational presentation is to be a three-dimensional solid. With regard to matters of existence, the Stoics are known to have assumed an essentially materialist position. However, the "things that are signified" somehow exist, but whether primarily as linguistic entities wedded to the phonetic sign and/or as some kind of mental entities comparable, perhaps, to the *ideas* of classical British empiricism or even as some kind of metaphysical entities existing independently from the mind remains to be seen.

So far it would seem perfectly right to say that in their analysis of meaning the Stoics anticipated the modern distinction between, say, "sense" or "connotation" on the one hand and "reference" or "denotation" on the other. And from what is generally known about Stoicism one would certainly expect the Stoics to have held that we usually intend to talk about something more than just our ideas.

It is not clear, however, if they actually had available to them a word for expressing our concept of denotation. For the traditional verb for semantic relations, *sēmainein*, on a par with our verbs "mean," "signify," "designate," and so on, in Stoic semantics stands exclusively for a relation that holds between the linguistic sign and its sense. The Stoics disliked linguistic ambiguities. And, unlike Aristotle, they would not have found it possible to say, for instance, "a particular something signifies substance." Aristotle's use of the term "signify" is at the very least highly ambiguous, and he certainly lacks a clear distinction between "sense" and "reference" or "connotation" and "denotation" respectively. In any case, as far as the evidence is concerned, *sēmainein* in Stoic usage never means "denote" but "connote" and thus invokes the notion of what appears to be a fundamentally nonreferential or rather intensional theory of meaning. Thus making the traditional and fairly general term *sēmainein* designate a relation that holds between the sign and its sense, the Stoics were quite likely to lack a word for expressing our concept of denotation.

To this it may be objected, however, that according to the testimony of Diocles Magnes as recorded by Diogenes Laertius (7. 58), Diogenes of Babylon, a later Stoic, when talking about the function peculiar to proper names, uses the verb *dēloun* ("reveal," "indicate"). In fact, he is reported to have held that what proper names do is to "reveal" or "indicate" an individual quality, whereas common names "signify" common qualities, that is, attributes belonging to more than just one individual. There is a curious switch from "reveal" or "indicate" to "signify" which may or may not be intentional. Now if what the proper name "Socrates" stands for in this context is what we call the denotation of a singular concrete term, *dēloun* ought to mean, of course, "denote." If, however, the so-called individual quality Socrates is something more akin to the sense of an individual expression ("teacher of Plato, married to Xanthippē," etc.) or to what may be called an individual concept, *dēloun* cannot be supposed to be on a par with our "denote." This would be true regardless of a possible ambiguity of the word "denote" which has been pointed out by M. White.[12] Now *dēloun* is a word Plato uses in the *Cratylus* when discussing the proposition that words do not merely "name" but also "mean": correct names supposedly convey the essence or true nature of the object referred to.[13] So *dēloun* does not really seem fit to express the concept of denotation. Rather it "means," in the sense in which G. Frege suggested that a word like "evening star" does not merely *denote* (the planet Venus) but also conveys the mode of the object's presentation. However, this does not yet solve our problem. For the so-called qualities were ordinarily thought of as physical bodies, capable of acting and being acted upon, whereas the linguistic content expressed by a significant sound was considered as an incorporeal entity. And as proper names were apparently held to indicate such qualities in the outside world, one may indeed be tempted to argue that the objects under consideration are, of course, denoted[14] rather than connoted and that, accordingly, the verb *dēloun* should be taken as a term expressing the concept of denotation. This would seem true particularly since Sextus's account of the semantic triad, in which the person Dion is introduced as the external object referred to by the expression "Dion," suggests that what proper names do is to name the external object. However, Sextus also records that according to Stoic theory the expression "Dion" signifies an incorporeal meaning. Moreover there is no bona fide evidence to the effect that the Stoics held that strictly what proper names do is refer to the external object.

On the contrary, there is evidence to the effect that proper names were not even considered as sufficient means of referring. This can be seen from the Stoic account of the truth of the basic type of singular propositions on whose truth depends that of others. The Stoics held that the "indefinite proposition" ("Someone is walking") and the "intermediate case" with a proper name or a common noun (i.e., "Socrates is walking," "A man is walking") become true when a corresponding "definite proposition" is true of a subject presently existing, indicated by *deixis* (i.e., "This (man) is walking"). In fact, Chrysippus is also known to have claimed that the proposition asserted by the sentence "This man is dead" is impossible since "this" always refers to something existing in virtue of the deictic pronoun. But the proposition asserted by the sentence "Dion is dead" is possible. If the sentence is true, there is no denotation for "Dion"; yet the sentence is significant.[15]

From this we may infer that only deictic pronouns were taken to refer in any strict sense, whereas names, as J. Pinborg asserts, always signify something along with their reference, in this aspect partaking in the properties of a predicate.[16] (While the deictic pronouns approximate B. Russell's notion of "logically proper name," the Stoic treatment of proper names reminds one of W. V. Quine's procedure for the elimination of proper names in favor of predicates[17] on the grounds that they are not needed for a language that is regimented so as to be lucid and to be able to express the truths of the sciences.) Accordingly, when Diogenes is said to have maintained that proper names "indicate" individual qualities, it seems reasonable to suppose that he did not mean to claim that proper names denote qualities, but held that the qualities under consideration are incorporeal meanings signified along with the reference. Accordingly, the verb *dēloun* would, on this interpretation, have to be taken as a term being on a par with our "connote" rather than as a possible term for expressing the concept of denotation.

Did the Stoics then have no available linguistic means of expressing what we would call denotation or reference? There are scholars who seem to imply that they did. The verb under consideration in *tynchanein* which in ordinary Greek occurs in two different types of grammatical environment. Used intransitively followed by a participle it means "happen to. . . ." Construed as a transitive verb with a direct object in the dependent genitive it could mean "get (something)," a name for instance.[18] It has been suggested that the external objects that were called *tynchanonta*— usually taken in the sense of "things happening to exist"—were so called precisely because they are the sort of things referred to by names.[19] Adopting the participle *tynchanonta* in this way rather than as short for "things happening to exist" seems ingenious and in a way more suggestive than assuming that the external objects were called *tynchanonta* for the very reason that "we happen to be talking about them."[20]

What we know, however, is that the Stoics may have used the verb *tynchanein* in the sense of "get (something)" to express the notion that something gets a *ptōsis*, that is, the type of meaning signified by a noun in the nominative case. This is something entirely different. For what they meant is then probably not that some object gets (and thus has) a name, but that something gets (and thus has) a linguistic content. No matter what the precise sense of the difficult term *ptōsis* may have been, thinking of external objects as getting a meaning "in order to be expressed" (Pinborg) does not seem to make much sense. Now at one place Sextus speaks of things as falling under a *ptōsis*, that is, under a concept (*Adv. math.* 11. 20). However, this does not yet make the expression "get a *ptōsis*" mean "be referred to."

The whole matter as it stands is in need of clarification. Some clarification can be gained, perhaps, from the controversial lines concluding a famous criticism of the Platonists' contention that there exist entities such as the ones called *ideas*. Roughly translated the crucial lines read as follows: "The ideas are without foundation; mental images we have, the meanings of nouns (*ptôseis*) belong to (i.e., are got by) what they [i.e., the Stoics] called common names" (SVF 1, 65). Read this way[21] the notoriously difficult piece of Greek suggests that the linguistic contents of general terms, that is, the meanings of expressions for predicates, do not exist as extralinguistic entities, and that the Platonist entities called *ideas* cannot exist as entities in their own right precisely because they are hybrids between the sense of a sign and its associated idea. They collapse into two kinds of things entirely different in nature. In any case, if the Stoic account of the Platonist notion of *idea* does in fact derive from the premise that Plato failed to distinguish between the sense of a sign and its associated idea, it would seem fair to infer that what the Stoics took the *idea* to be in the first place was some hybrid, a cross between what they considered to be a linguistic entity and a mental entity respectively. Therefore, the lines under consideration suggest that "get a *ptôsis*" is being used here to express the notion that the meaning signified belongs to the sound signifying it. In other words, it is not some external object referred to by name that "gets" a meaning but the sound uttered. Otherwise the Stoic argument would seem to be pointless.

Consider also the following sophism, not included in the collection of *Stoicorum Veterum Fragmenta*: " 'Whatever you say passes through your mouth' is true, as everybody will concede. 'You say house, thus a house passes through your mouth'—which is false. We do not say the house, which is corporeal, but the incorporeal meaning (*ptôsis*) which house gets" (Clement, *Strom.* 8. 9. 26. 1). It has been seriously doubted whether the solution offered by Clement is at all plausible. In fact, in view of a possible allusion to the same sophism in Augustine (*De Quantitate Animae* 32), where only a distinction between the thing denoted and the sound is mentioned, it has been suggested that the solution offered by Clement must be wrong, since what goes through the mouth is not the thought which is expressed by the noun but the noun itself; and that is a body, namely battered air.[22] This may be true, although it is hard to see how the objection can purport to be to the point. For the sophism clearly draws from a Stoic distinction between *utter* and *say*. According to this distinction what is being uttered are noises, that is, vocal sounds that are, of course, corporeal, while "say" was defined as "utter sounds which signify the thing thought" (cf. Sextus, *Adv. math.* 8. 80). However, what is *said* are not corporeal sounds signifying but things that are signified, that is, the incorporeal meaning which in the case of the noun "house" is a *ptōsis*. In other words, what is *said* is neither the linguistic sign "house" nor, of course, some spatio-temporal object to which this term may apply, but the linguistic content of the sign "house" which itself is not a house. And the house in question which is supposed to "get the *ptōsis*" is not the external object called house but the linguistic sign "house" to which the meaning is wedded. Yet the linguistic content of the sign "house" must, of course, not in turn be called house.

From what has been said so far it would seem that "get a meaning" is not at all likely to mean "be referred to"[23] and thus cannot be considered as a possible term for expressing the concept of denotation. Rather it expresses a relation that is supposed to hold between the linguistic sign and its content.

However, we still have not made up for the absence of a word for expressing the concept of denotation. If this peculiar absence is not simply due to bad philological luck, there should be some explanation for it. And there is. It is one that relates to the Stoic view concerning the truth of the basic type of singular propositions called "definite propositions" on whose truth depends that of the others. As the simple definite proposition is held to become true when the predicate, e.g., walking, belongs to the thing falling under the demonstrative, it is clear that proper names were not considered as sufficient means for referring. From this it would appear that the Stoics were inclined to employ a rather narrow concept of denotation, such as the one based on the notion of *deixis*. That is to say, *deixis* may be taken as the Stoic equivalent of our terms "denotation" and "reference" provided it is borne in mind that what this notion of reference amounts to is that only *deictic* pronouns refer in any strict sense. Accordingly the verb *deiknunai*, which in ordinary Greek could mean anything from "show" to "prove," may be taken to mean "refer to" (cf. Sextus, *Adv. math.* 8. 96). It is by no means sure, however, whether the

Stoics actually used this very verb in the sense in which we may say that an expression "refers" to something. This sense is surely intended in the use of the adjective "deictic" in reference to the demonstratives. But unlike *sēmainein* the verb *deiknunai* itself does not seem to have been used for expressing a semantic relation. In any case, the notion that strictly only deictic pronouns refer would seem to make sense inasmuch as it may be consistent with what is commonly referred to as Stoic nominalism. The Stoics did not like abstract entities such as the Platonic forms or Aristotelian universals. But unlike modern antiplatonic logicians who wish to avoid postulating abstract entities wherever possible and thus claim that what a general term denotes is not a class but each individual of which it is true, the Stoics may have believed that subscribing to a full-blown extensionalist theory would be tantamount to committing oneself to the position that what, say, "man" denotes is the corresponding class, and that what expressions for two-place-predicates stand for are classes of well-ordered couples that merely exist upon reflection. However we do not know this.

The Stoics, then, held a fundamentally nonreferential or rather intensional theory of meaning, one in which meanings in general are viewed as linguistic contents isomorphically related to the respective sign on the level of expression. The general term for such linguistic contents was *lekton*. Presumably this term was, at times at least, meant to apply to both the linguistic content of isolated expressions such as nouns and verbs and the various types of meanings expressed by different kinds of sentences, becoming thus a synonym of *sēmainomenon*. However, as there is evidence to the effect that *lekton* was used in the sense of that which is said or predicated of something as well as in the more general sense of that which is said or meant, peculiar inconsistencies are encountered. What they seem to suggest is that the term *lekton* underwent a semantic development that is not altogether easy to trace.

Now *lekton*, being the neuter gender of the verbal adjective of *legein* ("say"), can mean both "what can be said" and "what is said." This too leaves us with a problem. For taking *lekton* to mean "that which can be said" may seem tantamount to committing oneself to the position that the *lekton* exists regardless whether it is being expressed or not, whereas taking *lekton* to mean "what is said" seems rather to entail that the very entity in question exists only as long as the expression that asserts it. Although the second option is more likely to get us near to what the Stoics were aiming at, a correct understanding of the term *lekton* is quite difficult to determine. And it is hardly surprising to realize that, as to the question of what precisely the *lekton* was supposed to stand for, modern authors are no less divided than were the ancients. There is in the process of the Latinization of Stoic terminology evidence to the effect that *lekton* was indeed adopted either way. For that it could be taken to mean "dicibile," Augustine is one of our sources (*De Dialectica* 4). And in the *Corpus Glossariorum Latinorum* (ed. G. Loewe and G. Götz 2. 41, 48) there is a note "*lekton* = *dicibile*." However, the isolated character of this note makes it quite impossible to decide whether or not *lekton* is meant here in the Stoic sense, whatever that may have been. And as for Augustine, who believes that prior to and independent of speaking there is something in the mind that may be expressed by speech,[24] and who thus clearly assumes some kind of *ante vocem*-position, it is a notorious question whether the overall theory that he proposes is fundamentally Stoic in character at all. It is generally agreed that he draws heavily on Varro. But Varro himself is a source even more difficult to assess. In any case, John of Salisbury, who mentions Augustine's *dictio-dicibile-res* distinction in his *Metalogicon* (3. 5) takes it without hesitation as drawn from Aristotle.[25] Another place where *lekton* is taken to mean *dicibile* is William of Moerbeke's translation[26] of Aristotle's influential work *De Interpretatione*. In his commentary Ammonius asserts that the things expressed primarily and immediately by nouns and verbs are, according to Aristotle, thoughts (i.e., *noēmata*), and that it is not necessary to conceive of anything intermediate between the thought and the external thing—as did the Stoics by positing what they called *lekton* (cf. SVF 2. 169). Ammonius's account of the *lekton* may be a little bit misleading. However, inasmuch as he seems to realize that the *lekton* is neither the word nor, of course, the subjective thought, but is meant as some connection that we express through language, Ammonius clearly recognizes an important point of difference between the Stoic and the Aristotelian theory of meaning. But as it stands it does not really help us understand precisely why William of Moerbeke thought that he had to translate *lekton* by *dicibile*.

There are, on the other hand, passages that show that *lekton* was also translated by *dictum*. This tendency can be traced back at least to Seneca (*Ep.* 117. 13). Seneca's account implies that *lekton* tended to be taken to mean *enuntiativum*, *effatum*, or *dictum*. Nuchelmans points further to Isidore of Seville (*Etymologiae* 2. 22) and Alcuin (*De Dialectica*, ed. Migne, 101. 953A) where the term *dialectica* is explained by reference to the fact that what it designates is concerned with *dicta*; and the *lekton* is called *dictio*. In other texts *lekton* is declared to mean the same as *dictum*, but apparently taken as that which is uttered. Even though the Greek term certainly could have this meaning too, it is rather obvious that this later identification of the *lekta* as sounds or speech in general cannot be considered a likely way of making sense of what the Stoics meant by this term. For according to Stoic theory the *lekta* are to be distinguished from any spoken sound, words or sentences, the use of which merely serves the function of identifying them.

As Sextus asserts that every *lekton* must be expressed in words, its existence somehow seems to be tied to "being apprehended and being said." This notion fits the general account of *lekton* as "that which subsists in conformity with a rational presentation (and a rational presentation being one in which what is presented can be conveyed in speech)" (*Adv. math.* 8. 70), and as "that which subsists according to a rational presentation" (D.L. 7. 51, 63); hence it suggests that the *lekton* exists only insofar as it is expressed in words. In fact, in Stoic usage the Greek language equivalent to our "subsist" clearly signifies what may be called a subordinate or rather dependent mode of existence, one that is distinct from being real in the sense of being tangible and thus capable of acting and being acted upon. From this it would appear that the *lekta* do not exist as entities in their own right and that they are not something in the world. Contrary to what is asserted by many scholars, pointing to the fact that the *lekta* are occasionally regarded as "being real" and hence should be recognized as real entities, this way of conceiving of the *lekta* as something that "subsists" does not conflict with their being called "real," a notion expressed by the use of the verb *hyparchein*. For this word, usually taken to

mean something on a par with our "be real," need not be treated as
a verb of existence—although it is certainly true that quite often it
simply means "exist," particularly when its participle is being used
as a noun. However, *hyparchein* also tends to be used in contexts
where it is clear that the thing said to be real is either a predicate
that is true of a subject or else a proposition asserted by a sentence.
This distinction must not be overlooked. Now since there is in
Greek ontological speculation—ever since Parmenides' reflection
on the nature of what is—a rather strong tendency to treat properties of statements as properties of the things referred to by the subject term of the respective sentence asserting what is supposed to
be the case, one may be tempted to doubt that ancient thinkers
were prepared to recognize the peculiar ambiguity exhibited by
their use of the verb *hyparchein*. However, from the fact that the
Stoics, unlike earlier thinkers who held that even *that*-clauses
name some real complex in the world, stressed that the *lekton* is
something incorporeal, it would appear that they were not liable
to this kind of confusion. Speaking of the *lekta* as "being real"
either in the sense in which a predicate may be declared to be true
of a subject or in that in which a proposition expressed in a sentence may be called "true" simpliciter, does not commit them (per
se) to the position that the *lekton* exists independently of the mind.

Therefore it seems best to take the term *lekton* to mean "what is
said" or "what is meant"[27] rather than "that which can be expressed."[28]

It has been said that *lekton*, becoming synonymous with *sēmainomenon*, embraces the content of any isolated expression as well
as the statement expressed by sentences. Accordingly, the Stoics
also spoke of "incomplete" or "deficient" *lekta* and "complete"
lekta respectively. While a verb surely conveys a meaning, it does
not convey a full meaning. For when a person says "runs" or "is
running" and thus expresses what the Stoics were used to calling a
predicate (*katēgorēma*), we feel that something is missing, and
hence want to know *who*. Hence the predicate, which together
with the linguistic content signified by a subject expression (i.e.,
the type of meaning called *ptōsis*), makes up a proposition, is said
to be a defective *lekton* which can be constructed with a nominative case in order to get a proposition (cf. D.L. 7. 64). It seems that
a predicate was seen, on this interpretation, as a kind of schema

for propositions: by filling in the name position and the given predicate one forms a full blown assertion.[29] But what about the semantic content of nouns? As far as the sources go only predicates were called "defective" *lekta*. There is no evidence to substantiate the claim that the meaning signified by a noun was called a "defective" or "incomplete" *lekton*, as has been tacitly assumed by, for example, B. Mates, M. Kneale, or G. Watson. In other words, it looks as if the *ptōseis*, that is the meanings of nouns in general, were not considered as species of defective *lekta*. It is true, however, that Sextus mentions the *sēmainomenon* Dion as an instance of *lekton* (cf. *Adv. math.* 8.11, 75). And as the so-called proposition that is held to be a complete *lekton* assertoric in itself is said to consist of *ptōsis* and *katēgorēma*,[30] most students of Stoic semantics incline themselves to taking *ptōsis* to be one kind of deficient *lekton*, predicates another. In fact, it must not be forgotten that the *ptōsis* is definitely conceived of as something incorporeal, and in this respect is treated on a par with any *lekton*. Hence Sextus mentions the individual concept "Dion" as a *lekton*; and Augustine gives subject terms as examples of deficient *lekta* (cf. *De Dialectica* 2).

There is thus no reason to conclude that the Stoics regarded the meanings of nouns as something categorically different from those of verbs. Yet A. A. Long is probably right to emphasize the difference between subject and predicate. They do have different semantic roles corresponding to their different grammatical functions; nouns somehow enable reference to be made to things, whereas verbs signify predicates or *lekta* that have to be combined with a *ptōsis* if a *lekton* is to be complete.[31] Now a possible solution to the problem concerning the extension of the term *lekton* may evolve from a consideration of its semantic development. For if it is true that *lekton* originally was taken to mean what is said or predicated of something, and in this respect was employed as a synonym of predicate, that is, an asomatic action or passion which is held to be true of some agent or patient, then it would seem plausible indeed that the type of meaning signified by nouns was not thought fit to be considered as a state said of a body. And inasmuch as the Stoics may have confined the meaning of the term *lekton* to what is said or predicated of something with regard to the category called disposition, they are quite likely not to have

applied this term to the linguistic content signified by nouns or to
the various types of meanings expressed by different kinds of sentences. This attitude may have changed, however, both because of
the subsequent treatment of names as expressions signifying something along with their reference—in this respect partaking in the
properties of a predicate—and because of some conceptual assimilation of states of affairs expressed by sentences to the logical
status of predicates signified by verbs.

Such a conceptual assimilation is not at all unlikely. For distinguishing various types of meanings signified by different kinds of
verbs, the Stoics mention what they call *parasymbama* or *paraka-
tēgorēma* respectively, that is, an oblique case predicate, one that
is said of something signified by a noun in an oblique case (e.g., "It
grieves Socrates"). Yet this type of predicate without a subject in
the nominative case certainly has to be regarded as a complete
statement. So it seems that in this distinction there was indeed
some confusion between types of predicates and types of propositions. It is a confusion that is reflected in the highly ambiguous use
of the verb *hyparchein* for expressing both that what a true proposition asserts is the case and that a predicate said of the subject is
true of it. Moreover, both predicates and states of affairs were
indiscriminately called "things" and "facts" (*pragmata*) and alike
regarded as incorporeal. To clarify this matter some Stoics seem to
have brought in another distinction, one between "complete"
things/facts and "incomplete" *facts/things* respectively. But it is
hard to see how this distinction could have done away with the
basic confusion between types of predicates and types of propositions after all.

In any case, like *pragma,* the term *lekton* too seems to have been
extended to the meanings postulated of linguistic expressions other
than verbs. In fact, elaborating the well-known Protagorean and
Aristotelian distinction of various speech functions (cf. *e.g.,
Poetics* 1456b9 ff.) the Stoics came to develop rather detailed classifications of complete *lekta.* From the account given by the source
of D.L. 7. 66 we learn that apart from the complete assertoric *lekta*
called *axiōmata* which are in some respects reminiscent of the
"propositions" that many modern philosophers postulate as meanings of eternal assertoric statements, "interrogation" (i.e., a yes-or-
no question the answer to which is given by a sentence expressing

an *axiōma*), "inquiry," "imperative," "adjurative," "optative," "hypothetical," and "vocative" were distinguished as varieties of complete *lekta*.

Whether or not this distinction of types of meanings was elaborated from a system of questions that were to be asked in connection with every subject,[32] and whether or not the Stoic doctrine is that a number of distinct linguistic jobs can be performed by a single sentence, depending on which of the complete *lekta* associated with that sentence is actually communicated on a given occasion of its use,[33] is hard to determine. Many students also claim that there is only slight evidence that the Stoics actually established the category of mood. This may be true; in any case, there is no need to enter a lengthy discussion of the relevant material handed down to us by later grammarians. However, considering the close association of the various types of meanings distinguished as varieties of complete *lekta* with different moods, there is a small point that may be of some more general interest. It is one that gives rise to the notion that it was probably precisely because of this rather rigid association of the various types of meanings with, for example, the indicative, imperative, and so forth, that when the Stoics spoke of what they called "prescriptive sentences" (*logoi prostaktikoi*) as verbal expressions of the mental act of assenting to value judgments or ethical propositions (i.e., "Yes, it is the case that x ought to be done") and when they thus considered them as possible carriers of truth values,[34] they failed to realize that, despite being associated with the indicative mood, prescriptive sentences somehow entail imperatives and are thus in this respect similar to genuine commands. In other words, the Stoics apparently held that there was a categorical difference between imperatives (*prostaktika*) on the one hand and prescriptive sentences (*logoi prostaktikoi*) on the other. And whereas for obvious reasons genuine imperatives were not considered as carriers of truth values, prescriptive sentences were thought of expressing complete assertoric *lekta*. (As to the question of how the Stoics came to think that ethical judgments in general are of the sort of things that can be true or false respectively, one possible answer would be that they subscribed to what is commonly referred to as ethical naturalism and thus held that terms like "good" do not lack "cognitive" or "descriptive" meaning. But as there is also evidence that the Stoics found it possible to say, for instance, "The universal Law prescribes . . .," they may well have maintained, as well as ethical maturalism, some form of metaphysical moralism. Accordingly, they would have claimed that ethical judgments are disguised statements of fact, such as can be established by means of propositions either prompted by "noetic presentations," that is, "received through the mind itself, as is the case with incorporeal things" [D.L. 7. 51], or else apprehended as "the conclusions of demonstration, for instance the existence of gods and their providence" [D.L. 7. 52].)

In any case, the complete assertoric *lekta* called *axiōmata* are in some respects reminiscent of the "propositions" that many modern philosophers postulate as meanings of eternal assertoric statements. They resemble propositions in that they are expressed by complete indicative sentences, in that they are true or false in the basic sense, and in that they are abstract, or as the Stoics put it, incorporeal, and in that they, or at least some of them, seem to exist in some way whether we think of them or not.[35] In fact, it has been suggested that the Stoic *axiōmata* approximate what Bolzano and Frege came to call *"Satz an sich"* and *"Gedanke"* respectively.[36] Aligning the Stoics with Plato, Leibniz, Bolzano, and Frege, K. R. Popper proposed that the complete assertoric *lekta* be recognized among what he calls "the most important third-world linguistic entities."[37] This view as it stands seems to be in need of some qualification. Even if we leave aside possible objections that may be raised against the well-known notion of *proposition*, it is probably important to realize that the Stoic *axiōmata* differ from the meanings postulated of eternal assertoric statements in that many, if not most of them, are temporally indefinite rather than eternal, timeless or omnitemporal. In other words, unlike analytic sentences that abstract from reference to particular objects or groups, unlike the timeless sentences of mathematics, and unlike Law-sentences that are omnitemporal and refer, if at all, to open classes, most of the sentences mentioned as expressing complete assertoric *lekta* such as "Dion is running" or "It is day" are definitely not temporally unrestricted. They are not on a par with the sentences to which we assent or from which we dissent once for all. Rather they seem to be sentences whose meaning or content clearly depends on the circumstances in which they are uttered. To many modern philosophers and logicians who try to avoid using sentences of this kind wherever possible these Stoic *axiōmata* would be on a par with what is known as occasion sentences. In fact, the *axiōmata* seem to differ from propositions in that they are temporally indefinite in the same way as occasion sentences.

From this it followed, as was pointed out by J. Hintikka,[38] that the Stoics spoke freely of changes in the truth values of *lekta*. A complete assertoric *lekton* could not only change its truth but also cease to exist. One example of what was called "changing *axiōma*" is the conditional "If Dion is alive, then Dion will be alive" (SVF 2. 206). This *axiōma* is supposed to be true as long as both the antecedent and the consequent are true, but will become false once the antecedent still being true the consequent ceases to be true, thus making the whole conditional change from being true to false. (Note that the "criterion of truth" invoked here depends on the truth-functional definition of "if . . . then" that had been introduced by the Megarian Philo.)[39] As to the peculiar doctrine that certain *axiōmata* are being "destroyed," the sources refer to Chrysippus's argument against Diodorus to show that the impossible can follow from the possible (SVF 2. 202a, b). This argument somehow conveys the notion that, within the class of what they regarded as "definite" singular propositions, the Stoics recognized certain *axiōmata* such as "This (man) is dead" in respect of which the question of truth or falsity does not even arise. For as soon as Dion has died, the *axiōma* "This (man) is dead" ceases to be expressible. That is to say, once the sentence expressing this *axiōma* is being uttered, the proposition itself turns out to be inapplicable in the first place.

Did the Stoics hold that the *axiōmata* or *lekta* respectively exist in some sense whether we think of them or not? Those who emphasize that the *axiōmata* are kinds of objective and public thought-contents, thus aligning the Stoic notion of *lekton* with what may be called "*conceptus objectivus*" or "*sens objectif*,"[40] tend to argue that the answer to this question must, of course, be in the affirmative. However, there is not really any evidence to that effect. On the contrary, the arguments adduced for the theory that there are *axiōmata* that are neither expressed nor thought seem to be based on what can be shown[41] to be mistaken interpretations of the texts relevant to the discussion. One of the arguments under consideration is drawn from the Stoic theory concerning natural signification, that is, the doctrine that nonevident facts can, by way of proof, be established on account of the logical force of the premis(es) asserting what is the case: as for instance, if this man is wounded in the heart, then he will die. There are two *axiōmata* present in this conditional. Now it has been suggested that, since a "sign" or rather "signal" was defined as an *axiōma* functioning as the antecedent in a conditional that both begins with truth and ends with truth and serves to establish the nonevident consequent, the latter *axiōma*, which is the conclusion of the argument, therefore must exist in order to be revealed. But this is not really the point in question. For what is being revealed is certainly not the *existence* of either some object that the statement is about, that is, the object to which the referring part of the statement refers, or the fact it states but its *truth*. In other words, there may have been a dispute over the question of what precisely in the world makes the statement true. But the fact it states, being an abstraction, is not really something "in the world."[42] Neither is the *axiōma*. It certainly does not exist as an extralinguistic entity. The other argument under consideration is drawn from a remark made by Sextus (*P.H.* 2. 83; cf. *Adv. math.* 7. 42) who says that since *truth*, according to Stoic theory, is necessarily connected with knowledge, whereas *the true*, being a property of *axiōmata*, is not, there may exist true *axiōmata* although they are not known, in the sense that they may exist although no one is aware of them. Now this seems to be an argument rather difficult to assess. G. Nuchelmans says that what it yields is that not all true *axiōmata* are part of the system of knowledge possessed by the Stoic sage rather than that there may exist *axiōmata* that are not (yet) expressed in words.

This, however, leaves us with the question of how the Stoic sage can be supposed to know everything and precisely what accounts for this strict system of knowledge. Can he really be supposed to know everything both with regard to the past and the future? And does he have to know everything all the time? He certainly cannot articulate all of his knowledge at any moment. And as *axiōmata* supposedly are precisely the sort of things signified by the words in which knowledge is being articulated, they cannot really be held to exist unless someone actually expresses or articulates what he claims to be knowing, i.e., that something is the case. And what must not be left out of consideration is that after all the term *axiōma* derives from a verb which in philosophical language is on a par with our "claim," "lay down," "maintain," and thus conveys the meaning of "what is claimed (to be true)." Claims of this sort do not exist in a sort of third world waiting to be discovered and expressed in speech.

While it is clear that the *lekta* in general cannot be recognized as quasi-platonic entities, it is important to realize that they must not be identified with concepts qua psychical entities either. For acts of thought are, according to Stoic theory, as has been pointed out by A. A. Long, private physical modifications of the leading part of the soul, but the sense of words in which these concepts are expressed is immaterial, somehow objective and something others can grasp.[43] Rather it seems that meanings exist together with concepts just as they exist together with expressions.

This leaves us with the possibility that the *lekta* may also be regarded as conceptual contents of concepts. In any case, being correlative to concepts that are formed from impressions according to certain laws, meanings can probably be described in an analogous way. And inasmuch as some meanings are derivative in relation to others, this derivation was described in the same terms.[44] Now as the Stoics accepted a natural relation between expression and meaning, that is, some form of semantic isomorphism which was interpreted, however, etymologically, they seem to have held that linguistic change was something analogous to derivation of concepts and meanings. Most of the material relevant to the discussion of this natural relation or semantic isomorphism is to be found in Varro and Augustine: for example, that primitive words are to be distinguished from derivative words; that primitive words are imitations of the things signified; that derivative words denote things that have a semantic relationship to the things designated by primitive words; that processes in the expressions take place along with the "translation" of words for signifying one thing to signifying another; that through these processes words are more and more removed from their origin, and so forth. The question of how many of these theorems can be attributed to the Stoics is a difficult one[45] and remains to be answered.

As to the latent and rather unacknowledged conflict between the Stoic theory of meaning and the Stoic theory of etymology,[46] however, there is evidence that it was precisely because of some conflict of this kind that the Stoics came to hold positions that cannot be reconciled. As can be seen from both the phenomenon of anomaly and Chrysippus's doctrine that any word is ambiguous (cf. Gellius, *Noctes Atticae* 11.12), they maintained that a word qua expression is not necessarily connected with any meaning. Yet being eager to establish *Logos* as part of Nature and to find meaningful relations between language and reality, they tried hard on their etymological theory of similarity between meaning and expression to establish meanings even at the level of minimal vocal elements, in this respect following the famous theory referred to in Plato's *Cratylus*.

This, however, does not really help us understand how the Stoics may have argued that meanings somehow reflect facts of nature. Not only did they hold that what words mean are incorporeal entities that somehow belong to both the respective sign by which they are signified and the thought with which they coexist, but they also insisted that there holds no isomorphic correlation between thought on the one hand and things-that-are on the other. Unlike Aristotle who, because of the realist theory of meaning that he inherited from Plato, thought that there are real entities corresponding to words and that language mirrors relations that obtain between real entities existing independently from the mind, the Stoics implied that ontological analysis is bound to be subjective, or rather functional, in that it is man's mind that superimposes its concepts on reality. In other words, there is no Aristotelian thing-like body of complex entities corresponding to our statements. One of the key terms employed by the Stoics comes in with the expression *kat' epinoian*, that is, "upon reflection." It is upon reflection that we arrive at logical constituents such as "parts" and "wholes," "cause" or "event," even where the physical components are inseparable. And it is upon reflection that we arrive at a conceptual understanding of reality insofar as it can be articulated in meaningful discourse. "All that is real is existing substance," Posidonius is known to have emphasized, and "as far as reality is concerned this existing substance is different from matter only in thought."[47] He may have added that "God," too, is more of a

Fregean *sense*, that is, something connoted rather than denoted. In fact, structure (*logos*) and its demiurgic correlate matter (*hylē*) he seems to have recognized as contributions of functional thought. And there is even evidence that the so-called principles (*archai*) "God" and "matter" could, like Time, Space, and The Void, be regarded as incorporeals.[48] In other words while traditional ontology proceeded from the tacit assumption that terms like "matter," "form," "God," and "principle" have genuine denotations, some Stoics appear to have thought of them as indicating meanings and providing contributions of functional thought.

NOTES

1. *Understanding Language* (The Hague, 1975) 21.

2. On this most influential text in the history of semantics, see N. Kretzman, "Aristotle on Spoken Sound," in J. Corcoran, ed., *Ancient Logic and its Modern Interpretations* (Dordrecht and Boston, 1974) 3-21.

3. See B. Mates, *Stoic Logic* (Berkeley and Los Angeles, 1961) 11-26.

4. See e.g., J. M. Rist, *Stoic Philosophy* (Cambridge, 1969) 152-172.

5. Cf. A. C. Lloyd, "Grammar and Metaphysics in the Stoa," *in* A. A. Long, ed., *Problems in Stoicism* (London, 1971) 74.

6. G. Watson, *The Stoic Theory of Knowledge* (Belfast, 1966) 40.

7. W. and M. Kneale, *The Development of Logic* (Oxford, 1961) 153.

8. A. C. Lloyd, "Grammar and Metaphysics," 71.

9. Cf. G. Watson, *Stoic Theory*, 42 n. 1 with regard to SVF 2. 408, 409.

10. See J. Pinborg, "Das Sprachdenken der Stoa und Augustins Dialektik," *Classica et Medievalia* 23 (1961) 151.

11. See J. Christensen, *An Essay on the Unity of Stoic Philosophy* (Copenhagen, 1962) 48.

12. *Toward Reunion in Philosophy* (New York, 1963) 29-30.

13. Cf. *Cratylus* 393d3, 422d2, 423e7-9, and C. H. Kahn, "Language and Ontology in the *Cratylus*," in E. N. Lee, A. P. D. Mourelatos, R. Rorty, eds., *Exegesis and Argument* (Assen, 1974) 163.

14. See e.g., G. Nuchelmans, *Theories of the Proposition* (Amsterdam and London, 1973) 69.

15. Cf. B. Mates, *Stoic Logic*, 21 n. 53.

16. J. Pinborg, "Historiography of Linguistics: Classical Antiquity: Greece," *Current Trends in Linguistics* 13 (1975) 81.

17. B. Mates, *Stoic Logic*, 23 n. 67.

18. Cf. Sextus Empiricus, *Adv. math.* 8. 80; Aristotle, *Eudemian Ethics* 1241-a16.

19. Cf. J. Pinborg, "Das Sprachdenken der Stoa...," 84.

20. A. A. Long, "Language and Thought in Stoicism," in *Problems in Stoicism* 107 n. 9.

21. For an extensive discussion of the text, see A. Graeser, *Zenon von Kition. Positionen und Probleme* (Berlin and New York, 1975) 69-78.

22. See G. Nuchelmans, *Theories of the Proposition*, 73.

23. Cf. J. Pinborg, "Das Sprachdenken der Stoa...," 81 n. 25. His account of "get a *ptōsis*" is probably due to what must be considered a misunderstanding of the Greek. Instead of staying with the Stoic use of "say" he translates "We do not speak of the house which is corporeal but of the incorporeal *ptōsis*..," and thus misses the point.

24. Cf. B. D. Jackson, *Augustine. De Dialectica. Translated with Introduction and Notes* (Dordrecht and Boston, 1975) 127.

25. Cf. G. Nuchelmans, *Theories of the Proposition*, 116 n. 8.

26. Ed. G. Verbeke (Louvain and Paris, 1961), 32, 34; cf. N. Kretzman, "Medieval Logicians and the Meaning of *Propositio*," *Journal of Philosophy* 67 (1970) 773 n. 7.

27. Cf. B. Mates, *Stoic Logic*, 11; W. and M. Kneale, *Development of Logic*, 140.

28. G. Watson, *Stoic Theory of Knowledge*, 41.

29. Cf G. Nuchelmans, *Theories of the Proposition*, 57.

30. Cf. e.g., Plutarch, *Quaestiones Platonicae* 1009C, in the recent edition and translation (with notes) of H. F. Cherniss, *Plutarch's Moralia* XIII, I (Loeb Classical Library, London, 1976).

31. A. A. Long, "Language and Thought in Stoicism," 105.

32. Cf. J. Pinborg, "Das Sprachdenken...," 81.

33. Cf. N. Kretzman, "Semantics, History of," *in* P. Edwards, ed., *The Encyclopedia of Philosophy* vol. 7 (1971) 364-365.

34. Cf. SVF 3.171, 175.

35. Cf. W. and M. Kneale, *Development of Logic*, 156.

36. Cf. B. Mates, *Stoic Logic*, 19-25 and C. H. Kahn, "Stoic Logic and Stoic Logos," *Archiv für Geschichte der Philosophie* 51 (1969) 170-171 n. 25.

37. K. R. Popper, *Objective Knowledge. An Evolutionary Approach* (Oxford, 1972) 157.

38. J. Hintikka, *Time and Necessity. Studies in Aristotle's Theory of Modality* (Oxford, 1973) 84.

39. Cf. M. Frede, *Die Stoische Logik* (Göttingen, 1974) 47-48.

40. Cf. I. M. Bochenski, *La logique de Théophraste* (Fribourg, 1947) 39.

41. See G. Nuchelmans, *Theories of the Proposition*, 85-86.

42. Cf. P. F. Strawson, *Logico-Linguistic Papers* (London, 1971) 195.

43. Cf. A. A. Long, "Language and Thought in Stoicism," 83-84.

44. Cf. K. Barwick, *Probleme der Stoischen Sprachlehre und Rhetorik* (Berlin, 1957) 32-33.

45. See J. Pinborg, "Das Sprachdenken der Stoa...," 95.

46. Cf. A. C. Lloyd, "Grammar and Metaphysics," 65.

47. Fr. 92, ed. L. Edelstein and I. Kidd, *The Fragments of Posidonius* (Cambridge, 1972) 99.

48. Cf D. L. 7.134, and A. Graeser, *Zenon von Kition*, 94-107.

4

Dialectic and the Stoic Sage

A. A. Long

Most of the leading Stoic philosophers, from Zeno onward, divided their philosophy into three parts, logic, ethics, and physics.[1] The logical part was commonly divided into two "sciences," rhetoric and dialectic (D.L. 7. 41). Matters that a modern logician would recognize as his field were included in the study of dialectic, but this subject also covered epistemology, grammar, and even, in some treatments, literary style. In the fully developed Stoic system, dialectic was the general science of rational discourse and of language, while rhetoric dealt with the organization and construction of arguments for political, forensic, and panegyric speeches (D.L. 7. 42 f.).

Modern logicians have largely confined their attention to that part of Stoic dialectic which corresponds to the more formal aspects of contemporary logic.[2] This is perfectly legitimate, provided that the artificiality of the restriction is acknowledged: the Stoics' treatment of modality and their analysis of propositions and methods of inference have a permanent philosophical interest, which does not apply to some of their other work in dialectic. But for the understanding of Stoicism, throughout its history, it is worthwhile to ask how they conceived of dialectic in general, where they stood in relation to other ancient philosophers, what

101

value they attributed to it, and why, in particular, they held that "only the wise man is a dialectician." My purpose in this paper is to offer some of the answers to these questions.[3]

THE STOIC CONCEPTION OF DIALECTIC

At the beginning of his commentary on Aristotle's *Topics* Alexander of Aphrodisias notes the value of realizing that the term *dialectic* does not have the same meaning for all philosophers: "the Stoics define dialectic as *science of speaking well*, and make speaking well consist in speaking things that are true and fitting." He then observes that the Stoics "give this meaning to dialectic because they regard it as a property peculiar to the philosopher of the most perfect philosophy; and for this reason, in their view, only the wise man is a dialectician" (p. 1, 8 Wallies = SVF 2. 124). Alexander was writing at about the end of the second century A.D. when Stoicism was in decline. Five centuries earlier, at the origin of the Stoa, it was all the more pertinent to distinguish different senses of dialectic. The period of 300 B.C. was a time of great variety, vitality, and rivalry in Greek philosophy. At Athens, Academics, Peripatetics, Cynics, Megarians, and the newly founded schools of Zeno and Epicurus were competing for followers, and they differed from one another in their conceptions of dialectic and in their attitudes toward it. But all would have agreed that dialectic, however practiced and defined, undertook the posing and solving of logical paradoxes and also the provision of relatively formal techniques of argument between a questioner and a respondent on a variety of subjects. Cynics and Epicureans condemned such activities as worthless for the advancement of human well-being. They could not completely ignore them, and they were in a minority.[4]

The Stoic conception of dialectic was not developed in isolation from its treatment by other philosophers. But before considering its historical background, we must return to Alexander of Aphrodisias and statements by Stoics themselves about this subject. When we compare his definition of dialectic in Stoicism with other sources, it may seem that he has either confused dialectic with rhetoric or given a statement that applies to both of these together, that is, to "logical science" in general. The Stoic definition of dialectic which is most widely attested is "the science of things true and false and neither true nor false." It was equally standard for them to define rhetoric as "the science of speaking well," which Alexander ascribes to dialectic. But before castigating Alexander too severely, it is important to take account of a passage in the introductory section of Diogenes Laertius's account of Stoic logic:

(According to the Stoics) "rhetoric is the science of speaking well on arguments which are set out in narrative form; dialectic is the science of discoursing correctly on arguments in question and answer form; hence they also define it as the science of things true and false and neither true nor false" (D.L. 7. 42).

This text suggests that "the science of speaking well" is a truncated definition of rhetoric which might, with further explanation, fit dialectic as well; it also implies that method and style are what principally differentiate rhetorical from dialectical argument. These points are confirmed by a manual illustration attributed to Zeno: "when asked how dialectic differed from rhetoric, he clenched his fist and then opened it out." The clenched fist illustrated the "compactness" and "brevity" of dialectic, while the open hand with the fingers spread out was intended to simulate the "breadth" of rhetoric. (Sextus, *Adv. math.* 2. 7. = SVF 1. 75). For the Stoics in general rhetoric like dialectic is peculiar to the wise man. Neither subject is merely a skill nor technique.[5] As "sciences" both parts of Stoic logic demand, at least in theory, that infallible ability to distinguish truth from falsehood which is characteristic of the Stoic sage.

It is reasonable to suppose that Zeno and Cleanthes, as well as later Stoics, held this view. As the ideal reference of all human excellences the "wise man" in Stoicism fulfills many of the functions of Platonic Forms. In rejecting these incorporeal entities Zeno offered the wise man as the goal and standard of a perfectly rational life. But we may doubt whether the account of dialectic as "the science of things true and false" has a Stoic history before Chrysippus, or at least, before Cleanthes. There are several reasons for regarding this conception of dialectic as a later development in Stoicism.

Diogenes Laertius gives it as an *alternative* definition to "the science of discoursing correctly on arguments in question and answer form." This account of dialectic is almost certainly the older of the two. Far from being distinctively Stoic, it describes dialectic in a manner that fits the general conception of the term in the early Hellenistic period. Argument by question and answer was the most characteristic philosophical connotation of dialectic, deriving from the ordinary meaning of the word *converse* (*dialegesthai*), and from Socratic and sophistic methods of argument. The practice of this activity, however "correctly," is not prima facie equivalent to "the science of things true...," which makes such large claims for itself.

Furthermore, the detailed summary of Stoic logic in Diogenes Laertius has nothing whatsoever to say about how "to discourse correctly on arguments in question and answer form."[6] But its subject matter is entirely appropriate to "the science of things true...," or to use Chrysippus's language, "signs and things signified" (D.L. 7. 62).[7] First we are given an account of sense-impressions, the formation of concepts, and the criterion of truth—epistemology; next a discussion of dialectic under the headings of voice, elements of speech, types of style, genus, species, division, and amphiboly—broadly, the sign function of language; next, we have language as meaningful ("things signified"): *lekta* (what are said or meant), propositions, and arguments, including a brief section on logical paradoxes. At the end of this section Diogenes Laertius writes:

"Such then is the logic of the Stoics, which chiefly establishes their point that the wise man is the only dialectician.[8] For all things are brought to light through the study in rational utterances, both the subject-matter of physics and again of ethics (as for logic that goes without saying), and (?without logic the wise man?) would not be able to speak about correctness of names, how the laws have made arrangements for actions.[9] Of the two forms of inquiry which fall under the virtue (of dialectic), one considers what each thing that exists is, and the other what it is called." (7. 83)

A scope and a significance are here attributed to dialectic which go far beyond argument by question and answer and which do suit the "science of things that are true...." Diogenes Laertius speaks about a doctrine and a methodology that are not the common property of dialectic in any philosopher's usage and which may fairly be credited to Chrysippus.

For it is noteworthy that Chrysippus's name figures more frequently than any other in Diogenes Laertius 7.50-82 and no Stoic prior to him is mentioned at all. This may seem to be laboring the obvious, since it is regularly acknowledged that Stoic logic was primarily the creation of Chrysippus. But this point is generally related to his achievements in elaborating logical theory. I am now suggesting that he may have been the first Stoic to develop dialectic beyond argument by question and answer into a science that made epistemology, language and logic together an integral part of Stoic philosophy as a whole.

Here a few words are needed about his Stoic predecessors. The material has recently been examined by Michael Frede and I shall limit myself to points that bear on the history of dialectic in the early Stoa.[10] I agree with Frede that we have little reason to think that Zeno's strictly logical interests went much beyond the kind of puzzles, such as the Liar and the Hooded Man, which he would have encountered with the Megarians.[11] Plutarch tells us that Zeno "used to solve sophisms and recommended his pupils to take up dialectic for its capacity to do this" (*Stoic. rep.* 1034f = SVF 1. 50). He is said to have paid two hundred drachmas, twice the price demanded, for seven forms of the puzzle known as "the Reaper" (D.L. 7. 25) and he clearly thought that an ability to handle the stock paradoxes was a necessary part of the training of any would-be philosopher. Knowing "how to discourse correctly on arguments in question and answer form" suits Zeno's attested attitude to dialectic very well. He wrote a book of "solutions" and two books of "refutations"; his so-called *Technē* was probably a treatment of rhetoric, and some aspects of dialectic in Chrysippus's sense were doubtless treated in Zeno's other works, particularly *On Logos* and *On Signs* (D.L. 7. 4, 39-40). The basic theory of *katalēpsis*, "grasping" valid perceptual data, was Zeno's own invention; but we have no evidence that he presented his epistemology as the primary part of dialectic corresponding to the arrangement of Diogenes Laertius.

If dialectic for Zeno was largely restricted to knowing how to acquit oneself creditably in debates about logical puzzles, Aristo's attitude towards logic becomes more intelligible, as Frede observes.[12] This pupil of Zeno wrote three books "Against the dialecticians" in which he must have advanced the position, repeatedly attributed to him, that logic is completely without value, or even positively harmful.[13] Aristo's general tendency was to emphasize the Cynic elements of Stoicism, and this suits his dismissal of logic. It is more difficult, however, to understand his contempt for dialectic if this had already been adumbrated as "the science of things true...." Given his Cynic inclinations he may readily be supposed to have thought the solution of sophisms to be useless for the good life, and although Zeno saw some point in this activity, we should not overestimate the value that he himself placed on it.[14]

Of Zeno's other pupils only Sphaerus and Cleanthes are known to have written logical works. But the little that can be said about these is quite significant. Sphaerus's books included two "on the art of dialectic" and also works "on predicates" and "on ambiguities." (D.L. 7. 178). Cleanthes also wrote on the first two subjects and on "sophisms" and "forms of argument" (D.L. 7. 175). He made "dialectic" a sixth "part" of philosophy and his claim that "not everything past and true is necessary" (SVF 1. 489) was a contribution to the debate about the "Master argument" initiated by that most famous of dialecticians, the Megarian Diodorus Cronus.[15] While Frede is probably right to think that Cleanthes "had little interest in arguments as such" (p. 15), it may also be correct to see him as the Stoic who prepared the ground for the very large place that dialectic was to take in the philosophy of Chrysippus. It must have fallen to Cleanthes to defend Zeno's doctrines against attacks from the skeptical Academy of Arcesilaus;[16] and the importance of systematizing Stoic philosophy and making it competent to withstand skeptical criticism must have stimulated a greater interest in logic among some of Zeno's successors. I don't wish to overemphasize this point, but it seems to me insufficient to account for Chrysippus's conception of dialectic purely on the grounds of his personal interests.[17] Of course these must have played a major part. But if we need a Stoic who prompted the development of dialectic as a systematic science before Chrysippus, the most likely candidate is Cleanthes.

We may now return to the wise man and to Chrysippus's conception of dialectic, first recalling the relevant remarks in Diogenes Laertius. As a dialectician, the wise man knows how to investigate what each thing is and what it is called. These two functions of dialectic are hardly original to the Stoics. They associate the dialectician of Plato's *Cratylus* with his namesake from the *Republic*: in the *Cratylus* Socrates argues that only the dialectician —the man who knows how to ask and answer questions—is competent to evaluate the work of the "legislator," the giver of names (390 b-e). The influence of this dialogue is perhaps evident from Diogenes' reference to correctness of names and the laws' (*nomoi*) arrangements for actions, and more generally from the Stoics' principles of etymology.[18] But the reminiscence of the *Republic* is still more striking where (to cite just one passage) dialectic is the only "method of inquiry which systematically attempts in every case to grasp the nature of each thing as it is in itself" (533b, trans. Cornford). Both Plato and Chrysippus (to whom we may surely attribute Diogenes' statement) assert that dialectic is the science that investigates *ti esti hekaston*, 'what each thing is.'

I do not believe that these verbal similarities are accidental or insignificant, which is not to say that Chrysippus set out to reveal his allegiance to Plato explicitly. He certainly did not harness dialectic to the ideal metaphysics of Plato's Forms nor, as I shall argue later, did he assign an important heuristic function to discussion by question and answer. But he agreed with Plato that dialectic is the science indispensable to all philosophical inquiry, and this is important. It gives to logic or dialectic, whatever this connotes in practice, an independent scientific or epistemological status that it did not possess for Aristotle. This is indicated in Stoic sources by two points: first, the rejection of the Aristotelian term *organon* as the designation of logic and the substitution of 'nor contingent portion but part' (of philosophy) (SVF 2. 49); second, the use of the term *dialectic* with 'knowledge of demonstrative procedures' given as its goal (SVF 2. 49. 31). Both these points are totally incompatible with Aristotle's official description of 'dialectic', which is sharply distinguished from *apodeixis*, 'demonstration' or 'deductive proof.'[19] (See further below.)

Both the general principles of Stoic philosophy, which Chrysippus inherited, and the destructive criticism of the skeptical Academy can help to explain parts of his conception of dialectic. Further evidence on the *values* of dialectic needs to be considered here. We have seen that dialectic is a human excellence or virtue (*aretē*) and it belongs, as we should expect, to those virtues that

are *necessary* to the good life. Diogenes Laertius, who states this
(7. 46), continues with a list of the specific virtues of dialectic, and
these help to illuminate its general functions in Stoicism. First he
mentions *aproptōsia*, which means literally 'not falling forward'
and is defined as "knowledge of when one should give assent and
not" (give assent); next *aneikaiotēs*, 'unhastiness,' defined as
"strong-mindedness against the probable (or plausible), so as not
to give in to it"; third, *anelenxia*, 'irrefutability,' the definition of
which is "strength in argument, so as not to be driven by it to the
contradictory"; and fourth, *amataiotēs*, 'lack of emptyheaded-
ness,' defined as "a disposition which refers impressions (*phantasiai*) to the correct *logos*."

This catalog of dialectical virtues may fairly confidently be
attributed to Chrysippus. All four terms are neologisms of the
kind that he liked to make, and the definition of *aneikaiotēs* uses a
bogus etymological link between *eikēi* (the adverb from which
(*an*)*eikaiotēs* is formed) meaning 'at random' and *eikos*, 'probabil-
ity,' which is equally characteristic of Chrysippus. The four terms
are all privative nouns that denote a disposition *not* to behave in a
certain way, and what links them is the Stoic concept of knowledge, which Diogenes Laertius next proceeds to define; "secure
grasp or disposition in acceptance of impressions which is un-
changeable by argument." Dialectic is then asserted by Diogenes
to be a necessary condition of knowledge: without it "the wise
man will not be infallible in argument," and it enables him to do
three kinds of things—distinguish true and false, discriminate
what is persuasive and what is ambiguous, argue methodically by
question and answer.

The main points of this passage are confirmed and amplified by
a papyrus from Herculaneum which discusses dialectic in relation
to the wise man (SVF 2. 131).[20] *Aproptōsia*, and *aneikaiotēs* recur,
anelenxia is also expressed through its adjectival form *anele(n)k-
tos*, and much else is said about the sage: he is not subject to per-
suasion, he does not change, he does not err in respect of any sense
organ, he does not deceive and is not deceived; as before, the wise
man's dialectical qualities are expressed by negative predicates, or
largely so. But what they denote are meant to be read as positive
values, instances of the fact that "the wise do all things well" (SVF
2. 41. 25). As in Diogenes Laertius, the focus of the wise man's dia-

lectical virtues is on his "assenting correctly," and all the nouns or adjectives that describe him pick out particular types of situation, most notably philosophical arguments, in which precipitate assent would be the mark of folly. The main emphasis in both texts is upon dialectic in the limited, argumentative sense. We seem to be closer to the science of discoursing correctly by question and answer (Zeno's probable conception of dialectic) than to the larger, epistemological activity which I attributed to Chrysippus—dialectic as knowing how to investigate what each thing is and what it is called. Yet both our passages seem to point most clearly to Chrysippus.

This problem, I would suggest, is more apparent than real. Chrysippus did not abandon dialectic's traditional associations with formal debate and philosophical polemic. As the Stoa's chief protagonist against the Academic Sceptics he could not afford to do so. But he combined what we may call the defensive function of dialectic, as a weapon against rival philosophers, with its positive role as a systematic science of epistemology, language and logic. Another way of putting it would be to regard Chrysippean dialectic as incorporating both the Platonic and the Aristotelian conceptions of this term: it is Aristotelian in the sense that it provides its practitioner with the training necessary to cope with arguments for and against a given thesis; but it is Platonic in the sense that its overall purpose is the discovery and demonstration of truths.

In fact both passages just discussed include hints of a wider conception for dialectic than preservation of the wise man from unguarded assent in argument. Diogenes Laertius observes a connection between dialectic and ethics when he says that "precipitancy in assertions extends to actual events, so that those whose impressions are not trained tend to disorderliness and randomness" (7. 48). We may interpret him to mean that a man who gives his assent injudiciously, whether to a sense-impression or to a statement, will be unable to live in a consistent, purposeful manner. The Stoic goal of "living consistently with nature" presupposes the ability to make correct judgments about facts and values. So the wise man needs to possess a disposition to grasp the truth in every situation if his moral conduct is to be infallible. The Papyrus text —as supplemented by von Arnim—includes these interesting remarks, which follow its insistence that assent should always be linked to *katalēpsis,* 'grasping': "for in the first place philosophy, whether it is (practicing) correctness of *logos,* (or) knowledge, is the (same as business) concerning *logos;* (for) by being (within) the parts of the *logos* and their (arrangement) we shall use it with experience; and by *logos* I mean that which belongs by (nature to all) rational beings."[21] Here too the writer (SVF 2. 27-32, 41) is stepping beyond the narrower confines of dialectic into other well-known Stoic territory. He appears to be saying that thorough acquaintance with logic, "the parts of the *logos,*" is necessary for the cultivation of man's rational powers, his specifically human nature.

There are other texts that indicate Chrysippus's view that dialectic has both a defensive and a creative function. Plutarch devotes the tenth chapter of his treatise *On the Contradictions of the Stoics* to statements by Chrysippus about dialectic. The inconsistency that Plutarch seeks to detect has a bearing on the two functions of dialectic which I have suggested.

The main point at issue, for Plutarch, is Chrysippus's attitude toward "arguing the opposite sides of a question." Chrysippus recognized the value of this activity for skeptics whose aim is to promote "suspension of judgment" (*epochē*) in their audience (1036A). But he was at pains to qualify this approval in his advice to Stoic teachers, "those seeking to produce knowledge according to which we shall live consistently." Their task is not to argue with equal cogency on both sides but to "give their pupils basic instruction and to fortify them from beginning to end." They may, however, in appropriate circumstances, mention "the opposing arguments" as well, their justification being to "destroy their plausibility." Here then Chrysippus regards "arguing the opposite sides of a question" purely as an educational tool that must be used with caution (*eulabeia*). Much the same general position is stated in other quotations by Plutarch: opposing arguments must be handled in such a way that the inexperienced are not taken in by a plausible refutation—"for those who follow everyday experience in grasping perceptible things...(i.e., accepting the cognitive value of certain sensations) easily abandon these if they are carried away by the questions of the Megarians and a greater number of other more powerful questions" (1036E). This caveat is put still more positively in a passage from Chrysippus's work "On the use of the *logos*": (The faculty of reason) must be used for the discovery of truths and for their organization, not for the opposite ends, though this is what many people do" (1037B trans. Cherniss, *Moralia* Loeb. ed. XIII. 2). In these texts we witness the two aspects of Chrysippus's dialectic, its defensive function, where arguing both sides of a question may have limited value, and its creative role in the discovery of truths.

Plutarch's effort to detect inconsistency is based largely on one, apparently youthful, activity of Chrysippus. Under the influence of Arcesilaus, with whom he studied as a young man, Chrysippus published arguments for and against "Everyday experience" (1036C, 1037A).²² These were an investigation into the pros and cons of the conventional position that some sense experience provides demonstrably valid evidence about the world. Plutarch would have us believe that Chrysippus's arguments against the senses were far more effective than his defense of them and that his support for a position contrary to his own beliefs was grossly inconsistent with his published views about the use of contrary theses. There can be little doubt that Plutarch is here drawing upon a hostile biographical tradition, to which he himself gives the lie when he concludes his discussion with the words: "you do yourself confess that from ambition you are showing off by using the faculty of reason in ways unprofitable and harmful" (1037C, trans. Cherniss). Possibly Chrysippus's arguments for and against "Everyday experience" were an exercise set him by Arcesilaus (cf. D.L. 7.184). We certainly have no ground for thinking that his views on the value of arguing both sides of a question were inconsistent during his maturity as a philosopher.

Apart from its biographical interest, Plutarch's evidence shows that Chrysippus envisaged for dialectic the two complementary functions I have indicated. Arguing both sides of a question was the dialectical method of the contemporary Academy. Stoicism needed defense against this form of attack and the dialectical virtues, which we have studied, refer to the ideal armory of the Stoic sage who knows how to acquit himself excellently in disputation. Without his irrefutability and the like, as Diogenes Laertius says, "he will not show himself sharp and acute and generally skilful in arguments" (7.48). The titles of Chrysippus's logical works prove that he wrote at enormous length on techniques of argument and the handling of sophisms; in this respect he may be regarded as one of the heirs of Aristotle's *Topics*.

This brings us back to the whole question of what dialectic connotes for Chrysippus and the relation of this to Plato and to Aristotle. I have already drawn attention to points of contact and difference with both earlier philosophers and it is time to try to state these more precisely. Chrysippus agreed with Plato and Aristotle that philosophical argument, formally conducted, is the only proper procedure for the demonstration of truth. Like Plato he called the expert in this a dialectician which meant, for both philosophers, not merely a skilled logician but also, most important, someone who has knowledge of reality. In his conception of reality, however, and in his theory of knowledge Chrysippus differed sharply from Plato. In place of an investigation by question and answer which has as its goal to establish relationships between Forms, suprasensible realities, Chrysippus was interested in demonstrating the conditions that make it proper to assent to sense-impressions and propositions concerning material objects.

For Aristotle the scope of dialectic, argument by question and answer, is limited to subjects on which the majority of people have "opinions." Such matters, in Aristotle's view, not admitting of necessary truths, are appropriate for debate, which is not the case with the premises of the demonstrative syllogism that are "true and primary" (*Top.* 100a25-b23). We do not, on Aristotle's view, demonstrate truths by engaging in dialectical discussion. But this activity has value, both for clarifying the subjects it is competent to handle, and above all, for training the intellect.

Chrysippus's attitude toward dialectic in this sense seems not to have been very different from Aristotle's.[23] He too regarded training in handling contrary theses as a useful educational device provided it is not confused with the discovery of truths or treated as an end in itself. He certainly thought the wise man should be excellent at questioning and responding in formal debates, but nothing suggests that he shared Plato's views about the cognitive value of such encounters. They form a part of dialectic, as Chrysippus conceived of this, but not its positive role for the demonstration of truths. Though using the term dialectic much more broadly than Aristotle, Chrysippus agreed that in logic we should distinguish between demonstrative science and knowledge of how to conduct oneself in argument by question and answer.

DIALECTIC AND THE DISCOVERY OF TRUTH

Up to this point I have dwelt largely on statements by Stoics or Stoic sources on the nature and value of dialectic. These have helped to explain why the sage is a dialectician but not, perhaps, why he is the only dialectician. What about Chrysippus himself? He made no claims to be a Stoic sage yet it was popularly said of him, "if the gods had dialectic it would be the dialectic of Chrysippus" (D.L. 7. 180). The apparent paradox is partly resolved by pointing out that in statements of the form, "only the sage is a such and such," the predicate is evaluative as well as descriptive. It refers to what we might call supreme or perfect competence but with the fundamental proviso that no one who falls short of perfect competence can even qualify for the description. The Stoics admitted no degrees of virtue or vice, so banning the use of the comparatives better or worse, and they also regarded dialectic, itself a virtue, with the same complete lack of compromise. Either a man is wise and therefore a dialectician, or he is not wise and not a dialectician.

It may be said that this treatment of the term, dialectician, is merely one of the innumerable examples of the Stoics' practice in confining all knowledge, skill, and virtue to the wise man and that it is of no particular philosophical interest. I think this conclusion would be premature. The fact that dialectician, in Stoic usage, falls into the category of predicates peculiar to the wise man tells us something about the Stoic view of dialectic. Moreover, as we have seen, Stoic statements about dialectic lay great emphasis upon the wise man's unique competence.

He instantiates what dialectic is, the science of things true and false, and he is distinguished from other men, including would-be dialecticians, by his possession of truth (*alētheia*).[24] According to strict Stoic usage, truth is knowledge, a disposition of the wise man's *logos*, and it differs from "the true" in various ways. Above all, truth is something compound or complex whereas the true is uniform and simple. Dialectic, whether treating of assent to sense-impressions or to methods of inference, deals with the conditions that make particular propositions true or false. But a man can learn to formulate true propositions without grasping a complete structure of logical relationships, an ordered system of true propositions, which constitutes dialectic as such and therefore truth as a whole. The distinction between truth and the true helps to show the systematic character of the wise man's knowledge. He represents an ideal of language and rationality at one with reality, of truth discovered.

Chrysippus, it may be recalled, said that "the faculty of reason must be used for the discovery of truths and for their organization," and "the discovery of truth" occurs in Diogenes Laertius' introductory remarks on logic (7. 42). He speaks of a (sub-?) division of logic concerned with "canons and criteria" which has discovery of truth as its function, and says that it formulates rules about the differences of *phantasiai* (impressions presented to the sense organs or the mind). He also refers to a further part of logic, to do with "definition," saying that "they use this in the same way for recognition of truth; for things are grasped through general concepts" (*ennoiai*).[25]

In a treatise attacking Epicureans and Academics, Epictetus charges the latter, as skeptics, with trying to cast off or blind their own sense-perceptions (*aisthēseis*). He asserts that a man has natural endowments "for recognizing the truth" (Diogenes Laertius' phrase) but fails to "go on and take the pains to add to these (sc. measures and standards) and to work out additional principles to supply the deficiencies, but does exactly the opposite, endeavoring to take away and destroy whatever faculty he does possess for discovering the truth" (2. 20, 21, trans. Oldfather). Omitting for the present Epictetus's professed attitude to dialectic, I would suggest that this passage gives us a moral statement on the Stoic attitude toward discovering truth. Man is innately equipped to achieve this by reason of his own intellect and sensory faculties, but these require training in (we may interpret) the subject-matter and methodology of dialectic; hence what Epictetus calls elsewhere "the necessity of logic" (2. 25).

The orthodox Stoic doctrine, which he implies, takes us back to Diogenes Laertius on the discovery of truth. His "canons and criteria" and "definition" refer to the two primary aspects of the Stoic theory of knowledge. "Distinguishing between *phantasiai*," the scope of "canons and criteria," is the province of the human faculty to "assent correctly" and to "grasp" (*katalambanein*) the valid content of a sense impression or a sentence;[26] and we have noted those dialectical virtues that signify the wise man's capacity to do this. But assenting and grasping are activities of the *logos*, man's rational governing principle, and a fundamental fact about the *logos* is its being "a collection of general concepts and preconceptions" (SVF 2. 841).[27] Similarly according to Diogenes' analysis of the cognitive value of "definition," "things are grasped through general concepts." If we are to *know* what each thing is, we need to bring the particular percept or proposition under a valid general concept the basis of which, in Stoicism, is also sense experience and its organization by the intellect. As Gerard Watson has written, "the new piece of information must fit into the so far established picture, and *katalepsis* cannot be separated from *logos*, the particular act from the general disposition. For truth, then, there must be coherence."[28]

This last point is clearly hinted at in the dialectical virtue of *amataiotes*—"a disposition which refers *phantasiai* to the correct *logos*." But how are we to translate *logos* here? Hicks in the Loeb edition says "right reason." That is implied, no doubt, but it leaves the definite article untranslated. "Right reason" describes the *logos* of the wise man (and god) and it is his *logos* that pronounces judgment on the *phantasia*. But what intellectual process does this involve? Is it not more accurate and more informative to interpret *ton orthon logon* here as '*the* correct argument'?[29] An example, which might do justice to various items of our evidence, would be this: the wise man wakes up at 9:00 A.M. in a relatively dark room and his initial impression (*phantasia*) on waking is that it is still night. But before assenting to this impression he takes stock of his surroundings and realizes that it is light. His experience of the world has taught him the truth that "if it is night, it is not light"; he therefore withholds assent from his initial impression and infers that it is not night and therefore that it is day. This example seeks to bring together particular *phantasiai*, general concepts, Stoic methods of inference, and the sense of *orthos logos* in Diogenes. To possess an *orthos logos* implies the ability to reason correctly, and while we need not suppose that the Stoics were so humorless that they thought the wise man would subject all his experience to formal methods of inference, they should not be taken to regard reference to *orthos logos* as recourse to a mysterious intuition. The wise man has "right reason" because he has an infallible disposition to reason correctly. We should not perhaps forget Chrysippus's dialectical dog which infers the correct one of three possible roads for pursuit of its quarry by smelling only at the two roads that it did not take and then, without smelling at the third, rushes off along it (Sext. Emp. *P.H.* 1. 69)!

The wise man's possession of right reason relates him to the active principle of the universe which *is* right reason and identical with god. Consideration of this relationship can illuminate both the practical application of Stoic dialectic and the overriding imperative to live consistently in accordance with nature. This goal becomes more intelligible and practicable if it is seen to depend upon the systematic ability to grasp facts and to reason correctly. Life according to nature entails for the Stoic an attunement between his own attitudes and actions and the rational course of events. But how is a man to know whether he has achieved, or is progressing toward achieving, such a relationship? The answer is surely that the more he succeeds in grasping what is true the closer he comes to attunement with right reason in its cosmic sense.[30] For right reason (*orthos logos*) is logically equivalent to truth (*alē-theia*).[31] What truth means in this connection depends upon whether we are referring to the sage or to the *orthos logos* that is god. In the sage truth refers to his rational disposition, his systematic knowledge and ability to state all that is true. In reference to god truth seems principally to denote destiny, the causal nexus that determines all things. But this is an activity of *logos*; that is to say, it is both expressible and intelligible. The sage's systematic knowledge of particular truths is the human counterpart to the divine nexus of causes.[32]

The moral implications of the link between cosmic and human *logos* have been well understood by modern students of Stoicism. No one today would readily accept the view that logic in the mature Stoic system ranks below physics and ethics in importance.[33] But it is tempting to go further and to suggest that the study of dialectic itself, for Chrysippus at any rate, is an integral part of moral conduct. In analyzing the structure of language and its function to express true propositions, the Stoics were taking as their subject-matter fundamental aspects of the human *logos*, the rationality of human nature. Language and logic are not capacities of the human *logos* which can or should be isolated from its more obviously moral dispositions. The character of the wise man is sufficient proof of this point, and it can be confirmed by a wide range of Stoic texts. Chrysippus, as we have seen, was well aware that *logos* can be misused in dialectical activities. But when applied to the genuine discovery of truth, exercise of the *logos* must be an activity that accords with human nature; and this allows the most technical details of Stoic logic, and even the solution of sophisms, to be regarded as actions that contribute to the understanding of man himself and of the rationality of the universe. Thus dialectic may be regarded as a method of self-discovery.

That Chrysippus held such a view is implied by the catalog of his writings preserved in part by Diogenes Laertius (7. 189-202). This appears to have been arranged under the three headings, logic, ethics, and physics, and only the first of these is complete. The ethical catalog breaks off in the middle of a title, and physics is missing altogether. Now the titles of the works arranged under Logic give no indication of the broad significance for dialectic that I have sought to establish for Chrysippus. They cover in enormous detail a range of topics—types of proposition, aspects of grammar and style, methods of argument, and solutions to sophisms—which correspond to the summary of Stoic logic in Diogenes Laertius, with one major omission. Not one of Chrysippus's logical titles refers explicitly to epistemology, the first subject treated in Diogenes.

Then we turn to Ethics (7. 199-202). Like the logical titles the ethical books are arranged by sections. The first of these is headed "the classification of ethical concepts" and the books listed in its first series are mainly "Of definitions," e.g., "Of definitions of the good man, to Metrodorus, two books." But the most interesting item is the second main section, "concerning the common *logos* and the arts and virtues deriving from it" (7. 201). Its first series includes one of Chrysippus's books from which I have already quoted, "On the use of the *logos*," and all but one of the remaining titles concern topics that appear in Diogenes Laertius's treatment of Stoic logic: "On how we speak each thing and conceive of it," "On general concepts," "On supposition," "Demonstrations that the wise man will not hold opinions" (i.e., that his sole cognitive state is knowledge), "On grasping (*katalēpsis*) and knowledge and ignorance"—four books, and "On *logos*."

If we find it strange that these titles should appear under ethics, we have a further surprise in the second series of this section: I report this in full: "On the fact that the ancients admitted dialectic along with demonstrations, to Zeno"—two books; "On dialectic, to Aristocreon"—four books; "On objections brought against the dialecticians"—three books; and finally, "On rhetoric, to Dioscurides"—four books.[34]

The source of the catalog is not known, and we cannot be certain that Chrysippus arranged his works in this way.[35] But there can be no serious doubt that the arrangement has Stoic authority. It proves that some Stoics, if not Chrysippus himself, found it appropriate to classify under ethics some of his works that dealt quite explicitly with dialectic, rhetoric, and epistemology. If this appears to breach the recognized sphere of Stoic logic we should remember that "no part (sc. of Stoic philosophy) is separate from another part," according to some, "but they are mixed together" (D.L. 7. 40). Of great interest too is the heading for this section of ethics, which I quoted above. What is meant by "the common *logos*" from which arts and virtues are derived? Hicks translates *koinos logos* by "common view," which I fail to understand. I cannot see how "common view" could be a source for arts and virtues, but if we take *koinos logos* in a familiar Stoic sense the heading becomes intelligible and highly significant. The phrase should mean "the principle of rationality which is common to men and god." This is indeed the basis of virtue in Stoic theory and such a heading is fully appropriate to most of the titles of all three series in this section. But above all, it helps to explain the presence of dialectic in the treatment of ethics. As the science that handles language and logic, dialectic is concerned with *koinos logos* and therefore with ethics and with physics too. On the basis of independent evidence we have thus arrived at a conclusion already stated in Diogenes Laertius: the interdependence of dialectic, the wise man, and proficiency in physics and ethics.

THE SAGE AND DIALECTIC IN EPICTETUS

Up to the time of Chrysippus, Stoics differed in their conception and evaluation of dialectic and they continued to do so thereafter. It is likely that many, including Panaetius and Posidonius, accepted his view of the wise man as dialectician even if few Stoics apart from his immediate successors extended the study of logic and grammar. Historians generally associate the later Stoa with a decline of interest in logic, and up to a point this is correct. But it is important to distinguish professional Stoic teachers, with different views, from eclectic practitioners of Stoicism such as Seneca and Musonius Rufus. Seneca's attitude toward logic was dismissive, recalling the Cynic approaches of Aristo (*Ep.* 45. 5, 49. 5, 82. 19, etc.). But logic continued to form an important part of the Stoic curriculum during the imperial period, so much so that it was often regarded as mere pedantry and irrelevant to practice of the good life, thus explaining, if not justifying, a standpoint like Seneca's. Between these two extremes it was clearly possible to adopt a series of intermediate positions, and we have an interesting example of this in Epictetus. His statements about the value of logic are particularly relevant to our main theme since no Stoic was more insistent on the practical purpose of philosophy.[36]

Epictetus claimed no expertise as a logician and his discourses, as recorded by Arrian, make only passing reference to the more formal elements of Stoic dialectic. But his terminology and his methods of argument suggest quite considerable familiarity with logical textbooks by Chrysippus or other Stoics. Several of his discourses (1. 7; 1. 17; 2. 12; 2. 25) are specifically concerned with the value of logic, and the subject recurs in many others. When all of these passages are put together they show that Epictetus's general conception of the role of dialectic was broadly in line with the position of Chrysippus. Many of his remarks on this subject are related to the two extreme positions that he rejected. Epictetus constantly attacks pretentious display of logical techniques which is unrelated to practical conduct. "The books of the Stoics are full of quibbles. What then is the thing lacking? The man to make use of them, the man to bear witness to the arguments by what he does" (1. 29, 56). It is not the mark of a man making true progress to want to know "what Chrysippus means in his books on the *Liar*" (2. 17, 34) or to pride himself on posing the Master argument (2. 17-18, 18).[37] A man might analyze syllogisms in the manner of Chrysippus and still be wretched (2. 23, 44). Taken in isolation such statements as these (and there are many more of the same kind) seem to treat logic as a trivial activity which has no function for the serious-minded. But Epictetus's purpose is different. In these statements he is not rejecting logic as such but misapplications of it and erroneous views about its intrinsic value. He is rejecting the idea that a would-be Stoic who gets first-class marks on Chrysippean logic has achieved anything worthwhile if this is unrelated to the structure and plan of his life as a whole; and with this Chrysippus would have agreed.

Epictetus's positive attitude to logic is quite consistent with his negative posture. "Logic is necessary": not as an end in itself but as the "measuring instrument" of our *logos*, our rational faculty (1. 17). The faculty of reason is our innate instrument of judgment, and it is through logic alone that we can come to understand and refine this power. We should read and try to interpret Chrysippus, not for its own sake, but in order to "follow nature" and to enlarge our understanding of ourselves. It is the interpretation, not the interpreter, which has value.

In discussing Chrysippus I suggested that he might have regarded dialectic as a means of self-discovery, but I could not prove this from any surviving quotation. In Epictetus this is stated explicitly: he compares Chrysippus's achievement in logic to that of a diviner who predicts the future from inspecting entrails (1. 17, 18-29). Chrysippus is someone whose analysis of *logos* has yielded true indications of human nature.

In this treatise Epictetus moves rapidly from an assessment of logic to psychological and ethical conclusions, and this is characteristic of his methodology. But there is one discourse that deals at some length with the theme, "On the use of equivocal premises, hypothetical arguments and similar subjects" (1. 7). Epictetus's purpose here is to show that dialectic in the more restricted sense —knowing how to argue by question and answer—is a field in which the wise man will be proficient. It is not enough to have knowledge of particular facts. "One must learn how one thing follows as a consequence upon other things . . . if a man is to acquit himself intelligently in argument...and is not to be deceived by quibblers as though they were conducting a proof" (1.7, 10-12).

Having established the wise man's need of dialectical competence, Epictetus turns to particular problems that arise in formal debates. If the premises of an argument are equivocal how is a man to deal with an inference that is valid but false? Or if an argument is built on hypothetical premises, under what conditions should a man give his assent to the hypothesis and how far does his acceptance of it commit him to granting all its consequences? Epictetus raises these questions, and argues that a training in formal argument to deal with them is presupposed by the Stoic conception of the good man (1.7, 25-29). He then infers the need for ordinary men to work at the perfection of their own reason. It is no excuse to claim that an error in reasoning is not equivalent to parricide. Reckless assent to a sense-impression and inability to follow an argument are errors in themselves and signify an untrained reasoning faculty (1.7, 30-33). We are reminded once again of Diogenes Laertius's dialectical virtues. The wise man is infallible in all respects. His dialectical prowess is both a faculty to reason correctly in debate and a means of conducting himself without error in all the occasions of life.

This discourse by Epictetus—the seventh of Arrian's first book —is the nearest thing we possess to a Stoic equivalent of Aristotle's *Topics*. It shows us that formal argument by question and answer was still being practiced in the first century A.D. and it also recalls Zeno's interest in the ability to cope with sophisms. The Stoic sage was always a dialectician, but it is remarkable that his dialectical prowess and significance under Chrysippus have remained so prominent in Epictetus.

NOTES

1. D.L. 7.39. This division of philosophy and the use of the term *logic* probably go back to the Academy under Xenocrates, cf. M. Frede, *Die stoische Logik* (Göttingen, 1974) 24-25.

2. So Frede cited in n. 1, Benson Mates, *Stoic Logic*[2] (Berkeley and Los Angeles, 1961) and W. and M. Kneale, *The Development of Logic* (Oxford, 1962).

3. Several recent studies have touched on these topics in emphasizing the close relationship between aspects of Stoic logic and the Stoic system as a whole:

G. Watson, *The Stoic Theory of Knowledge* (Belfast, 1966); Ch. Kahn, "Stoic Logic and Stoic Logos," *Archiv für Geschichte der Philosophie* 51 (1969) 158-172; A. C. Lloyd, "Grammar and Metaphysics in the Stoa," *Problems in Stoicism*, ed. A. A. Long (London, 1971) 58-74; A. A. Long, "Language and Thought in Stoicism," *Problems in Stoicism* 75-113 and *Hellenistic Philosophy* (London, 1974) 121-147.

4. On Epicurus's method in dealing with certain Megarian sophisms, cf. David Sedley, "Epicurus, On Nature book XXVIII," *Cronache Ercolanesi* 3 (1973) 71-77.

5. Sextus Empiricus (as cited above) notes this as the difference between Xenocrates' account of rhetoric and the Stoic definition that uses the same words as Xenocrates.

6. 7. 49-82. This section begins with a quotation from Diocles Magnes (first century B.C.) which probably extends beyond chapter 49, but cf. F. H. Sandbach, "Ennoia und Prolēpsis," in *Problems in Stoicism*, ed. A. A. Long, 33.

7. So too Diogenes' opening remarks about the contents of dialectic, 7. 43-44.

8. I follow von Arnim's text for this line (SVF 2. 39. 39) and not H. S. Long in the Oxford edition with a reading: "the wise man is always a dialectician."

9. The text of this sentence is very difficult and almost certainly corrupt. My question marks frame words that are absent from the Greek, but I conjecture with von Arnim (SVF 2. 130) that a subject (the wise man?) is needed for the infinitives *echein eipein*. The subsequent reference to "considering what each thing is called" seems to imply that the wise man is an expert in the correct use of names. For a different translation, cf. Hicks in the Loeb edition, who takes "virtue" in a general sense and not as a reference to the virtue of dialectic.

10. *Die stoische Logik*, 12-26.

11. Cf. the Megarian style of Zeno's argument against the proposition, "do not pronounce judgment until you have heard both sides," Plutarch *S.R.* 1034E. It is probable, as Frede argues (*Die stoische Logik*, 23-26), that Zeno's logic was also influenced by the Academy, though the most likely date for his arrival in Athens (c. 311 B.C.) rules out the report of D.L. 7. 2 (accepted by Frede, *Die stoische Logik*, 23 n. 8) of lengthy study under Xenocrates.

12. Op. cit. p. 13. I doubt whether we can learn much about Zeno's logic from Epictetus, *Disc.* 4. 8. 12 (SVF 1. 51) but cf. Andreas Graeser, *Zenon von Kition* (Berlin/New York, 1975) 11 ff.

13. D.L. 6. 103; 7. 160, 163; Sextus Emp., *Adv. math.* 7. 12, etc.

14. Cf. Stobaeus, *Ecl.* 2. 22, 12 Wachsmuth (SVF 1. 49): "Zeno used to liken the arts of the dialecticians to the right measures which do not measure wheat or anything else worthwhile but chaff and dung."

15. For the evidence, bibliography and discussion, cf. Klaus Döring, *Die Megariker* (Amsterdam, 1972) 39-44, 132-138.

16. This is a valid inference from the chronology: when Cleanthes succeeded Zeno as Head of the Stoa in about 261 B.C. Arcesilaus was already Head of the Academy and Chrysippus hardly more than twenty years old. Cleanthes may have had little competence in logic (cf. Frede, *Die stoische Logik*, 26-27), but not much credence should be rested on the ancient biographical tradition, cf. R. Hirzel, *Untersuchungen zu Cicero's philosophischen Schriften* II.1 (Leipzig, 1882)

85-88. D.L. 7.182 reports that Chrysippus diverted a dialectician's attack from Cleanthes to himself.

17. The same point is made by J. B. Gould, *The Philosophy of Chrysippus* (Leiden, 1970) 9 and by Frede, *Die stoische Logik*, 26-27.

18. Cf. H. Steinthal, *Geschichte der Sprachwissenschaft*[2] (Berlin, 1890) I, especially 334, 344. Stoic principles of etymology and the grammatical part of their dialectic fall outside the scope of this article; for two recent discussions that raise points about their general philosophical position, cf. A. C. Lloyd, cited in n. 3, and my remarks in *Hellenistic Philosophy*, 131-139.

19. On the general background to Aristotelian dialectic, cf. Fr. Solmsen in *Aristotle on Dialectic. The Topics*, ed. G. E. L. Owen, (Oxford, 1968) 49-68 and Owen's paper, "The Platonism of Aristotle, *Proceedings of the British Academy* 51 (1965) 142-145.

20. Von Arnim is responsible for this text which he first published with a commentary in *Hermes* 25 (1890) 473-495. It should be emphasized that he established his readings on the basis of the Naples and Oxford apographs without inspection of the papyrus itself (cf. 473). That is not an adequate basis for an authoritative edition of any of the Herculaneum material, and it is virtually certain that new work on the papyrus would reveal some errors in his text, which should be regarded for the present as provisional. His attribution of the papyrus to Chrysippus is highly probable.

21. I have bracketed those words of which the Greek equivalents are missing or seriously defective in the text as reported by von Arnim. But this does not imply that I have serious doubts about the validity of his restorations or the sense of the passage.

22. It is these works that are included by Diogenes Laertius, along with their addressees Metrodorus and Gorgippides, in his catalog of Chrysippus's writings, 7.198.

23. Cf. Paul Moraux in *Aristotle on Dialectic* (cited in n. 19) 304, and more generally E. Bréhier, *Chrysippe et l'ancien Stoïcisme*[2] (Paris, 1951) 62-65.

24. For evidence and discussion, cf. my remarks in *Problems in Stoicism* (cited in n. 3) 98-102.

25. In the last sentence of 7.41 *D.L.* says: "but some omit what has to do with definition." That these did not include Chrysippus seems clear both from our general accounts of Stoic logic and from Chrysippus's list of writings.

26. On the meaning of the terms and the Stoic doctrine they help to express, cf. J. M. Rist, *Stoic Philosophy* (Cambridge, 1969) 133-141; F. H. Sandbach, "Phantasia Katalēptikē," in *Problems in Stoicism*, 9-21; Andreas Graeser, *Zenon von Kition*, 39-55.

27. A quotation by Galen from Chrysippus.

28. *The Stoic Theory of Knowledge*, 37. The importance of general concepts (*ennoiai*) in the Stoic theory of knowledge is very well argued by Watson.

29. This also suits the other occurrences of *logos* in D.L. 7.46-47, three of which Hicks rightly translates by "argument."

30. This goes some way toward resolving the question I raised in *Proceedings of the Aristotelian Society* 1970/71, 102, where I alleged that the Stoics gave no

satisfactory answer to the question how a man might know whether his reason accorded consistently with Nature.

31. *Alētheia*, as 'knowledge,' is a disposition of the 'governing principle' (*hēgemonikon*) or *logos* such that the *logos* is upright or correct (*orthos*); cf. SVF 2. 132 with other descriptions of the wise man. For *orthos logos* and *alētheia* as cosmic principles cf. SVF 2. 913 and 3. 4; Marcus Aurelius 9. 2.

32. I am not of course denying knowledge and consciousness to the Stoic deity; Cleanthes and Chrysippus are said to have claimed "the same virtue and truth belong to man and god," SVF 3. 250.

33. As is implied by E. Zeller, *Die Philosophie der Griechen*[4] (Leipzig, 1909) 3. 1. 60 f., and M. Pohlenz, *Die Stoa*[3] (Göttingen, 1963) 33.

34. Notice also that logical subjects and etymologies predominate in the later series of the first ethical section, 7. 200.

35. For bibliography on the catalog, cf. Marcello Gigante, *Diogene Laerzio*[2] (Rome-Bari, 1976) 2, 541 n. 233. Bréhier's claim that logical works have "surreptitiously" contaminated the ethical catalog (*Chrysippe* 21) raises more questions than it resolves.

36. A. Bonhöffer has a well-balanced account, *Die Ethik Epiktets* (Stuttgart, 1894) 122-127.

37. Epictetus is however our principal source for the Master argument, 2. 19, 1-5.

5

What Does the Wise Man Know?

G. B. Kerferd

Early Stoic theory divided mankind sharply into two classes, the wise and the foolish (SVF 1.216), and there was no overlap between these two classes. No one who is foolish has knowledge; this is possessed only by the wise man (cf. SVF 1.66; 3.552, 657, etc.), and it seems clear that the wise man is wise in virtue of the knowledge that he possesses. So it is important to ask *what* is it that the wise man knows. We are told a good deal, even if not always as clearly as we might wish, in the ancient sources about the ways in which the Stoics distinguished between knowledge and lesser cognitive states such as opinion and sense-perception. But if we ask, not how does the wise man's knowledge differ from these lesser cognitive states but what is the content of his knowledge, we seem at first sight to find no clear statement in the ancient sources, and either no answer or differing answers in modern writers.

This is a problem that goes back at least to the Socratic doctrine that virtue is knowledge. But in what follows I discuss only the Stoic position. It will be convenient to begin by distinguishing a number of different possibilities, not all mutually exclusive, and then to consider some of the ancient evidence.

A. One extreme view would be that the wise man simply knows everything, i.e., he is omniscient. Thus Johnny Christensen writes

125

"It is thus (logically) possible to imagine a man whose knowledge and understanding is co-extensive with the complete structure of the Universe, the 'objective content' (the *lekton*) of his systems of cognitions being identical with the objective content of an ideal account of Nature. . . . This man is the famous Stoic Sage."[1]

B. It is possible, however, that the wise man's knowledge is in some way selective in content, i.e., he knows some things, but not all things.[2] Two versions of this view may be distinguished: (1) he needs to know the fundamental principles upon which the Universe is based, and so the basic principles of Physics and Logic, but not every detail, or indeed any of the details at all. Moreover while he must know the general laws of the universe, he cannot for example be sure that the content of a particular action corresponds to these general laws, though he can give reasonable grounds for so supposing.[3] On this view knowledge of Physics is indeed essential for the Stoic wise man, but only of its general principles or laws, i.e., the principles of the Stoic Logos; (2) but it is possible that the range of the wise man's knowledge was not as wide as this, but was still further restricted, namely to knowledge of which things are good and which things are bad, either in detail, or at least in their general principles.[4]

C. Another possibility is that the knowledge of the wise man does not really depend at all upon content. While it is not without content what its content is does not matter—in itself it is content-free. This could be the case in either of two ways. (1) Cicero, in a famous passage (*Prior Academics* 2. 144 = SVF 1. 66) dealing with Zeno's account of the knowledge of the wise man, says nothing about content, but distinguishes knowledge from lesser cognitive states by using the analogy of the tightly clenched fist itself tightly clasped by the other hand. The implication is that the content of the hand can be the same for knowledge and for other cognitive states—the difference arises because of the firmness or lack of firmness with which the content is grasped. This might imply that the knowledge of the wise man could apply indifferently to all or any of the cognitive experiences available to the foolish. When converted to knowledge these experiences acquire a certainty, security, and firmness that was previously lacking, but otherwise they are not changed. (2) Finally it would be possible to maintain that the knowledge of the wise man is content-free because the wise man is not concerned with the What of his knowledge but only with the How. More specifically it is the aim of acting rationally, i.e., acting in accordance with reason, which is the distinguishing mark of the wise man, and it is this which constitutes his knowledge.[5]

Before approaching the ancient evidence, certain general considerations may be mentioned. Since the Stoics were uncertain whether there ever had been any actual wise men (or else felt that there could only have been one or two in all), it would not be inconceivable for the (theoretic) Wise Man to have been regarded as omniscient—this would accord with their view of him as constituting an ideal limit of perfection, beyond which there could be no further progression in knowledge or in any other respect. Moreover I take it as common ground that the ultimate ideal, and consequently the essence of the Wise Man, is life in accordance with Nature, which Nature is identifiable with the rational principle found both in the Universe and in the individual man. There can be no conflict between nature in the universe and in the individual, since our individual natures are parts of the nature of the whole (D.L. 7. 87 = SVF 3. 4). But it does not follow that one who knows the part (sc. his own nature) therefore knows everything that can be known about other parts. Moreover the view that the Sage is literally omniscient has to face both general and particular difficulties. First the general difficulties. For the Sage to be omniscient would involve him in knowing everything that is the case—future as well as past, the contents of other people's minds, the minutest details about the most trivial of facts—whether the total number of the stars or the number of hairs on each man's head is odd or even, and so on. This would involve the Wise Man's reason becoming coextensive in its content with the content of the rational principle in the universe. The wise man would have to be the ultimate computer memory bank, the repository of all the information there is, and there is nothing to suggest that the Stoics thought of their Wise Man in these terms. In fact the best historical candidates for the claim to have been Wise Men were for the early Stoics such men as Socrates, Antisthenes, Diogenes the Cynic, Heracles, and Odysseus, none of whom were remarkable either for their detailed knowledge of physical phenomena or for the encyclopedic nature of their knowledge of facts.

There are also specific difficulties arising out of Stoic doctrine which confront the view that the Wise Man is omniscient. The most important are two. First while virtue is acquired as the result of learning (SVF 3. 223, 225) the step from being foolish to being wise is sudden and complete. Only the wise man has knowledge. If his knowledge is knowledge of absolutely everything, then the illumination at the moment of conversion becomes a kind of factual revelation covering all the contents of the universe. There is in the tradition nothing to suggest that this was the kind of conversion which the Stoics had in mind. Nor is the difficulty avoided if we suppose that the Wise Man does not *acquire* information at the moment of conversion which he did not previously possess, but rather converts previously gained opinions into certain knowledge. There is nothing to suggest that the range of previously possessed opinions either had already been or become comprehensive and all-embracing, or that it somehow became so at the moment of conversion.

The second difficulty arises out of the fundamental contention of Stoicism that the particular kind of right action, the *katorthōma*, which is the action of the Wise Man as such, is independent of all external circumstances and considerations. It depends solely on the attitude of mind with which it is done, being determined not by the What or objective content of the action but by the How, to use Nebel's formulation. In such a case the objective content of the Wise Man's knowledge might seem to be irrelevant, and certainly there would be no point in having his mind filled with millions of factual details about the universe.

When we turn to the actual evidence we find, I believe, essentially one statement (repeated a number of times) which suggests omniscience, and a whole series of statements which suggest at least some limit to the range of content of the Wise Man's knowledge. There is first the statement that the Wise Man is "ignorant of nothing"—*mēden agnoein* (SVF 3. 131. p. 41. 12-13). Now there can be no doubt that thus translated into English and taken as an isolated proposition the words *mēden agnoein* do imply omniscience. Moreover it comes from a papyrus from Herculaneum which may well preserve actual words of Chrysippus (cf. *Hermes* 25 (1890) 494-495). But the passage continues with the assertion that ignorance together with supposing, absence of belief, and similar states are foolish and so have no part to play in the case of the wise man. Cicero seems to be proceeding at least indirectly on the basis of this passage when he says "Error, rashness, ignorance, opinion, suspecting, and in a word all the things alien to firm and steady assent, Zeno set apart from virtue and wisdom" (*errorem autem et temeritatem et ignorantiam et opinationem, et suspicionem et uno nomine omnia, quae essent aliena firmae et constantis adsensionis, a virtute sapientiaque removebat* [*Ac. Post.* 1. 42 = SVF 1. 60]) and *his* interpretation suggests that the meaning may have been, not that the Wise Man is omniscient, but that the wisdom of the Wise Man is such that *in it* there is no place for ignorance, i.e., simply that knowledge excludes ignorance. This would not then tell us anything about the *range* of the knowledge of the Wise Man, merely the nature or quality of this knowledge.

The positive evidence for some restriction on the range of knowledge of the Wise Man is of a number of different kinds.[6] Zeno had declared that the education in the various arts and sciences which had become known as the Encyclical or General Education (*Enkuklios Paideia*) was useless (D.L. 7. 32 = SVF 1. 259). Chrysippus did find use in it (D.L. 7. 129 = SVF 3. 738) but there is nothing to suggest that this kind of knowledge was in any way *part* of the wisdom of the wise man (cf. SVF 3. 739, 740). Certainly he seems to have maintained that virtue did *not* arise from any skill or art (*Technē*) and certainly not from Encyclic or Encyclical Education (*SVF* 3. 224). The basic position is as outlined in the first part of Seneca's 88th letter: the Liberal arts (*artes liberales*) are useful only as a *preparation* for philosophy, they are not part of it, and in *Ep.* 117 he lists a whole series of studies that are of no use whatsoever. Stobaeus classes all such studies including the Encyclic Arts as Practical exercises (*Epitēdeumata*), not branches of knowledge (SVF 3. 294).

In the last part of letter 88 (from par. 21 onward) Seneca gives us a somewhat different approach to the problem, based on Posidonius. The arts fall under four headings—(1) *vulgares*, vulgar and sordid; (2) *ludicrae*, sports and theater; (3) *pueriles*, the encyclic arts; and (4) *artes liberales*, properly so called, these being the arts concerned with virtue (*quibus curae virtus est*). In par. 24 the letter continues with a statement (introduced by "he says" *inquit*)[7] that philosophy has as parts natural philosophy, moral philosophy, rational philosophy, and the crowd of *artes liberales*. Mathematics and geometry for example *are*, on this view, a part of philosophy because they are helpful *to* philosophy. To this Seneca objects (and there is good reason to suppose that he is objecting on behalf of Posidonius)[8] that the fact that A is helpful to B does not make A a part of B, (88. 25). Moreoever (88. 26) the aims of philosophy and mathematics are different—philosophy is concerned with causes whereas mathematics is concerned with numbers and measurements. He goes on (88. 28) to say that philosophy is entirely independent of the special sciences—"Philosophy asks no favours from any other source—it builds everything on its own soil."

At the end of this passage Seneca seems to have moved to a view of wisdom that equates it with knowledge of good and evil exclusively, the third view distinguished earlier in this paper. But until this he seems to be operating with a rather different view of wisdom, and this involves the problem of two other formulations of some importance and interest, which it has proved convenient to label the "short" formula: Wisdom is knowledge of things divine and things human (*Sapientia*) *divinorum et humanorum scientia*, and the "long" formula: Wisdom consists in knowing things divine and things human and their causes *sapientia est nosse divina et humana et eorum causas*.[9] It has been thought probable that the reference to causes was specifically introduced by Posidonius,[10] but it hardly alters the doctrine from that required by the short formula, since, as Seneca points out (*Ep.* 89. 5), "The causes of things divine and human are a part of things divine" (*causae divinorum humanorumque pars divinorum sunt*). Nonetheless Seneca's way of putting things does seem to imply that he, at least, regarded the long formula as developed later in time than the short formula, and presumably by addition to it. At the end of the passage discussed earlier (*Ep.* 88. 26 = Posidonius F 90 Edelstein-Kidd) we are given what I call the "restricted" formula, namely, the wise man investigates and has come to know the causes of natural phenomena (*sapiens causas naturalium et quaerit et novit*), restricted because it seems deliberately to restrict the wise man to knowledge of causes, leaving the facts themselves to the geometer and other similarly specialized scientists. This makes it clear that it is not the same as the long formula, despite the fact that both involve reference to causes.

It looks then as if we can distinguish three separate formulations in Seneca—the restricted formula—wisdom is knowledge of causes; the short formula—wisdom is knowledge of things divine and things human; and the long formula—wisdom is knowledge of things divine and human and their causes. We do not have materials to enable us to reconstruct the full history of these formulations before Seneca. The long formula could be explained by the addition of the restricted formula to the short formula,[11] although as Seneca saw such an addition might very well have been by way of exposition rather than involving any modification of the meaning of the short formula. But what of the restricted formula? If the analysis suggested above is correct it also is likely to come immediately from Posidonius. But while the long formula looks very much like a development from the short formula, the restricted formula does not look like this, but rather like an alternative and perhaps more precise formulation of the short formula (cf. Sen. *Ep.* 89. 5 just quoted). Certainly the view that knowledge is knowledge of causes was clearly stated already by Aristotle (*Met.* A.981a23-b6). The distinction between the Encyclia and philosophic knowledge is developed at some length by Philo (*De Congr. qu. erud. gratia* 798, 140-151) in terms of a double antithesis, first that of Seneca in *Ep.* 88, between contributory or preliminary studies and philosophy itself, and then in terms of the contrast between skill or art (*Technē*) and knowledge (*Epistēmē*). The basis of the second antithesis is clearly stated—knowledge is distinguished by the presence of a sure and unshakeable grasping of what is known (*Katalēpsis*)—but this grasping or *Katalēpsis* is not found in the case of mere arts or skills (par. 141 = SVF 2. 95). Now it is clear that this distinction between *Technē* and *Epistēmē* was fully developed in Chrysippus and the early Stoa (SVF 2. 93, 94, 96, 97). It is reasonable to conclude that when Philo distinguished between the Encyclia and philosophic knowledge in terms of the distinction between *Technē* and *Epistēmē* he was not simply applying a distinction made by Posidonius, but rather the basic distinction already familiar to the early Stoa.

So far, we might suggest, it begins to look as if the Stoics may have been operating with a basic distinction between a kind of fundamental knowledge (e.g., of causes and principles) and other ways of acquiring and holding information. Another approach altogether may lead us in the same direction. The wise man is defined as he who possesses knowledge of the true (SVF 2.132). Sextus Empiricus expounds at some length on two occasions (*Pyrrh. Hyp.* 2. 80-84, *Adv. Math.* 7. 38-45, cf. SVF 2. 132) the basic Stoic distinction between truth and the true. Truth is corporeal since it is "knowledge declaratory of all true things" and as such is a particular state of the corporeal *Hēgemonikon*—that is to say, Reason or Logos as the authoritative part of the human soul. But the true (whether singular or plural) is incorporeal, because it is a statement (*Axiōma*) about something and as such is incorporeal. The full nature of this Stoic doctrine has not yet received definitive treatment or explanation.[12]

The particular corporeal state of the *Hēgemonikon* which is Truth, is knowledge or *Epistēmē*, and it is a mark of the wise man. Only the Wise Man (among men) possesses knowledge, but it is found as well in the gods, who are also wise (SVF 3. 245-254). But the gods and the divine are for the Stoics the active rational principle in the Universe, and to this active principle are assigned the terms cause, nature, necessity and, finally, truth (SVF 2. 913). So truth is not simply a particular state of the Hēgemonikon of the (human) wise man; it is also a corporeal property of the active principle in the Universe as a whole. This truth is the Nature of the Universe, and is the first cause of all true things (Marcus Aurelius 9. 2). Just what this truth is which is equated with the Nature of the Universe is unclear, but it would seem to be a state, or rather the state, of the active rational principle that is found both in perfected individuals and in the Universe as a whole. It is not the whole of reality, but in some sense the causal, organizing, rational, or logical principle underlying reality; and it is the principle of knowledge in the wise man just as it is the structural principle of the universe. A fully specific formulation of this principle may be seen in Posidonius's declaration (F 186 Edelstein-Kidd) that the goal for man is to live in the contemplation of the truth and ordering (*Taxis*) of all things and in helping to establish this so far as is possible. The truth that is in all things *is* the *Taxis* or principle of order, and what the wise man, who alone achieves the goal, is doing is contemplating, not the details of the universe, but its organizing principle which is also the structure. In so doing he joins in bringing this structure into being (in himself).

Some further light may be shed if we approach the problem

from still another point of view, that of the Stoic doctrine of the virtues. The virtue known as *Phronēsis* seems to have had a two-fold application for the earlier Stoics. For Zeno it is the most fundamental virtue of all (which I will call Sense I), identified by him with *Epistēmē* (SVF 1. 201); and as such, both for him and for all the early Stoics, it was a condition or state of the *Hēgemonikon* (SVF 1. 202; 3. 198). The various "virtues" are on this view aspects, no more, of *Phronēsis* which is the one unique virtue[13]—thus justice is *Phronēsis* in things that are to be distributed, courage is *Phronēsis* in things that are to be faced without retreating, and so on. This one ultimate unique virtue Ariston supposed was knowledge of things good and things bad, and it acquired different names, i.e., the names of the particular virtues, when operative in different spheres. But Ariston did not call this ultimate virtue *Phronēsis*, he treated *Phronēsis* as simply *one* aspect of this knowledge, parallel with courage and justice, i.e., he used *Phronēsis* in a more limited sense than that used by Zeno (cf. SVF 1. 374), a sense that I shall call Sense II.

For Chrysippus Ariston's position was not satisfactory—he wrote a book against him to show that though all the virtues were indeed related to a single power or function of the soul (SVF 3. 257), nonetheless each really did possess its own independent sphere (SVF 3. 256). But the only way in which such a differentiation of virtues could arise is in terms of the objective content of each of the various subordinate virtues. In other words virtue in general, and particular virtues as well, can always be looked at from two aspects. There is first of all that which makes a virtue virtuous and there is second that which differentiates one virtue from another and makes it be the specific virtue that it is. This second or differentiating feature Galen does not hesitate to call, in Aristotelian language, the Matter (*Hylē*) of the virtue (SVF 3. 256. p. 61. 18-20).

This is the background against which we should consider two statements that otherwise might seem inexplicable. (1) The activities that constitute virtue are right actions in the strict sense—*Katorthōmata* (SVF 3. 501)—and included among these activities are *Phronēsis* and Temperance and so on (SVF 3. 501, 284, 297; 2. 1005). (2) The virtue of *Phronēsis* is concerned with appropriate actions—*Kathēkonta* (SVF 3. 264. pp. 64. 16 and 65. 1). The basic

distinction between *Katorthōmata* and *Kathēkonta* being that the
latter are defined in terms of the objective content of the actions—
the What as opposed to the How—it follows that virtues that are
distinguished from one another by their content or sphere of action
are being distinguished within the sphere of *Kathēkonta*—in the
sphere of *Katorthōmata* no such distinctions are possible. So when
Diogenes Laertius (7. 125 = SVF 3. 295) distinguishes each of the
main virtues as dealing with a particular subject, and treats *Phronēsis* alongside Courage and other virtues, he is clearly using *Phronēsis* in Sense II. When therefore he declares that *Phronēsis* is concerned with acts to be done, acts not to be done, and acts that fall
under neither head (sc. Adiaphora), he is likewise speaking within
the sphere of *Kathēkonta* (so also in SVF 3. 262, 263, 268). But the
formula relating *Phronēsis* to acts to be done and acts not to be
done is not confined to *Phronēsis* in Sense II, it is also found for
Phronēsis in Sense I in the sphere of *Katorthōmata* (SVF 2. 1005,
1181; 3. 284).

I want to suggest that there is no inconsistency of any kind here.
I take it as basic to our understanding of the Stoics that for them
every *Katorthōma* is also a *Kathēkon*, although of course it is not
the case that every *Kathēkon* is a *Katorthoma*. In other words, the
right action done by the wise man, which is right in virtue of How
it is done, is also always an appropriate action and it is appropriate in virtue of the What, or the objective content of the action.
Everything that the wise man does will consequently have these
two aspects, the How and the What. This explains the twofold
application of *Phronēsis*: in Sense I it functions as the source of
Katorthōmata, in Sense II it functions as a (i.e., one) source of
Kathēkonta. In each case it is a manifestation of the activity of the
rational element in the soul striving to act, according to nature, in
accordance with the active principle in the universe and in the soul
itself. This in turn enables us to suggest a solution to the question,
What does the wise man know? He knows what is in accordance
with nature: at the highest level this is knowledge of what acting
rationally is or consists in, in other words knowledge of the How
in relation to action. But it also includes knowledge of what is
Kathēkon in various circumstances, and so it includes knowledge
of the What, not in the sense of the detailed specifications, or the
specific *praecepta* or precepts, but the principle that determines

the What. More simply, the rational principle can be seen both (1) as a purely formal principle, constituting the How, the *Katorthōma;* and (2) as the formal principle expressing itself in the What, i.e., as *Kathēkonta.* The first aspect is concerned with intensionality and the second with extensionality, but the virtuous activity is one, seen from two different aspects.

NOTES

1. Johnny Christensen, *An Essay on the Unity of Stoic Philosophy,* (Copenhagen, 1962) 68-69, cited with approval by Gerard Watson, *The Stoic Theory of Knowledge* (Belfast, 1966) 63.

2. So A. A. Long, *Problems in Stoicism* (London, 1971) 101: "The sage is of course neither omnipotent nor omniscient." The denial of omniscience is found already in Justus Lipsius, *Manuductio ad Stoicam Philosophiam* (1604) III, viii taken by me from the text in *Senecae Opera,* ed. M. N. Bouillet, Vol. I (Paris, 1827) cxcii-cxciv.

3. Cf. M. Van Straaten, *Panétius, sa vie et ses écrits* (Amsterdam, 1946) 149-150, following G. Nebel, *Hermes* 70 (1935) 447-449 and I. G. Kidd in *Class. Quart.* n.s. 5 (1955) 194 = *Problems in Stoicism,* 167.

4. So apparently Josiah Gould, *The Philosophy of Chrysippus* (Leiden, 1970) 172-176, cf. also 168-169. Close to Gould's position is D. Tsekourakis, *Studies in the Terminology of Early Stoic Ethics (Hermes, Einzelschriften* 32) (Wiesbaden, 1974) 76-77.

5. P. Barth-A. Goedeckemeyer, *Die Stoa*⁶ (Stuttgart, 1948) 27; E. Zeller, *Philosophie der Griechen* III. 1.⁵ (1923) 242.

6. In what follows I draw considerably upon W. Ganss, *Das Bild des Weisen bei Seneca* (Inorg. Diss. Freiburg im Schweiz, 1948) 11-14, 14-24.

7. This shows that we are concerned with an unnamed objector to what has just been stated—so earlier in this letter, par. 12. For a statement on this usage, see W. C. Summers, *Select Letters of Seneca* (London, 1910) 196 (note on *Ep.* 28. 8).

8. Reinhardt, *Poseidonios* (Munich, 1921) 50 wanted to make the content of this objection (though not the objector himself!) an expression of the views of Posidonius. But the special sciences, which the objector wants to include in philosophy, formed part of the Encyclic Arts and so the third class in the Posidonian classification given just before. In this classification only the fourth class, not the third class, constitutes a part of the concern of the wise man. This has been pointed out to me by I. G. Kidd, to whom I am deeply grateful for preventing me from going badly astray here.

9. The "short" formula in Seneca, *Ep.* 88. 33 and 89. 5, Cic., *De Fin.* 2. 37, Sextus, *SVF* 2. 36, Cic. *De Off.* 1. 153 as well as in later writers; the "long" formula in Seneca *Ep.* 89. 5, Cic., *De Off.* 2. 5, *Tusc.* 4. 57, 5. 7, Philo, *De Cong. qu. Erud. gr.* 79.

10. So Reinhardt, *Poseidonios* 58; Pohlenz, *Die Stoa*, I, 214; II, 106, as against Hirzel, *Untersuch.* II. 512. 1; cf. Sen. *Ep.* 95. 65.

11. But it is worth pointing out this is *not* what Seneca says Posidonius did. What Seneca says Posidonius did (*Ep.* 95. 65 = Posidonius F 176 Edelstein-Kidd) was to add the search for causes to *"praeceptio"*—the offering of moral precepts.

12. See in the meantime the suggestive treatment by A. A. Long, *Problems in Stoicism* (London, 1971) 98-104, *Hellenistic Philosophy* (London, 1974) 130-131.

13. See for what follows E. Bréhier, *Chrysippe*² (Paris, 1951) 235-245.

6

Monism and Immanence: The Foundations of Stoic Physics

Robert B. Todd

Monism and immanence are the central ideas in Stoic physical theory. They are associated in any monistic system because the One must in some sense be present in all that is derived from and dependent on it. In Stoicism this recurrent metaphysic is expressed in materialistic terms with the One being a physical element Fire, and the sphere of its immanence the cosmos that evolves from it; Fire is immanent both by being the self-moving source of a cosmogony, and by a continued presence in the created cosmos. In this paper I shall examine the attempts of two Stoics, Zeno and Chrysippus, to formulate a physical theory adequate to these basic intuitions. In order to cover the relevant material in the present space my discussion will inevitably be schematic and speculative. I cannot hope to give full attention to the numerous problems in the source material, to treat adequately the question of the influences on Stoic physics, nor of course to discuss with any fairness the views of other scholars.[1] My hope is that by concentrating on this central theme in Stoic physical theory I can suggest something of the overall structure and continuity of thought in this part of the Stoic system, while raising the major problems of interpretation.

The Stoics were not original in formulating a theory of physical monism, but were the first to recognize that such a system required

137

a specific physical theory to explain the immanence of the primary element. Thus Heraclitus (fr. 30) asserts the capacity of Fire to undergo change into the other elements, or Diogenes of Apollonia (fr. 5) claims that Air is "present in" everything, but neither formulates a physical theory to express this immanence. In this way the broader metaphysics of their systems, in which the primary elements have a divine character and a controlling force over the universe, are not satisfactorily sustained in their physics. Whatever the actual success of Stoic physical theory in meeting its own aspirations, it certainly cannot be accused of this deficiency. It was undoubtedly influenced by conceptions of immanence introduced by Plato and Aristotle. Plato had developed the concept of a self-moving soul pervasive throughout the universe, and this idea was reflected in Aristotle's theory of nature as a similarly self-moving principle in bodies that underwent natural change.[2] The precise degree of influence on Stoic cosmology from either of these sources is disputable.[3] What is clear is that the Stoics used many inherited conceptions to express the immanence of the primary element in materialistic terms. Self-motion for them was always the motion of a body and not that of an immaterial force of formative principle; immanence was therefore the presence of this body in bodies derived from and dependent on it.

I shall explore the details of the theories through which the Stoics expressed these ideas by considering physical theory in a narrow sense than did they themselves. *Physis* or Nature in Stoic philosophy was an evaluative category that served as the basis of ethical theory. The primary element of Stoic monism was seen as divine and rational, and what I have termed its immanence also represented a causal process specifiable as fate and providence, and expressing a teleological view of nature. These conceptions are ultimately derived from a condensed analysis of the relation between monism and immanence in what the Stoics called their theory of first principles (*archai*). In this paper I shall be concerned only with the problem of the relation of this theory to the body of qualitative physics that Zeno and Chrysippus developed to demonstrate the immanence of the primary element. Thus after discussing in Part I the character of these first principles, a common ground to both philosophers, I shall try to show how first Zeno (Part II), and then Chrysippus (Part III), sought to embody them in cosmogonical and cosmological theories. My object will be to decide how successful they were in providing a physical theory adequate to the metaphysics of the theory of first principles. In the final part of the paper (IV) I shall raise briefly some of the implications of this discussion for an assessment of the status of physical theory in Stoic philosophy.

I. MONISM AND IMMANENCE: THE GENERAL THEORY[4]

The Stoic theory of first principles perplexed many ancient critics because it did not describe an element or set of elements that served as the source or constituents of secondary compounds, but two abstractly characterized notions, That-which-acts (*to poioun*) and That-which-is-acted-on, or is passive (*to paschon*), that in turn are regularly referred to as God and matter respectively (SVF 1. 85, 86; 2. 299-303). Now since Stoicism is a monistic system the two first principles must be physically inseparable (SVF 1. 88), so that this duality is reached by a logical, or conceptual, distinction. This means that each principle is either only active or acted on, and that they are both identifiable only in relation to one another; they cannot, like the qualitative powers of Aristotelian physics, separately act or be acted on under different conditions.

To give sense to these abstractions we must first establish the physical context of this relationship between the principles. We can begin with the basic conception of Stoic physics, that there is a finite material continuum. Acting and being-acted-on can then be regarded as logically distinguishable aspects of this single body, whatever qualitative forms it might assume in cosmology and cosmogony; and this accords with a general Stoic definition of that which acts or is acted on as body (SVF 1. 90; 2. 387). Put otherwise, this single body with two such aspects must be one that acts on itself, a notion that, as we shall see, is carried over into the qualitative physics of Stoic cosmogony which describes the action of a self-moving primary element.

But if these first principles are to be aspects of a single body, it must also follow that they cannot be bodies themselves. That they have such an incorporeal status is conveyed only by one much disputed reading in the Suda, a Byzantine lexicon, where a standard

report of this doctrine is quoted (SVF 2. 299). This is an attractive
alternative to that in the manuscripts where the *archai* are said to
be bodies, if only because in general an aspect, or logically distinguishable feature, of a body cannot itself be a body. The atomic
structure and insolubility in water of lead, for example, are similarly aspects that are interdependent and therefore incapable of
separate physical existence. Now some ancient authors (SVF 1. 98,
2. 310) do speak of the first principles as bodies, but in one of these
cases (SVF 2. 310) the report also characterizes them as separately
identifiable bodies. The latter view clearly misrepresents the
Stoics, and is probably itself the basis of the claim that the *archai*
are bodies rather than derived from it. In general then the interdependence of the *archai* seems to require that they be incorporeal,
for the Stoics can give no sense to the notion of separate bodies
that just act, or are just acted on. We should also, I think, accept
that this interpretation must be valid even where a qualitative distinction can be drawn between the active and passive aspects of
body, as in the cosmogonical process when secondary elements
are derived from the primary element. Otherwise the Stoics would
have no safeguard against the criticism that they believed that two
bodies could occupy the same place. Part of that safeguard must of
course be the form that their physics takes in giving qualitative
values to activity and passivity, and this we shall examine in detail, but ultimately it will rely on the theory that these aspects are
not themselves bodies. Finally our interpretation need not conflict
with the general Stoic doctrine that qualities are bodies (e.g., SVF
2. 377); for this applies to the qualitative form that things in the
Stoic universe assume as the result of the copresence of the active
and passive principles, and is therefore dependent on their being
incorporeal.

The Stoics' conception of their first principles has, I would
argue, been to some extent misunderstood by ancient and modern
critics alike because a crucial term in the reports of this doctrine
has been misconstrued. The passive principle is regularly described
as matter, a substance that is *apoios*. The Greek term has been
understood to mean "qualityless," one of its senses, so that a critic
could then, for example, ask how God could produce everything
from such a substance (e.g., SVF 2. 323a), as though it were a separate body on which a purely active principle acted. But a rarer

though perfectly possible sense for *apoios* is "inert," or "not acting," its literal meaning. If we grant this sense to the Stoics, as indeed Seneca's apparent translation of the term into Latin as *iners* (SVF 2. 303) suggests that we should, then the logic of their monism is directly sustained. Inert matter is simply one aspect of body that complements its other aspect, its activity; as activity requires a medium to act on, so that medium can itself be identified, trivially and reflexively, as not acting. There is no "mysterious qualityless matter" (Sextus Empiricus, *P.H.* 3. 31), but only the inert aspect of a body that acts on itself. These aspects are, as we have seen, only logically distinguishable features of body, and the language in which they are identified should be understood as compatible with this position. Thus there is no absurdity, as Plutarch (SVF 2. 380) thought, in the claim of some Stoics that matter is *apoios* because it is the source of all qualities. This is simply to claim that body that acts on itself does so in virtue of its having an aspect that does not act; qualities are then produced in the cosmogonical process that we shall consider shortly by this action and not by the action of one body on another.[5]

It is time to draw this abstract account further in the direction of qualitative physics. I shall try to show that in this context the theory of first principles has two functions. First, it provides a groundwork for a cosmogonical account of change in which the activity of the active principle on itself is the creativity of the primary element in establishing the cosmos. Second, it serves as an analysis of the universe as a whole, or of any of its parts, at any point in its history, and shows that the object of analysis will have two inseparable aspects, the active and the passive, or God and matter. In this second role it confirms the immanence of the One that its first use must demonstrate through specific physical theories.

The more general of the roles is of course the second.[6] Its validity in Stoicism can best be appreciated by reconsidering in more detail the text (SVF 2. 299) in which the *archai* are said to be incorporeal. This reports that the Stoics "say that *archai* and elements differ in that the former are not created and destroyed, while the latter are destroyed at the conflagration (*ekpyrōsis*)." It then goes on to describe the *archai* as formless and incorporeal in contrast to the elements that have to be formed. In this distinction between *archai* and the process of elemental change from the primary element Fire, and back to it at the periodic conflagration of the universe, we can, I think, see the role of the principles as analytical concepts. They apply to the universe at any stage in this evolution, and can perhaps be identified with what the Stoics called *lekta*, or incorporeal statements made about bodies,[7] an attractive view in the light of our earlier interpretation of the *archai* as incorporeal on the basis of the present text. The full nature of the *archai* as analytical principles can only emerge in our discussion of the details of physical theory. For the moment we may further establish that they have this role by considering the reports (SVF 1. 81 = 2. 316, 317) in which the Stoics are said to distinguish the "primary matter," or substance (*ousia*) from which the universe evolves, from its constituent parts, with the former remaining quantitatively the same whatever the quantitative variations in the parts. The whole to which these parts belong can, I think, be understood as the single body of which there are active and passive aspects,[8] and the theory here is thus the classical monistic view that there is only one whole to which all parts are relative. This, I would suggest, is also complemented by the analytical use of the theory of first principles; for if either the whole or any of its parts can be analyzed into an active and passive aspect, then when this analysis is applied to a part it will entail that this part is part of the whole to which an identical analysis could also be applied.

In its other use the theory of *archai* has to partner this analytical function by providing a cosmogonical theory leading to a universe of which such an analysis could be given. This is achieved, initially at least, through a specific value being attached to the notion of the active principle acting on itself in terms of the behavior of the primary element Fire. Nature we find regularly defined as "Fire, acting like a craft [or like a craftsman—*technikos*] proceeding on a course toward change" (SVF 1. 171; 2. 1027). Now such activity requires some material on which the craft can work, and by the terms of the theory of first principles this could only be Fire itself; like body in general, Fire must use itself as its own matter. Thus Fire's "self-crafting," as we may term it, becomes a qualitative version of the abstract notion of body acting on itself, or having both an active and an inert aspect. In the next section we shall see that this model of craftsmanship leads directly into the biological model that Zeno uses in his cosmogony to describe how Fire actualizes itself in the formation of the cosmos. For the moment we may simply note an evident and revealing antecedent to it in Aristotle's claim in his general discussion of teleology (*Physics* 2. 8. 199b28-29, cf. 199a12-13) that if the crafts followed the processes of natural change then they would be self-moving; wood, he for example says, would naturally grow into a ship if the craft of shipbuilding were in the wood. In their conception of "crafting Fire" the Stoics have retained the same inseparability of a self-moving craft and its matter as Aristotle envisaged, but transposed it to a cosmic level.[9] But they differ, as we shall see, in regarding this crafting force as body that continues to act within the matter derived from it.

The two applications of the theory of first principles that I have discussed are of course equivalent. It is, that is, a matter of indifference whether we choose to analyze the universe, or any of its parts, into their active and passive (or divine and material) aspects, or whether we describe how the activity of the one is being exercised on the passivity of the other. In the first case we convey the general fact of immanence, while in the second we specify how the primary element achieves and maintains this state. It must however follow that if in both cases the notion of immanence is not the same then there should be some reason for the divergence in the relevant physical theory. For example, a cosmogony may entail that the primary element is immanent in different degrees in different parts of the universe, and that there are different balances between the active and passive principles; this will mean that the results of using the *archai* analytically will vary because of the way that they have been applied in the cosmogony. Physical theory would have to take account of this, and in the next two sections we shall assess Zeno's and Chrysippus's success on this and other counts in their attempts to express in physical terms the immanence of the primary element of which they had given a metaphysical formulation in the theory of first principles.

II. ZENO: IMMANENCE AND COSMOGONY[10]

A typical version of the cosmogony attributed to Zeno is as follows (1. 102):

In the beginning God, being independent, transformed the whole of substance through air into water; and as the [male] seed is enveloped in the embryo, so also is God, as the seminal reason of the universe, left behind in the moisture, adapting matter to himself for the next development. Thereafter he first brings to birth the four elements.

This and similar accounts can be related to the depiction of the primary element of Stoic physics as "self-crafting" Fire. First, as we see, this element transforms itself (i.e., "the whole of substance") into water through the intermediary element air. Fire is often itself compared to a seed (SVF 1. 98, 107) and here we see it creating a seedbed or cosmic embryo by associating itself with moisture in a traditional combination of generative matter. Whatever medical sources this cosmobiology may have, the Aristotelian theory of sexual generation offers the philosophically most illuminating background. Aristotle compared the male seed to a craftsman (*Generation of Animals* 1. 22 *passim*), and also described the action of this seed on the female menses as the contact of an active with a passive principle (*Gen. An.* 1. 21, 729b9-22). Zeno's cosmogony can be read as an adaptation of this account. Fire as the primary element is a self-moving seed that creates from itself passive matter on which to act in bringing to birth the elements of the cosmos; it is therefore never separate from matter but actually present, or "left behind," in it. This contains two important differences from Aristotle's account of generation. First, in his system the male seed is simply a moving or formative principle in its action on the female matter (*Gen. An.* 2. 1 *passim*), and is dispersed after the formation of the embryo (*Gen. An.* 2. 3, 737a8-16). Secondly, Aristotle regarded this seed as a substance formed by the concoction of nutriment in the body (*Gen. An.* 1. 18); Zeno however must regard the seminal Fire as itself the source of the bodies derived from it. In this way his notion of cosmic genesis jointly expresses the theory of generation known as *pangenesis* (that the semen is drawn from all parts of the body), as well the theory of preformationism (that the embryo is a microcosm of the fully grown organism), both of which were attacked by Aristotle (*Gen. An.* 1. 17; 2. 1). Not surprisingly they are paralleled in Zeno's own theory of sexual generation (SVF 1. 128): that the male seed is drawn from (an *apospasma* of) the faculties of the male soul, and acts on passive female matter.

This embodiment of the theory of first principles in a biological model serves Zeno's purposes very well. The notion of Fire as a self-generating seed explains how matter in the universe is differentiated, while retaining the requirement that the primary element (or active principle) be inseparable from the bodies derived from it. Thus in the cosmic embryo Fire and moisture are the qualitative equivalents of the active and passive principles but cannot be separately identifiable bodies; in this, and in all subsequent cases in the evolution of the elements, there is only one body with two aspects. In the embryo moisture can be said to be an aspect of Fire because it is derived from it; its passivity is its physical dependence on this generative source, and its inseparability is just the relation that exists between any part of a grown organism and its seed.

The subsequent evolution of the elements must be understood then in terms of this biological foundation. Although the traditional strata of earth, water, air, and fire emerge by a process of condensation and rarefaction from the original embryo (SVF 1. 102), they are dependent on the self-generating property of the primary element. The cosmogony is completed when this element reemerges as the uppermost element, the matter of the heavenly bodies (SVF 1. 116); this indicates that it was actually present in the preceding process, and must now reestablish itself in the final cosmology as the substance of the self-moving stars and planets, as distinguished from other bodies in the sublunar area of the universe that are self-moving to the degree that this element is present in them. In other words there are two levels to Zeno's cosmos; the fire of the heavens, which is self-moving, has circular motion (SVF 1. 115) and is God's location in the cosmos (SVF 1. 154), and the sublunar bodies whose essential motion must be rectilinear. In terms of the theory of first principles, Fire will not be distinguishable from its matter at the former level, while at the latter there will be the same kind of qualitative distinction between active and passive aspects, as we noted in the case of the cosmic embryo. The presence of the primal element in this sublunar world can be noted particularly in the case of organisms (SVF 1. 120) where it is a principle of life; indeed Zeno defines the soul as a combination of this heat with breath (a *pneuma enthermon*, SVF 1. 135). Otherwise it is to be distinguished from the destructive fire of our ordinary experience.[11]

Such in brief outline is Zeno's cosmology. It represents an economical application of the theory of first principles both as a groundwork for a cosmogony, and as an account of the immanence of the primary element. The model adopted for the cosmogony explains in terms of an organic development the different degrees to which the primary element is immanent in the universe. The analysis of different parts of the universe into active and passive aspects will vary in qualitative terms because the original seed has so distributed itself. But at this point a difficulty arises. The theory of first principles prescribes only a general theory of immanence and not a full account of the development and structure of the universe. The elements that evolve in the sublunar world, for example, must themselves be formed into compounds, and in the case of organisms specific differences be established and maintained. But Zeno's concept of immanence does not provide a satisfactory explanation of such phenomena. As we have seen, the primary element reemerges as the matter of the heavenly bodies and is not further distributed physically in the cosmos. Its immanence thereafter is expressed as permeation of divine reason (SVF 1. 161, 162), where this seems to cover the causation of seasonal change (SVF 1. 165). Physical immanence must therefore be an implication of the cosmogonical process itself; the sense in which compounds in the sublunar world are permeated by the primal fire is simply that it is their generative source. Thus if the heat of an organism is identical with the "crafting" heat of the heavenly bodies (SVF 1. 128) this does not mean that any form of emanation from the latter occurs, but only that fire is present in an organism as a result of the cosmogony. In this sense God is to be taken as the "seminal reason" of the universe; the reason that emanates from the heavens has no physical correlate. But the difficulty with this account is that a seed is not the life-principle of an organism. If there is a constantly generative heat in the universe it still is not clear how in itself it differentiates matter into different types of organisms. The universe as a whole is identified as animated (SVF 1. 110-114) by the God that is located in the heavens, but his influence on the sublunar world is not expressed through any direct physical influence. Zeno may therefore have a theory of immanence adequate to the requirements of the theory of first principles, but still not satisfactory as a general theory of nature; some extension of Stoic materialism seems called for.

There are indications that some of these difficulties were already felt in antiquity. In Cicero's *On the Nature of the Gods* (1. 36-38) an Epicurean critic wondered about the compatibility of Zeno's identification of God both with the heavens, and with an all-permeating reason. His remarks are polemical, but his point seems to be that Zeno had detached God from the universe and only provided a vague account of his relation to it. An answer of sorts is given later (2. 27) by a Stoic spokesman who emphasizes that organisms in the universe are permeated by a life-giving heat that seems to be distributed from the location of the uppermost element; the latter theory is certainly not Zeno's and can probably be attributed to Cleanthes, if not later authors.[12] What is interesting is that this response is couched not in the terms of a more precise theory of the growth of the cosmos from a seminal fire, but with reference to the final stratification of the elements. The notion of a life-principle in the universe which we have claimed was missing from Zeno's cosmogony is provided by inserting an additional distribution of the primary element from its cosmological position as the matter of the heavenly bodies.

Zeno presumably regarded his cosmogony as itself an adequate account of the differentiation of compounds; a seed he must have felt could cause growth into a living organism, and impose structure on the elements that evolved in the cosmogony. But even so such a creative force hardly explains the variety of compounds; indeed Zeno is left with a crude animism that he could only have refined if he had made more precise some of the concepts in his cosmobiology. We can perhaps see this if we recall his modifications in Aristotelian genetic theory. Aristotle had explained reproduction in an eternal universe where the actuality of the male preceded his inseminating the female and establishing an embryo as a potential organism. He could thus be sure of the result of this process—man would beget man. In Zeno's cosmogony, however, a single seminal element was in potentiality the universe and created it by actualizing itself; that process of actualization has to be explained through to its conclusion in the evolution of the cosmos, but it is just such completeness that is lacking from his physics. Organic growth on the one hand, and an immaterial reason pervading from the heavens on the other, do not jointly provide a theory of immanence that explains the identity and variety of physical bodies in the universe.

Stoic physics was not to develop by revising Zeno's cosmogony. It was to make the theory of immanence a more precise account of the individuation and differentiation of matter by showing that the primary element in its cosmological role as the matter of the heavenly bodies was distributed in the sublunar world. The account that appears in Cicero is a vaguely articulated version of such a theory. Its most elaborate form was assumed in Chrysippus's theory of immanence. Whether his revision could also retain the model of organic change on which Zeno's cosmogony was built, and what difficulties a deviation from this might present, we shall consider in the next section.

III. CHRYSIPPUS: PNEUMA AND IMMANENCE[13]

Chrysippus's theory of pneuma has been the most discussed part of Stoic physics in recent years, but it has not often been presented as the successor to Zeno's cosmology. I shall argue, against the generally held view, that it must be seen as reform of that earlier system rather than a radical break with it. As such it provides the comprehensive theory of immanence missing from Zeno's physics, though whether in this way it more successfully embodies the combination of monism and immanence established in the theory of first principles will have to be considered.

Pneuma literally means breath, but the Stoics drew on a medical tradition in which this substance was represented as a principle of life organisms and a combination of both heat and air. Zeno, as we saw, defined the soul as "heated pneuma" (SVF 1. 135). It would be unlikely that this body replaced the Zenonian primary element of "crafting Fire" in a revised cosmobiology, since Chrysippus accepted a cosmogony almost identical to Zeno's (SVF 2. 579), as well as the doctrine of a cosmic conflagration (*ekpyrōsis*) in which everything returned to the primal Fire (e.g., SVF 2. 596). Although Chrysippus regarded pneuma as part of the content of the male sperm along with moisture (SVF 2. 741; cf. *Gen. An.* 2. 2, 736a1-2) there is no evidence that either he or Zeno associated it with the combination of heat and *moisture* that formed the cosmic embryo. And finally those texts that equate or juxtapose pneuma and the primal fire are vague doxographical reports (SVF 2.774, 1027) that scarcely allow us to see this Chrysippean innovation as supplanting Zeno's primary element. Here I shall try to establish that the two are indeed closely related but that pneuma enters the cosmogonical scene at a later stage as the continuator of the action of that element, with the basic framework of Zenonian cosmology left intact.

If pneuma was not a primogenitive element, what was it? For Chrysippus it clearly has cosmic significance since it pervades the whole univers (SVF 2.441, 473), and this is generally understood[14] to be a transposition of Zeno's identification of the soul with this substance to a macrocosmic level. In this role it also retained the properties of air and heat that had made Zeno's full definition of the soul *pneuma enthermon* (heated air). This leads some sources to define it as a compound of the two elements fire and air (e.g., SVF 2.442), though this is somewhat misleading. Fire here must presumably be fire with the creative or "crafting" properties possessed by Zeno's primary element if pneuma is to be immanent in the universe, but it would be strange if it were also associated with the sublunar air that does not possess the same property of self-motion. Again we know that one of pneuma's activities was to pervade the air when the soul-pneuma extended from the senses into the medium between a perceiver and the object of his perception (SVF 2.866).[15] This makes it unlikely that air was one of its constituents. If, however, pneuma is not heated air in virtue of a blend of two of the four elements, there is only one candidate that could serve as its substance, the *aithēr* that formed the matter of the heavenly bodies. *Aithēr* may have been already used by Zeno to characterize this matter (cf. SVF 1.154), but it was certainly the term used by Chrysippus (SVF 2.579). It is heated air simply because it results from the rarefaction of air in the cosmogony; to define it as *aithēr* seems to be an effective way of distinguishing it from the primary fire whose properties of self-motion and divinity it nonetheless retains. Pneuma is nowhere explicitly identified with this body, but if we build on that *prima facie* likelihood then I believe that considerable sense can be made both of its physical properties and cosmological role, and also of some of the confusing evidence about it.

Aithēr then as the substance of the heavenly bodies is self-moving and has circular motion (SVF 2. 579), and we know that Chrysippus located God in its "purest" part (SVF 2. 644). This admission that the primary element in its cosmological role is immanent in the universe in different degrees establishes a common ground with Zeno, but Chrysippus, I shall try to show, is innovative in constructing a further theory of physical immanence on this foundation. For although, as I have suggested, pneuma was to be identified in substance with *aithēr* it was specifically assigned the function of distributing this physically, and metaphysically, superior element throughout the universe. Pneuma will not pervade the *aithēr* itself since that body is inherently self-moving, but it will move out from it into bodies that require such a property. These bodies will be the sublunar elements that have evolved in the cosmogony that in relation to pneuma constitute matter that is "inherently inert and unmoved" (*argon ex heautēs kai akinēton*, SVF 2. 449). Thus Chrysippus would not explain the formation of compounds by the theory of a seminal reason immanent in the universe from the cosmic embryo, but would show how the organic growth of the universe is completed by inserting into Zenonian cosmology a principle of life associated with the primary element in its intracosmic role. The degrees of divine immanence in the cosmos will then be specified, as we shall see, by the different manner in which pneuma pervades different parts of the sublunar world.

I shall try to confirm this outline with reference to the physics of pneuma before considering its relation to the theory of first principles. Pneuma's motion is of a peculiar sort; it is described as "tensional" (*tonikē*, e.g., SVF 2. 448) and as a form of oscillation "from itself and into itself" (SVF 2. 442, 471). Its own identity in distinction from the *aithēr* would follow from the fact that it can "contain itself" (*hauto synechon*, SVF 2. 440) or cause its own "containment" (*synektikē aitia*, SVF 2. 440). This evidence can I think be rationalized by the interpretation of pneuma that I am proposing. Pneuma's motion is tensional, and it has its own tension (*tonos*, SVF 2. 447), because it has to move away from a body that has circular motion, the *aithēr*, in a rectilinear fashion. It extends out *from this source*, but is also drawn back to it; its motion is for this reason oscillatory in character. In this way pneuma can also be regarded as a force; it has its own tension, and self-containment, sufficient to overcome the inherent and contrary motion of its physical source and to pervade the matter of the sublunar world, while by its oscillation retaining contact with that body. Its peculiar motion thus ensures that it can be immanent in its medium while being the carrier, as it were, of the divine self-moving body whose immanence it is the purpose of this theory to explain. The formation of compounds is then a simple implication of this physics. Pneuma transmits its inherent powers of containment (i.e., its tension) to the inert matter of the sublunar bodies and thus qualities can in general be described as "air tensions" (*tonoi aerōdeis*, SVF 2. 449). Specifically, pneuma's individuation and differentiation of matter is reported as a tripartite effect; organisms acquire souls, plants their nature (*physis*), and other compounds a "state" (*hexis*) of unity (SVF 2. 714-716, 1013). The cosmos so permeated in these different degrees (cf. SVF 2. 634) is thus made "sympathetic with itself" (SVF 2. 473), another biological concept that refers both to the interrelationship of the bodies acted on by pneuma, and to the relation between the matter of the heavenly bodies and that of the sublunar world that pneuma links by its mediating action (SVF 2. 543). The latter role probably complemented, or even supplanted, Chrysippus's account (2. 555) of the stability of the cosmos as the dynamic balance of the two light elements (Fire and Air) with the heavy pair (Earth and Water), a view closely allied to Zeno's (SVF 1. 99).

A reconstruction along these lines provides a response to some of the criticisms of pneuma by ancient authors. Alexander (SVF 2. 442), for example, wondered how pneuma could form elements into compounds when it was itself a secondary body formed from two of the four elements; but, if our interpretation is correct, pneuma is a primary element since it is allied with the one self-moving element in the universe, and its formative activity is a continuation of that body's predominant role. Again Galen (SVF 2. 440) was concerned that pneuma could not be self-containing but would require a separate physical cause to unify it, and that cause another such cause, and so on ad infinitum; this we can simply answer by restating pneuma's affiliation to an inherently self-moving element whose properties it retains in performing its distinct cosmological function. Both these critics then found difficulties in understanding pneuma's relation to the elements. Given the state of our source material for Stoic physics we can perhaps infer from the direction of their attack that a reconstruction that makes sense of just this relation is at least valid in principle.

In this regard the most striking confirmation of our interpretation may be provided by critics who claimed that if pneuma was not identified with any of the elements then it must be a fifth body (SVF 2. 310, 389; cf. 2. 416). This is true in that pneuma is not an element but a body that operates in the context of the elemental system by linking the element of the heavenly bodies with those of the sublunar world. We can thus understand why such a "fifth body" should be perceived by a Peripatetic like Alexander as a challenge to Aristotle's theory of the *aithēr, his* fifth body (*de mixtione* 10. 223. 6-17). That substance was detached from the sublunar bodies, like Chrysippus's *aithēr*, but its causal influence on the sublunar world was simply through its transmitted motion; pneuma's actual immanence from such a body would obviously destroy the physical divisions of this cosmos, as it would reform an analogous division maintained in Zeno's cosmology. Alexander was in fact prepared to admit the validity of the general theory of immanence but wished to restate it in his own terms; he suggested that the sympathy between parts of the universe could be better explained by the motion of (his) *aithēr* than by the physical "bond" of pneuma (SVF 2. 441). Indeed earlier in the Stoicizing treatise *On the Cosmos* (late first century B.C.-early second century A.D.) attributed to Aristotle we find the language of immanence (397b33, 398b23), and even the expression "containing cause" (*synektikē aitia*, 397b9), used to describe divine influence transmitted through the heavenly bodies in the context of an Aristotelian cosmology. At issue between Stoics and Peripatetics was not the concept of immanence itself, only its expression by Chrysippus in physical terms.

More important though than any difficulties that it presented to philosophical opponents are the internal problems that the theory of pneuma raises when we examine it, not, as we have, in the terms of its own physics but as an embodiment of the metaphysical theory of immanence expressed in the theory of first principles. Clearly pneuma accomplishes a great deal by explaining in physical terms the unity of the cosmos and the diversity of entities in it. If a general problem in monism is demonstrating the relation between the One and the many then the theory of pneuma deals with it more successfully than the notions of immanence developed in Zeno's physics. In this way it can probably be regarded as providing a more satisfactory basis for Stoic ethics by showing in what specific sense man was part of the universal nature by reference to which he was enjoined to live. But these and other advantages (notably in psychological theory) are offset by some general difficulties that this theory raises.

By our reconstruction pneuma's motion is the continuation of the action of the primary element of Stoic physics that had produced a universe of stratified elements through a cosmogony. Just as Fire was an active seed within passive matter derived from it, so pneuma is active within the passive sublunar elements as the agent of the primary element in its intracosmic status as the matter of the heavenly bodies. Pneuma was probably explicitly identified as active and its medium as passive; the reports (SVF 2. 416, 418, 439, 444, 473) that distinguish the four elements into active or "tensional" (fire and air), and passive or "tensionless" (earth and water) pairs result, I suspect, from a common confusion about pneuma's relation to the elements, and a failure to identify its qualities of heated air in terms of the properties of *aithēr* rather than two of the four stratified elements. There is thus the cosmobiological continuity of pneuma assuming the role of a life-principle from the seminal Fire, and a theoretical continuity through its equally being an active principle in the universe. This is, I think, the aspiration of Chrysippus's theory of immanence, but the problem is whether it is adequately realized in his physics.

There are two areas in which we might question the success of his attempt to graft the theory of pneuma onto Zenonian cosmology. First, it would seem that if pneuma moves out from the *aithēr* through the sublunar elements then it is physically distinguishable from them since *aithēr*, its substance, has evolved at a later stage. An answer to this presumably is that there is a continuity between the active seminal element from which the sublunar bodies have evolved and this immanent body. Its sole function is to pervade these bodies and it is therefore never physically located in the *aithēr* but is always present in its medium. However, the plausibility of such cosmobiological continuity depends on the account given of pneuma's motion, and this introduces the second of our

difficulties. The theory of this body's motion which we have discussed is not itself based on any biological model of organic motion, whatever the medical origins of the concepts of pneuma and
"tension." It is a theory of motion in a continuum where a qualitative distinction can be drawn between the body in motion and its
medium. The nature of this distinction however is quite different
from that to be drawn between the seminal primary element and
bodies derived from it. There the logic of the model ensured the
inseparability of that element and *its* medium. But in the case of
pneuma's motion there is no equivalent support. Indeed our reconstruction of pneuma as force oscillating from the peripheral *aithēr*
serves to undermine the requirement, derived from the theory of
first principles, that the active and passive aspects of body be
inseparable. Oscillation itself suggests a physical separability of
the moving body from its medium, for such a body has a source
from which it emanates and to which it retreats; and this is doubly
so where such motion is forced, as where pneuma's rectilinear
oscillation is achieved by a diversion from the circular motion of
its physical matter. The introduction of a force, in this specific
sense, into Stoic physics is indicative of the discontinuity between
Chrysippus's theory of immanence and the Zenonian cosmology
founded on a model of organic change. It also, I think, implies an
admission that pneuma could not naturally (or organically) pervade the sublunar bodies without possessing the physical property
necessary to overcome their resistance. For although relative to
pneuma this matter may be inert (SVF 2. 449), it still has a quasi-
independence through having evolved in the cosmogony, and is
not therefore identical with the concept of matter, prescribed in
the theory of first principles, as a logically distinguishable aspect
of a single body.

Our assessment of Chrysippus's innovation in relation to Stoic
metaphysics must therefore depend on whether we are prepared to
regard his theory of immanence as part of a continuous account of
the organic development and establishment of the universe, or
whether we see it, for all its use of biological concepts, as essentially breaking with Zenonian cosmobiology and introducing a
physical dualism inconsistent with Stoic monism. When the issue
is put in these terms Zeno's apparent conservatism in cosmology
can be accorded a certain respect. He maintained the traditional

division between the divine matter of the heavens and the sub-lunar elements, and had no theory of physical emanation from the former sphere; direct physical immanence was only a result of the organic growth of the cosmos from an elemental seed. In trying to explain the unity and variety of the cosmos by providing a physical link between the divided levels of Zeno's universe, Chrysippus, as we have seen, enriched Stoic physics and metaphysics. At the same time this innovation placed strains on the theoretical coherency of Stoic monism which are reflected most clearly in the recurring polemic in antiquity against Stoic physics for holding that body could go through body, or that two bodies could occupy the same place. I have discussed elsewhere[16] the sources of this critique and the various forms that it assumed; it was usually directed against the theory of "total blending" (*krasis di' holōn*) which, I have argued, was part of an empirical rationalization of pneuma's motion through matter. In the present context we can see that this criticism exaggerates the central difficulty in Chrysippean physics: that the agent of immanence in the universe could be seen as separated from its medium. It reemphasizes sharply that although the innovative theory of pneuma was based on the metaphysical program of the theory of first principles, and succeeded in richly elaborating Stoic monism, its very complexity and comprehensiveness led to a strain between Stoic physics and Stoic metaphysics.

Whether through the difficulties discussed here, or simply because of its complexity, the theory of pneuma plays a minor role in later Stoic philosophy. It is, for example, mentioned only in vague terms in Diogenes Laertius's major epitome (cf. 7.138-139, 156). Its neglect can also be gauged from the version of Stoic theology offered in Book 2 of Cicero's *On the Nature of the Gods* that has as its physical basis a theory of immanence as the omnipresence of a vital heat, and is probably derived from Cleanthes. Chrysippus's interest in carrying forward the abstract program of the theory of first principles into a novel theory of motion in a continuum was not much shared by his successors. Stoic ethics and theology were influential without close attention to this most elaborate version of the associated physical theories. It has taken the efforts of modern students of Stoic physics, notably Sambursky,[17] to give the theory of pneuma some place in the development of Western scientific thought.

IV. STOIC PHYSICS AND STOIC METAPHYSICS

My opening claim that the central theme in Stoic physics was the immanence of the primary element was hardly novel. I do however hope to have shown that this truism is sustained not merely by the familiar details of Stoic cosmogony and cosmology, but also by the systematic relation that they have to the general program for monistic physical theory expressed in the doctrine of first principles. In this relation between abstract principles and qualitative physics we find what may be called the rationality of Stoic physics, its status as an explanatory system. One scholar has recently said of the scientific character of Stoic physics that it is "rational speculation that advances a tradition based on Hesiodic myth."[18] This seems too extreme a view just because it overlooks the theoretical basis of Stoic physics in a monistic metaphysic. If there are limitations to Stoic physical theory, and if we want to assess its scientific character, then we must explore the area of these metaphysical assumptions. In conclusion I offer a few brief observations based on a reconsideration of these assumptions, discussed earlier in Part I, in the light of our subsequent examination of their embodiment in physical theories.

At the outset we must recognize that Stoic monism contains two components not strictly essential to a monistic system: materialism and cosmogony. That is, the One of Stoic monism is both a body and the primary element in a cosmogony, but had the cosmogony been rejected then the theory of first principles could have been retained in a materialistic system that would have been broadly similar to that of Spinoza. The first principles would have simply had an analytical function, and revealed that the universe, or any of its parts, could be described as having an active and a passive aspect. The question of how it reached this state from a primary element would be eliminated, and one cannot help thinking that the Stoics would have benefited from the economy. Their greatest problems in physical theory came, as we have seen, from their attempt to ensure that their cosmogony yielded a universe to which their theory of first principles applied. Indeed the rejection of cosmogony, and in particular its associated theory of an eventual conflagration of the universe, by Boethus of Sidon (SVF 3. 265) and Panaetius (e.g., fr. 165 Van Straaten) in the second century B.C. perhaps indicates that these later Stoics perceived that their philosophical system lost nothing by eliminating these features of physical theory. It seems in principle possible for a Stoic, without seriously impoverishing his metaphysics, to claim that God has always pervaded the universe as a body inseparable from and acting on matter. It is of course another question whether the early Stoics whom we have studied would have regarded such revision as theological impoverishment because it deprived God of the power to create and destroy, or perhaps endowed him with too great a power by freeing him from the causal processes of cosmic evolution.[19]

But a broader issue is raised by this discussion of the range of physical theories necessary to embody satisfactorily the theory of first principles; and that is whether such an abstract theory as the latter prescribes any specific physical theory at all. We have seen the grounds on which cosmogony could be eliminated from Stoic physics, but there are equally good grounds for the elimination of what I have suggested was the other contingent aspect of their monism—their materialism. This is seen most clearly in the assimilation of Stoic conceptions of immanence into the matrix of Aristotelian cosmology by later authors. The Aristotelian God at the periphery of the universe could be seen as the source of an immaterial force that pervaded the universe. In the *On the Cosmos* his action can be compared to that of a puppeteer pulling strings (398b16-23), a mechanical model of transmitted motion that can be contrasted with the Chrysippean theory of pneumatic motion as the direct physical immanence of one body in another. The balance between monism and immanence in the Aristotelian version is of course different, but on the other hand the assimilation of the fundamental concepts of Stoic physics into another system only shows the contingent character of their embodiment in Stoicism in a materialistic and cosmogonical form. It also reflects the Stoic debt in the construction of their physical system to both Platonic and Aristotelian models of immanence as the motion of an immaterial force.

Stoic physics is indeed an excellent illustration of Pierre Duhem's dictum that from no metaphysical system can we derive "all the elements necessary for the construction of a physical theory."[20] For we have now seen that Stoic metaphysics prescribes only the general principles of Stoic physical theory and not its detailed form. In the case of Chrysippus's theory of pneuma a comprehensive theory of nature conflicted somewhat with the theory of first principles just because the latter could not anticipate all the requirements of physical theory. As we can now see, Chrysippus could have eliminated cosmogony from his system and thereby the problem of the separability of pneuma from its medium would never have arisen. It would have been its eternal function to pervade matter, and the difficulties created by the cosmogonical priority of its medium would be removed. Again, from these same general considerations, we can perhaps formulate another reason why in antiquity Stoic naturalistic ethics could flourish, and yield as its most influential doctrine the celebrated theory of natural law, without detailed attention being given to the physical theories through which the concept of nature was articulated. Nature as an ethical absolute could be derived from Stoicism without the associated doctrines of qualitative physics that we have studied just because those doctrines were not essential to its expression in metaphysical terms.

It is valuable for us to recognize the relation between Stoic physics and metaphysics if only to assess the balance between their originality and their debts to predecessors in this area. We can see at once, for example, the kernel of truth in the traditional, if often overstated, view that the Stoics were heavily dependent on pre-Socratic natural philosophy. This can surely be retained as an insight that reveals that whatever special debts they owed to other thinkers the Stoics had an exact precedent for their peculiar combination of monism, materialism, and cosmogony in the systems of Heraclitus and Diogenes of Apollonia. We can also perhaps assess the manner in which the various special theories of Stoic physics are a satellite of the central doctrines of their monism that we have discussed in this paper. The question needs more investigation, but I think it can be claimed that these theories are original to the extent that they reflect those basic doctrines closely (e.g., the theories of causality, the categories, and time) rather than simply complement them (e.g., the infinitely divisible continuum, place, the infinite extracosmic void).

Finally we can acknowledge that the greatest originality of Stoic physics, and perhaps its greatest interest for the modern student, lies in its attempt, paralleled most closely in Plato's *Timaeus*, to make physics the embodiment of metaphysics. The Stoic God, it has often been noted, is like a Platonic demiurge who does not however copy a pattern but brings himself as a pattern to the creation and structuring of a universe that directly embodies his identity. This inspiring notion of the physical immanence of the deity is at the root of a Stoic's self-confidence about his place in nature, and receives its most eloquent expression in the Stoic moralists of the early Roman Empire. This paper will have achieved its purpose if it shows that that familiar rhetoric is worth complementing by the study of the early Stoics' attempts to express the same notion through a unique development in Greek physical theory.[21]

NOTES

1. On the source material see R. B. Todd, *Alexander of Aphrodisias on Stoic Physics* (Leiden, 1976) 22-23. The references to SVF do not constitute all the evidence on a given subject but usually only indicate a representative passage on which my interpretation is most closely based. As a whole the present paper represents only an interim synthesis of my continuing work on the source material for Stoic physical theory, much of which remains to be evaluated thoroughly.

2. F. Solmsen, *Aristotle's System of the Physical World* (Ithaca, 1960) 95.

3. H. J. Kramer (*Platonismus und hellenistische Philosophie* [Berlin, 1971] 108-131) strongly emphasizes the Platonic background, while A. Graeser, *Zenon von Kition: Positionen und Probleme* (Berlin/New York, 1975) 94-108 and M. Lapidge, "*Archai* and *Stoicheia:* A Problem in Stoic Cosmology," *Phronesis* 18 (1973) 240-278, give more attention to Aristotelian antecedents. On influences on Stoic physics from post-Aristotelian Peripatetics, see J. Longrigg "Elementary Physics in the Lyceum and Stoa," *Isis* 66 (1975) 211-229. A study entitled *The Origins of Stoic Cosmology* by David E. Hahm is, I gather, to be published shortly by the Ohio State University Press.

4. The most extensive recent discussion of the *archai* is by Graeser (*Zenon von Kition,* 94-108); see also E. Weil, "Remarques sur le 'matérialisme' des Stoiciens," *Mélanges A. Koyré* (Paris, 1964) II, 556-572 and Lapidge ("*Archai* and *Stoicheia,*" 240-262. On some of the ancient criticism, see Todd, *Alexander* 221-222.

5. *Apoios* might mean "qualityless" in the sense of "undifferentiated"; cf. D.L. 7. 137 (SVF 2. 580) where the four elements are described as matter that is *apoios ousia* "when taken together" (*homou*), that is, when the primary element is in an undifferentiated state before the cosmogony described just before at 136. I think that this can be regarded as a complementary rather than an alternative sense to that proposed here.

6. F. H. Sandbach (*The Stoics* [London, 1975] 74) seems to regard this as the only function of the *archai*, since he denies the identification of God with the primary element Fire, a view with which I obviously cannot agree.

7. C. M. Kahn, "Stoic Logic and Stoic Logos," *Archiv für Geschichte der Philosophie* 51 (1969) 168.

8. M. Lapidge, "*Archai* and *Stoicheia*," 243.

9. Solmsen, *Aristotle's System*, 102 n. 35; 115 n. 91.

10. Lapidge, "*Archai* and *Stoicheia*," 265-267 is the fullest recent discussion of Zenonian cosmogony.

11. Lapidge, "*Archai* and *Stoicheia*," 267-270.

12. F. Solmsen, *Cleanthes or Posidonius? The Basis of Stoic Physics* (Mededelingen der Konsnklijke Nederlandse Akademie van Weteschappen, Afd. Letterkunde, N.R. 24, no. 8. [Amsterdam, 1961], 265-289 = *Kleine Schriften* [Hildesheim, 1968] I, 436-460).

13. For recent discussions of pneuma, see S. Sambursky (*Physics of the Stoics* [London, 1959] 1-48), J. Christensen (*An Essay on the Unity of Stoic Philosophy* [Copenhagen, 1962] 23-38), J. B. Gould, *The Philosophy of Chrysippus* [Albany, 1970] 99-102), L. Bloos (*Probleme der Stoischen Physik* [Hamburg, 1973] 52-113), A. A. Long (*Hellenistic Philosophy* [London, 1975] 152-163), Lapidge ("*Archai* and *Stoicheia*," 273-278) and Todd, *Alexander*, 34-39 and 211-219. On the Chrysippean authorship of this theory, see especially Lapidge, "*Archai* and *Stoicheia*," 274-276.

14. Cf. Solmsen, *Cleanthes*, 286.

15. Cf. Todd, "*Sunentasis* and the Stoic Theory of Perception," *Grazer Beiträge* 2 (1974) 251-261.

16. Todd, *Alexander of Aphrodisias*.

17. Cf. also M. Hesse, *Forces and Fields* (London, 1961) 75-77.

18. Bloos, *Probleme der Stoischen Physik*, 151.

19. Cf. L. Edelstein, *The Meaning of Stoicism* (Cambridge, Mass., 1966) 32.

20. Pièrre Duhem, *The Aim and Structure of Physical Theory*, trans. P. Wiener (New York, 1962) 18.

21. Some of the research for this paper was supported by a grant from the Canada Council, herewith gratefully acknowledged.

7

Stoic Cosmology

Michael Lapidge

For the Stoics, the final goal in life was to live harmoniously with nature (*physis*). But the question of what constituted this nature was the subject of considerable discussion among the Stoics themselves, as one would expect: was one to live in harmony with universal nature (= the external world), as certain Stoics, such as Cleanthes, insisted—or rather, ought one to live in harmony with one's own human nature? The distinction is largely a matter of emphasis, inasmuch as one man's nature was considered to be a mere living cell—to borrow an appropriate metaphor of F. H. Sandbach—in the universal organism. In any case, in order to live in harmony with nature in either sense it was essential to understand the behavior of universal *physis*, and that is why all the early Stoics (excepting only Ariston of Chios [SVF 1. 351]) commended the study of *physics* as propaedeutic to the study of virtuous behavior. The universal *physis* was defined by the Stoics both as the generative force in the universe, causing life and growth, and as the force that held the universe together and in order (SVF 2. 1132); in its role as ordering force, *physis* is equivalent to the "true order" (*orthos logos*) of the universe and is responsible for its "orderly arrangement" (*dioikēsis*). Accordingly, the study of the "order of the universe"—which is the proper meaning of the word *cosmology*—is the central concern of Stoic physics. Given the Stoics' insistence on universal natural order and man's relationship to it, one may fairly say that cosmology was the cornerstone of the Stoic system, and that cosmology played a more fundamental— even if less obviously prominent—role in Stoicism than in any other ancient philosophical system.

One looks in vain, however, through the surviving Stoic fragments for any detailed explanation of *how* man was to live in harmony with universal nature: what lesson, for example, should the wise man who is contemplating suicide draw from the fact that the universe is spherical or that the tides move in concert with the moon? Presumably the mere fact of universal order would be a sufficient incentive to the man aspiring to wisdom; and it may be that the statement of Posidonius, a later Stoic of the first century B.C., concerning man's goal—that man should "live in *contemplation* (my italics) of the truth and order of the universe, cooperating as far as possible in bringing it about" (fr. 186 Edelstein/Kidd)—is a more realistic assessment of man's potential contribution to universal order than any of his predecessors. Furthermore, once man is reduced to a mere observer of, rather than participant in, cosmic order, the study of cosmology loses its theoretical justification. This may be one of the reasons why, when after Posidonius Stoicism was transplanted to Rome, cosmology ceased to be a prevailing occupation of Stoic philosophers. But during the period of the early Stoa—from its founder to Chrysippus—cosmology was a vital interest to the Stoics, and it is unfortunate that modern scholarship has often tended to underestimate the importance of Stoic cosmology.

Earlier scholarship was content to view Stoic cosmology as a rather unsophisticated system having many features in common with the pre-Socratics: such was the view of Eduard Zeller and E. Vernon Arnold, for example, both of whom stressed the Stoics' similarities to Heraclitus. This view was encouraged by the statements of the doxographers as well as by the early Stoics themselves, who were often pleased to find an antecedent, and thus support, for a particular theory of their own in Hesiod or Heraclitus. More recently, however, the anachronism of such a view has become increasingly apparent, and it is now realized that many Stoic theories were arrived at through criticism of, and contact with, Platonic and Aristotelian physics. I would suggest that another avenue of approach to Stoic cosmology still requires careful investigation, namely, the debt of Stoic cosmological theory to earlier and contemporary Greek biological and medical theory. For the early Stoics, the universe was a living being, a *zōon* (SVF 2. 633 ff.), and its behavior was frequently to be explained in terms of biological theory. Other philosophers, such as Plato in the *Timaeus* (30b), had described the universe as a *zōon;* but none had applied the analogy as extensively as the Stoics. In their cosmology, the universe, like a living being, was born, lived an allotted span of life, and died; like a living being it reproduced itself. The universe, like a living body, was animated by vital heat or vital breath that passed through its entire extent; again, as with an animate body, all its parts were interconnected. In the account of Stoic cosmology which follows, some parallels with the Sicilian medical writings, with Aristotle's biological treatises, and with the works of Theophrastus, will be indicated. But I would stress that the relationship between Greek medicine and biology on the one hand, and Stoic cosmology on the other, is susceptible of much fuller treatment than can be given here.

Let us first consider the Stoic theory of cosmogony, that is, the generation or creation of the universe. The Stoics could not believe in a creation *ex nihilo*, and therefore they were obliged to posit an eternally existing substance (*ousia*) out of which universes arose and into which they dissolved. Had the Stoics not proceeded beyond this point, they might justifiably be said to resemble the pre-Socratics, most of whom argued that the universe arose from one of the various prime substances—earth, air, fire, and so on. However, between the time of the pre-Socratics and the Stoics, Plato and Aristotle had investigated closely the process of genesis and had demonstrated that genesis could only take place from the interaction of opposite forces. In the light of this demonstration, the early Stoics were led to design two opposite forces which, interacting, would bring about a universe. They called these forces "principles" (*archai*) and—again using Aristotelian terminology—designated one as active (*poioun*) and one as passive (*paschon*). Although these principles were two in number, in theory at least they were inseparable: an active force in action cannot exist without something to act upon. It need not be surprising, therefore, that many Stoic testimonies stress the inseparability of the two principles (SVF 2. 308, 313 etc.); and although the Stoics considered them to be corporeal, they used their *archai* to some extent as methodological principles like those of Aristotle. Hence the apparent paradox, that whereas the early Stoics conceived the universe as arising from one primary substance of fixed mass (SVF 1. 87), they needed to posit two further principles in order to account for the process of genesis. Logically speaking, Stoic theory would require us to speak of one primal substance with two aspects, one active, one passive.

In theory, then, the two principles ought to have been inseparable aspects of the one substance. But when the Stoics came to describe the behavior and properties of their two principles, they tended to forget the theoretical inseparability and resorted to biological terminology and metaphor to describe them. The active principle was otherwise called *theos* (god) or *Zeus* in Latin sources, and it was defined as a "mighty and continuous fire" (SVF 2. 1045). One source reports a doctrine "according to the Stoics, who say that the fiery and hot substance is the command center of the universe, and that god is corporeal and is the creative force itself, (being) none other than the energy of fire" (SVF 2. 1032). It will be seen that this divine fire is something quite unlike the fire that we know from daily life (a distinction that will emerge more clearly from the following discussion). Thus the Stoics described the "nature of things" (*physis*) as a "creative fire (*pyr technikon*) going methodically about the business of creation" (SVF 1. 171; 2. 1133-1134). In this definition the "nature of things" is apparently equivalent to god: and in fact one witness reports that "the Stoics defined god as endowed with mind, a creative fire, going methodically about the business of creation of the universe" (SVF 2. 1027). *Theos* has replaced *physis* of the earlier definition and the two terms are therefore interchangeable. In short, the Stoics' active cosmic principle, called *theos*, consisted in creative fire.

The properties of the second, or passive, principle are less easily defined. It is said to consist in "unqualified matter" (*apoios hylē*) (SVF 2. 300-301); that is, *hylē* is the shapeless stuff which is shaped or "qualified" by the active principle into a universe. It is evident that the Stoics were indebted to Aristotle for their conception of *hylē*, but the exact nature of this debt still requires careful study. At all events, *hylē* is the passive aspect of the primal substance; it is theoretically inseparable from *theos*. In effect, the separation of *theos* and *hylē* is a mental process only, and therefore the study of the properties of each per se is metaphysical, not cosmological. For the purposes of cosmogony it is enough to stress that, since *theos* and *hylē* are the ingredients from which universes are fashioned, they must precede these universes in time. The fact that *hylē* is precosmic may allow us some further understanding of how it was conceived by Zeno. There is a report that Zeno "interpreted" Hesiod's *Theogony*, and in particular, that he explained Hesiod's precosmic "chaos" (*prōtista chaos: Theog.* 116) as deriving its name "from its being liquid" (*apo tou cheesthai*) (SVF 1. 103); this report is corroborated by a statement elsewhere that, according to Zeno, Hesiod's precosmic chaos was simply water (SVF 1. 104). The Stoics were not given to etymologizing as an idle entertainment: etymology was used by them to bolster key points of their doctrine. Accordingly, we must take very seriously the reports that Zeno conceived of a precosmic moisture along the lines of Hesiod's primeval chaos. We have seen that, before the creation of a universe, all that existed for Zeno was a primal substance with two aspects, one active, one passive; and we have also seen that Zeno conceived of the active aspect as consisting in "creative fire." It is reasonable to suppose that, for the purposes of his cosmogony, Zeno conceived of the passive aspect as consisting in moisture or water.

Why should Zeno have wished to describe his two precosmic principles as fiery and watery, respectively? It was a widely accepted notion in antiquity that both fire and water were instrumental in creation. Theophrastus, for example, a contemporary of Zeno, stated that "everywhere nature generates life by mixing heat with moisture, the moisture acting as matter (*hylē*) for the heat" (*de caus. plant.* 3. 23. 3). This notion was particularly applied to the process of reproduction in animals and humans. Aristotle explains at length that the male semen consists both in hot spirit (*pneuma*) and moisture, and that reproduction takes place from the combination of this hot male semen with the liquid female secretion (*de gen. anim.* 2. 2. 735a30-737b7). Zeno followed Aristotle in his explanation of human reproduction: for him also sperm consisted in hot *pneuma* (plus moisture) which combined with the moist female secretion—called by Zeno, interestingly, *hylē* (SVF 1. 126-129). It is clear that Zeno conceived of the process of cosmogony as being analogous to that of human and animal procreation: the universe was generated by the hot fiery *theos*-principle acting on the moist *hylē*-principle. This is what is meant by the statement of Arius Didymus that, for Zeno, divine reason (i.e., *theos*) moves through the universe "just as sperm moves in the womb" (SVF 1. 87), and by the similar report of Diogenes Laertius concerning Zeno's cosmogonical theory:

And just as [in human/animal procreation] the sperm is enveloped in the womb, so the *theos*, which is the seminal reason of the universe, remains as such in the moisture, modifying to its ends the *hylē*, with a view to the next stage in the cosmogonical process. [SVF 1. 102]

So although in theory the two "principles" were strictly inseparable, in Zeno's biological account of cosmogony they assumed very distinct and separate properties, and it is not surprising that later Stoics should have pursued the implications of Zeno's biological model by describing the active principle as male, the passive as female (SVF 2. 1070), or again, as Zeus and Hera (SVF 2. 622, 1074). These later accretions reemphasize the biological aspect of Zeno's cosmogonical theory.

The first stage of the cosmogonical process, then, is accomplished by the action of the fiery spermlike *theos* operating on precosmic moisture. This interaction in turn brings about the second stage, namely, the generation of the four elements (earth, air, fire, water) from which the visible universe is constituted. Although there are some small variations, surviving accounts of cosmogony attributed to the three most important early Stoics—Zeno, Cleanthes, Chrysippus—agree in the description of this two-stage cosmogonical process. So for Zeno, after the operation of creative fire on precosmic moisture, the coarser part of the resultant mass condenses to form earth, some remains as water, some through vaporization turns into air, and part of this again by continuing rarefaction goes on to produce fire (SVF 1. 102). Cleanthes retained Zeno's conception of the role of creative fire and moisture, but apparently discarded Zeno's subsequent process of condensation and rarefaction, substituting instead a sort of chain reaction between the outermost and innermost parts of the cosmic mass (SVF 1. 497). Chrysippus's cosmogony was traditional and Zenonian: beginning with fire and water, earth condenses, water remains, air evaporates and, by becoming rarefied, produces *aithēr* (SVF 2. 579).

There are several problems inherent in the Stoics' cosmogonical scheme. One such problem is occasioned by Zeno's attempt to describe his two *archai* in terms of his biological model as well as in theoretical (or metaphysical) terms. The two *archai* are theoretically only the active and passive aspects of one substance. But once they are conceived—even metaphorically—as fiery and watery, the strict monism becomes difficult to maintain. Another problem arises with respect to terminology. By the action of creative fire on precosmic moisture the four elements are generated; but one of these elements is fire. There is a tendency among commentators of Stoicism—ancient and modern—to assume that these two fires are really one. The Stoics themselves, however, distinguished carefully between them: fire the *archē*, that is, the *theos*, was described as "creative fire" (*pyr technikon*), whereas fire the element (*stoicheion*) was described as "destructive fire" (*pyr atechnon*) (SVF 1. 120). In other words, the elemental fire we know from daily life is "destructive" in that it consumes whatever is placed in its path; but the fire of the sun and stars and of the *theos* itself is "creative," being identical with the vital heat in all living things which preserves them and causes them to grow. Failure to apply this distinction with rigor reduces many features of Stoic cosmology to confusion. But it might have made for greater clarity if the Stoics themselves had been able to devise a more satisfactory terminology for their two distinct fires.

At all events, the sublunar world as we see it is made up of the four created elements in various combinations; the heavens, on the other hand, consist in pure creative fire or *aithēr*. As is clear from the accounts of cosmogony, these four elements are mutable, and may change into each other through rarefaction or condensation. It remains to consider how these four sublunar elements together with the *aithēr* are arranged in the universe, and how the universe maintains its coherency and stability. But before these questions may be satisfactorily answered, another feature of Stoic cosmology must be discussed: the conception of the cosmic *pneuma*.

Like the theory of cosmogony, the Stoic theory of cosmic *pneuma* had its origin in biological thought. The word *pneuma* means simply "wind" or "breath." By the fourth century B.C. Greek medicine, and in particular the Sicilian medical school, had recognized the importance of breathing in animate creatures: Philistion, for example, had demonstrated that the air that was breathed was vital to the health of the entire body (fr. 4 Wellmann). Aristotle, in his biological treatises, had extended the Sicilian medical theory concerning *pneuma:* he distinguished between external air which was breathed and an "inborn" *pneuma* (*de gen. anim.* 2. 3. 737a9 ff.). This inborn *pneuma* in Aristotle's biological system absorbed the traditional associations of the vital bodily heat (*thermon*) which had been taught, for example, by Empedocles; for Aristotle the inborn *pneuma* was spread throughout the body and was the agent both of bodily growth (*auxētikon*) and generation (*gonimon*). In Aristotle's system, then, the inborn *pneuma* was virtually the source of bodily vitality—I say "virtually" because, for Aristotle, this *pneuma* could never replace or be identical with the soul; for him the *pneuma* was corporeal, the soul incorporeal.

Zeno was apparently much influenced by Aristotle's conception of an inborn bodily *pneuma*. And because Zeno was a thoroughgoing materialist, he had no hesitation in making the bodily *pneuma* identical with the soul (*psychē*) (SVF 1. 135-138); and in this Zeno was followed by all the major Stoics. As for Aristotle, so for Zeno *pneuma* was spread throughout the entire body, thus vitalizing it. It would seem that Zeno explained bodily sensation (*aisthēsis*) as the movement of *pneuma* from the soul's "command center" (*hēgemonikon*) to other bodily regions (SVF 1. 151). But because of the paucity of surviving testimonies, we do not know the details of Zeno's theory of bodily *pneuma*. However, Galen has preserved for us an extract in Chrysippus's own words—one of the rare occasions when an ancient Stoic is able to speak directly to us—concerning the properties of bodily *pneuma*, and Chrysippus's views may be taken as representative of the school as a whole. Chrysippus wrote in his treatise *On the Soul:*

The soul is *pneuma* [which is] inborn in us, continuous, extended throughout the entire body, as long as there be the breath of vitality in the body. Its parts are extended to each part of the body: we describe its extension into the windpipe as voice, that into the eyes as sight, that into the ears as hearing, that into the nostrils as smell, that into the tongue as taste, that extended to all the flesh as touch, and that extended into the testicles—with a slightly different meaning—as spermatic. The command center of the soul is the part where all these things come together, and is located in the heart (SVF 2. 911).

It will be seen that, although some of Chrysippus's terminology is traditional (and Aristotelian), his extensive application of the concept of *pneuma* to account for all bodily phenomena is very remarkable.

To return to Stoic cosmology: it will now be clear that the Stoic conception of a cosmic *pneuma* was simply that of the bodily *pneuma*, penetrating all parts of the body and vitalizing it, applied by analogy to the universe. There is nothing surprising in this analogy. As I mentioned earlier, the Stoics believed that the universe was a living being (*zōon*); it would have been a small and reasonable step to extend the biological notion of the body, pervaded and animated by *pneuma*, analogically to an animate universe. Furthermore, several pre-Socratic cosmologists—notably Anaximenes and Diogenes of Apollonia—had recognized air or *pneuma* as the source of life and hence as equivalent to God. All early Stoics taught the existence of *pneuma* in the body: but which Stoic first drew the analogy in full and endowed the universe with vital *pneuma*? Although there is abundant evidence that Zeno taught a bodily *pneuma*, there is none whatsoever that he taught a cosmic *pneuma*. For him the principal cosmic agent was the creative fire that was the source of vitality in the universe; no testimony explicitly referring to Zeno mentions a cosmic *pneuma*. One might add that it is not easy to see how Zeno might have squared his conception of *pyr technikon* with that of a cosmic *pneuma*, even if he had conceived of one. A similar situation obtains with respect to Cleanthes: no surviving fragment or testimony in his name refers explicitly to a cosmic *pneuma* (although like Zeno he clearly taught a bodily *pneuma* [SVF 1. 521, 523]). For Cleanthes, the prime cosmic agent was a creative fire or heat which had its principality in the sun (SVF 1. 499, 530). Even when Cleanthes would seem to have anticipated a notion that was more extensively developed by Chrysippus in terms of *pneuma*-theory—the theory of tension (*tonos*) which I shall discuss presently is a case in point—the theory is explained in terms of fire, not of *pneuma* (SVF 1. 563).

All the surviving evidence points to Chrysippus as the probable "inventor" of the Stoic theory of cosmic *pneuma* in its full form. Whereas no ancient source explicitly attributes a theory of cosmic *pneuma* to Zeno or Cleanthes, there are abundant attributions to Chrysippus (SVF 2. 439-462). When, as frequently happened, an ancient commentator wished to quarrel with the Stoic theory of *pneuma*, if anyone was named as the representative of that theory it was Chrysippus. Even if he was anticipated by one of his predecessors (and we have no evidence that he was), it was Chrysippus who realized the great versatility of the concept of bodily *pneuma* as well as its applicability to cosmology, and it was he who worked out the full complexity of the theory of cosmic *pneuma*. In Chrysippus's system, *pneuma* became equivalent to god and equivalent to divine reason: either *nous* (SVF 2.634, 1027) or *logos* (SVF 2.1091). In certain contexts at least, Chrysippus's *pneuma* replaced the creative fire of his predecessors Zeno and Cleanthes. Chrysippus's theory of cosmic *pneuma* is of such importance for the study of Stoic cosmology that several features of this theory require detailed discussion.

First, the doctrine that *pneuma* pervaded the entire universe, just as bodily *pneuma* had pervaded the entire body (as was clear from the passage of Chrysippus's *On the Soul* quoted earlier). In order to describe the pervasive motion of cosmic *pneuma*, Chrysippus employed the same term—*diēkō* ('to pervade')— as he had used for bodily *pneuma* (SVF 2.310, 414, 416, 475, etc.). With their penchant for etymologizing, the Stoics explained that God (*Dia*) derived his name from the fact that he "pervades" (*diēkō* < *dia* + *hēkō*) the universe (SVF 2.1021, 1063). The pervasion or interpenetration of *pneuma* was total; there was no gap nor empty space in the universe where *pneuma* did not enter. This theory allowed later commentators of Platonic or Christian inclination some amusement: that the godhead might be thought of as entering even the most debased and shameful of things was considered ridiculous (SVF 2.1037, 1039-1040). But for the Stoics no part of the universe, insofar as it was all equally permeated by the divine *pneuma*, could be considered as debased or odious. Also, the fact that *pneuma*—which was corporeal (*sōma*)—could be thought of as pervading or passing through other bodies, perplexed some ancient commentators extremely. We learn from these commentators, and particularly from Alexander of Aphrodisias, that Chrysippus had worked out an intricate theory of mixture to explain the interpenetration of body and body (SVF 2. 463-481). There is no need to examine that theory here, save to mention that for Chrysippus the "total mixture" (*krasis di'holōn*) of cosmic *pneuma* was a theoretical necessity and a technical possibility.

The cosmic *pneuma*, pervading the universe in various strengths, is responsible for the various shapes and kinds of things (SVF 2. 310). Diogenes Laertius has preserved an argument from Chrysippus's treatise *On Providence* which explains this aspect of the functioning of the divine mind (*nous*)—a term that, as I mentioned earlier, is exactly equivalent to *pneuma*—by means of an analogy (yet again) with the human body. The universe is said to be ordered by the divine mind because,

(this) mind pervades every part of it, just as the soul does in our bodies. But through some parts it pervades more, through others less. Through some parts it passes as a "hold" or "grip" [*hexis*], functioning as the bones and sinews in our bodies; it pervades other parts as mind, functioning as the command center [*hēgemonikon*] in our bodies. [SVF 2. 634]

This theory, attributed specifically to Chrysippus but reported only partially by Diogenes Laertius, is explained more fully in other sources. Philo at one point explains that *nous* (again one may understand *pneuma*) has a variety of motions, of which *hexis* is stable, is found in stones and all other inanimate objects, and is analogous to the bones in our bodies; *physis*, however, is a movable *hexis*, is found in plants, and is analogous to our hair and fingernails (presumably because these parts evidently grow and replace themselves); *psychē*, moreover, is *physis* which has acquired the capacity for mental images and desires and is common to all animals including human beings; finally, the capacity for thought—*pneuma* in its greatest concentration—is the property of the human and divine mind (SVF 2. 458). Thus there are four stages of being which are differentiated by the degree to which they possess *pneuma* and by the sort of motion that this *pneuma* has. A somewhat different explanation of the various forms of being is attributed to the Stoics by Galen: both *physis* and *psychē* were said by them to consist in *pneuma*, but the *pneuma* that is *physis* (i.e., that found in plants) is colder and more humid, whereas that which is *psychē* is hotter and drier (SVF

2. 787). These two variant explanations—the one physical, the other chemical—are apparently not mutually exclusive, and were probably considered to be complementary by the Stoics themselves.

A more important function of the cosmic *pneuma* is that it imparts coherence to the universe. The role of *pneuma* in cosmic coherence is again, one may suspect, derived by analogy from a Stoic biological theory. Both Zeno and Cleanthes had taught that the solidity or firmness of the body was due to the "exhalation" (*anathymiasis*) of the soul (SVF 1. 139, 520) which for them consisted in *pneuma;* and it may be that a similar exhalation was in their view responsible for the solidity of the universe (even though no surviving testimony states this explicitly). Once again it seems to have been Chrysippus who addressed himself most concertedly to the question of the universe's solidity and coherence. Chrysippus explained cosmic coherence by means of a certain internal tension (*tonos*) which was created in the universe by the interpenetrating cosmic *pneuma* (SVF 2. 447, 546). This notion of tension, too, was in origin a biological one. There is evidence that all Stoics taught some theory of a bodily tension: Zeno, for example, allegedly taught that speech consisted in *pneuma* which was "stretched" or "in tension" (*diateinon*) between the heart or command center and the pharynx and tongue (SVF 1. 150; but the attribution to Zeno is not beyond suspicion), and various sources attribute a theory of bodily tension to Cleanthes as well (SVF 1. 525, 563). But to judge from the abundance of surviving testimony, it was Chrysippus who worked out the theory of bodily tension in detail. For Chrysippus, all bodily sensation occurred as the result of the transmission of impulses from the peripheral sense organs through the medium of *pneuma* to the command center (SVF 2. 826). This transmission could best take place if the *pneuma* were "extended" or "taut" throughout the body. The eight parts of the soul as taught by Chrysippus (i.e., the five senses plus speech, generation, and the command center itself) were compared by him to the eight tentacles of an octopus, where sight was *pneuma* "stretched" (*diateinon*) from the command center to the eyes, hearing to the ears, and so on (SVF 2. 836; cf. the passage from Chrysippus's *On the Soul* quoted above, p. 168). Elsewhere Chrysippus explained bodily tension by means of an image of the spider

in his web: if any small insect landed in the web, the impulse would
be transmitted to the spider at the web's center as a result of the
tension in the web (SVF 2. 879). And so Chrysippus applied his
theory of tension to explain a wide variety of bodily phenomena:
sight, hearing, locomotion, sleep, and death. He even applied the
theory beyond the realm of physiology to that of ethics: desire or
appetency, for example, was said by Chrysippus to result from the
"tensional force" of the soul (SVF 2. 844; 3. 220, etc.).

What is important for Stoic cosmology is that Chrysippus
applied this elaborate theory of bodily tension analogically to the
universe. There is considerable debate as to how far Chrysippus
was anticipated by earlier Stoics in his theory of cosmic tension.
Although Zeno may perhaps have taught a theory of bodily tension, there is again no evidence whatsoever that he taught a cosmic tension; the one testimony that is frequently adduced in support of such an attribution (SVF 1. 99) states only that air and fire
are somehow "extended" (*teinesthai*) around the center of the universe, their lightness offsetting the heaviness of earth and water at
the center. This statement manifestly has nothing to do with the
tension (*tonos*) created by an all-pervading cosmic *pneuma*. In
fact the absence of any reference to cosmic tension in Zeno corresponds to the absence of any mention of cosmic *pneuma*, and cor-
roborates the suspicion that Zeno did not apply his theory of
bodily *pneuma* and tension to the universe. With Cleanthes a
more complex situation obtains. Like Zeno, Cleanthes clearly
taught a theory of bodily tension. Unlike Zeno, he also seems to
have conceived of some sort of cosmic tension: the universe, he
thought, would exist so long as its tension did not cease (SVF 1.
497). From another source we learn that tension (in the body at
least) is a result, in Cleanthes's words, of the "impact of fire" (SVF
1. 563). It would therefore seem to follow that, for Cleanthes, cosmic tension did *not* result from the agency of an all-pervading cosmic *pneuma*. One may conclude that it was Chrysippus who first
fully realized the possibilities of applying the theory of bodily
pneuma analogically to the universe, and that it was Chrysippus
who worked out fully the implications of pneumatic tension for
the theory of cosmic coherence.

The theory of cosmic tension occupied so important a position
in Chrysippus's cosmology that one must consider how this ten-

sion operated. Already Alexander of Aphrodisias—one of the Stoics' earliest and most trenchant critics—had asked how *pneuma*, which consisted in fire and air (both divisible substances), could impart coherence rather than divisibility to the substances it pervaded (SVF 2. 441). The Stoic reply to this criticism would presumably have been formulated in terms of two complementary theories: that of tensional movement, and that of the coherency of air. "Tensional movement" (*tonikē kinēsis*) consisted in the simultaneous movement of *pneuma* in a body from the interior outward and from the periphery inward (SVF 2. 451; cf. 2. 448, 450, 452-453). As Philo explains, the coherency of bodies consists in this *pneuma* "turning back upon itself, being thus in tension between the center and the periphery" (SVF 2. 458). This tensional movement in a body is continuous; when it stops, the body ceases to cohere.

Coherence in a body is also maintained by means of inner air. This aspect of air is described by Plutarch in an account of the chemistry of freezing:

Freezing, moreover, which is the most excessive and violent effect wrought by cold in bodies, is what water undergoes but what air produces. For in itself water is fluid, not firm and not cohesive; but when it is bound by air as a result of its coldness, it is in tension and consolidate. [SVF 2. 430]

It is difficult to assess how much of this is Plutarch and how much Stoic, but the idea that air was cold is one that Plutarch shares with the Stoics, rather than (for example) with Aristotle, for whom air was warm. Elsewhere, Plutarch quotes from Chrysippus's treatise *On Bonds* to the effect that there is no coherence in bodies without air, since it is air which holds bodies together (SVF 2. 449). Apparently, then, Plutarch's account of freezing derives from Stoic sources. And given that *pneuma* consists in fire and air, it would appear that air imparts to *pneuma* its cohesive force. This supposition is confirmed by another passage of Plutarch (again quoting Chrysippus) which states that matter by itself is inert, but is activated by "qualities" which are described as *pneumata* or "aerial tensions" (*tonous aerōdeis*), and these aerial tensions are responsible for giving form and shape to all things (SVF 2. 449). For Chrysippus, apparently, the tension created in a substance by air and that created by *pneuma* were identical. This identity is reflected too in Plutarch's statement that air and fire (the constituents of *pneuma*) are said to have cohesive force and tension (*euto-nia*), and that air and fire are responsible for holding together earth and water (SVF 2.444). Plutarch's report is corroborated by Alexander of Aphrodisias who states that, for the Stoics, air and fire are *eutona* ("tensional") whereas earth and water are *atona* ("untensional") (SVF 2.473; cf. 2.844).

Cosmic coherence derives from pneumatic tension. As a result of the all-pervading *pneuma* the universe is unified; this unity implies a tensional connection between all parts of the universe. There are three important consequences from this Stoic theory of cosmic coherence:

1. A tensional connection between all parts of the universe implies in particular the tensional connection between heavenly and terrestrial phenomena. Consequently, there is in Stoicism a "scientific" explanation for the correlation of the moon and tides; there is also a theoretical justification for astrology, since the events of a man's life may, as a result of cosmic tension, be connected with astral movement.

2. There can be no void within the universe itself, or the continuity of the tensional connection would be broken. This proposition is explained by Diogenes Laertius (who is here summarizing two treatises of Chrysippus—*On the Void* and *On Natural Systems*):

Within the universe there is no void, but rather it is unified. This is necessitated by the common vitality and common tension (*syntonia*) between heavenly and terrestrial things. [SVF 2.543]

This necessary absence of any void within the universe is more fully explained by Cleomedes in his treatise *On Circular Motion*. (Although Cleomedes does not mention Chrysippus by name, the tenor of the discussion is unmistakeably Chrysippean, as will be seen by comparing the following passage with that of Diogenes Laertius cited above):

Such are the characteristics of the void, that it is not found within the universe at all. This is clear from the phenomena. For unless the substance of the universe were wholly coherent, it would not be possible that the universe be held together and ordered by nature, nor would there be a sympathy of its parts with one another; nor unless there were one tension holding it together and unless the *pneuma* were all-pervasive, would it be possible for us to see and hear. [SVF 2.546]

It is interesting to note that the common tension ensures a "sympathy" (*sympatheia*) of parts. This notion is ultimately of medical origin: the Hippocratic treatise *On Nourishment* explains that there is "one confluence, one common vitality" and that "all things are in sympathy" within the human body (DK 22. C2). Chrysippus applied this medical notion to his cosmology (as Alexander of Aphrodisias reports):

Chrysippus assumes that the universal substance is unified, with a certain *pneuma* pervading it entirely, by which everything is held together and remains together and is in sympathy with itself. [SVF 2. 473; cf. 2. 475]

Independent reports by Plutarch (SVF 2. 912) and Philo (SVF 2. 532) confirm that the notion of cosmic sympathy was Chrysippean; once again, it is an example of the Stoic application of a biological notion to cosmology.

3. If the universe is unified spatially and contains no void, and if all causation is corporeal, it necessarily follows that all parts of the universe are connected temporally as well as spatially. That is to say, if cosmic *pneuma* had spatial extension, it also had temporal extension; and this is what is meant by Chrysippus's definition (in his treatise *On the Universe*) of fate as a "pneumatic force" (*dynamis pneumatikē*) (SVF 2. 913). Just as all cosmic parts are interconnected, so all events are linked to one another. Hence arises the Stoics' notion of a chain of fate; and this chain of fate, held together by pneumatic force, is the cosmological and theoretical basis of the Stoics' determinism.

It has been necessary to consider Chrysippus's theory of cosmic *pneuma* at some length because this theory, more than any other Stoic cosmological conception, commended itself to a long posterity, and numbered among its descendents the Holy Ghost itself. With Chrysippus's cosmic *pneuma* in mind, we may return to Stoic theory concerning the shape and structure of the universe. The shape of the Stoic universe is easily described: it was spherical (SVF 2. 547), and hence it was finite in extent, not infinite. More problematical is the question of what surrounded this spherical universe. It is stated by several ancient authorities that the Stoics taught an infinite void (*kenon*) surrounding the universe (SVF 2. 535, 539); consequently the Stoics are said to have distinguished between "the whole" (*holon* = the universe) and "the totality" (*pan* = universe plus void) (SVF 2. 522-524). And accordingly modern commentators have pictured the Stoic universe as a finite ball floating in an infinite void. But the Stoic view may not have been so simple. For the Stoics everything which existed was corporeal; they admitted only four types of incorporeal things, which had no real existence but were only "things said" (*lekta*) (SVF 2. 331). One of these four incorporeals was "nothing" (*kenon*) (SVF 1. 95; 2. 331). Presumably the *kenon* or void beyond the universe was conceived by the Stoics as this sort of incorporeal; the conception is tantamount to saying "there is nothing outside the universe." However this may be interpreted, it is clearly far different in conception from the Atomists' void. I suspect that the Stoics strictly posited a finite spherical universe and nothing else. When asked by detractors what surrounded this universe they replied, "*kenon*"; whereupon the detractors interpreted this *kenon* in Atomist, not Stoic, terms. Such a misunderstanding of Stoic terminology would explain the confusion in Plutarch's account of the extracosmic void (SVF 2. 525); it might also suggest that the distinction between "the whole" and "the totality" was an addition of later doxography—or at least of later Stoics who chose to overlook the original theory.

What of the arrangement within the universe of the four elements that were created during the process of cosmogony? As in other ancient cosmologies, the four elements were arranged in spherical tiers, with earth in the center, then water, then air, and finally fire at the periphery of the sphere (SVF 2. 555). The more pressing question is: why did these four tiers maintain their stations? Whence did the universe derive its stability? A passage in Achilles Tatius suggests that some Stoics answered this question by recourse to the gravitational tendencies of the four elements: all four elements "tend" (*neuei*) toward the center, and because of this "the universe does not shift" (SVF 2. 554). This would seem to have been the view of Zeno, for a passage from Arius Didymus explicitly ascribed to Zeno gives a slightly more detailed account of the same theory: of the four elements two are heavy (earth and water) whereas the other two are "weightless" (*abarē*) by comparison. All four elements nonetheless have a natural inclination toward the center of the universe, but most of all the heavy elements. The stability of the universe results from the balance of light and heavy elements (SVF 1. 99).

This scheme of each of the four elements having a natural (=gravitational) and rectilinear motion toward the center, is deceptively simple, as becomes apparent as soon as one looks more closely at the outermost element, fire. Insofar as it is listed among the four created elements, one might expect that this element would consist simply in destructive (*atechnon*) fire. But Zeno specifically maintained that the fire of the sun, moon, and stars was creative (*technikon*) (SVF 1. 120). As such this fire was equivalent to the *theos* that, according to Zeno, consisted in *aithēr* (SVF 1. 154). Presumably this *aithēr* was pure *pyr technikon* (= the *archē*) which had not been converted into elements during cosmogony. Now Aristotle in his work *On the Heavens* had argued that there were two simple elemental motions: rectilinear (*eutheia*) and circular or peripheral (*peripherēs*). In Aristotle's cosmology, earth and water tend downward rectilinearly, air and fire upward; the *aithēr*, however, is a sort of fifth body that encloses the other four elements and revolves peripherally around them (*de caelo* 1. 1-2). It is worth asking if Zeno's cosmology was influenced by this Aristotelian theory. Certainly Zeno did not teach a fifth element: Cicero on two occasions denies that the Stoics envisioned any such fifth element (*Acad. post.* 1. 39; *de fin.* 4. 12). Whether or not Cicero's express denial could refer to the Stoics' *aithēr*—technically not an "element" but a "principle"—is not clear. In any case, Zeno seems to have adopted something of Aristotle's theory of elemental motions: at one point he argues that fire moves rectilinearly, and elsewhere that "terrestrial light" moves rectilinearly whereas "aethereal light" moves peripherally (SVF 1. 101). This must mean that sublunar fire or light moved rectilinearly and consisted in "destructive" fire, whereas the stars, sun, and moon—the *aither*—moved peripherally. The problem is: how can this view be squared with that mentioned earlier, whereby all four elements "tend toward the center" (SVF 2. 554)? Either the outermost layer of the four is fire that tends (rectilinearly) toward the center, or it is aethereal fire that moves peripherally: I do not see how it can be both. Perhaps—in spite of Cicero's testimony—Zeno did teach something resembling the "fifth element" arrangement: earth, water, air, and then "destructive" or "terrestrial" fire, all tending toward the center; and then beyond these a peripherally-moving *aithēr* consisting in "creative fire." The question of the arrangement of the elements and of their natural tendencies is therefore a confused one; but this confusion results as much from the paucity of surviving testimony as from the inconsistencies within it. Furthermore, the theory of cosmic stability being due somehow to elemental tendencies towards the center was no doubt quickly rendered obsolete by Chrysippus's more satisfactory theory of internal coherence created by the all-pervasive *pneuma*. One may suspect that Chrysippus's revolutionary theory commended itself so well to later Stoics and commentators that the pre-Chrysippean theories of elemental tendency were dimly remembered or else forgotten.

We have seen that, according to all the early Stoics, the *pneuma* that was spread throughout the body had a "command center" (*hēgemonikon*), usually located in the heart, where presumably *pneuma* was most densely concentrated. If the analogy of bodily *pneuma* was accurately applied by Chrysippus to cosmic *pneuma*, one might well ask if the universe similarly had a "command center," and if so, where it was located. Various other Stoics had located the cosmic "command center" variously. A difficult and disputed passage in Arius Didymus (SVF 2. 642) would suggest that certain Stoics located the *hēgemonikon* in the earth, but this view must surely arise from a textual corruption. Cleanthes taught that the sun was the *hēgemonikon* (SVF 1. 499). Antipater of Tarsus held the *aithēr* to be the "command center," and according to Diogenes Laertius, Chrysippus in his treatise *On Providence* had also located the cosmic "command center" in the *aithēr*. Diogenes Laertius adds that later in this same work Chrysippus gave a slightly different account, namely that the *hēgemonikon* is the "purest" (*katharōtaton*) part of the *aithēr* (SVF 2. 644). Apparently the purest part of the *aithēr* consisted in *pneuma* and so was equivalent to god or *theos*. This raises the difficult question of relative purity: if the *hēgemonikon* is the purest part of the *aithēr*, there must by implication be a more impure part. If so, what would account for its relative impurity? As far as I am aware, no surviving testimony offers any explanation of the relative purity or impurity of Chrysippus's cosmic *pneuma*, and one can only imagine an explanation. Possibly the relative impurity of *pneuma* would derive from its mixture with the created elements, and thus it would only be pure if it were totally free of these elements. Relatively impure *aithēr*, therefore, would seem to imply some mixture of *pneuma* with either terrestrial fire or air. But in the absence of Stoic testimony on this point, further speculation is unwarranted.

The theory of relative purity and impurity is interesting because it seems to underlie the Stoic theory concerning the dissolution of the universe into fire (*ekpyrōsis*). Each of the early Stoics taught that the universe, after certain definite periods of time (whose duration is never specified), dissolves into fire and so "purifies" itself. This process of purification was apparently called *katharsis* by the Stoics (SVF 2. 598); it was a purification in the sense that, at *ekpyrōsis*, the universal substance consisted in nothing but pure fire. We can see how this process would have been outlined by Zeno: the universe originally generated from creative fire (*pyr technikon*); after a period of time it resolved itself once again into pure fire, whence another universe was in turn generated from the pure creative fire. The cosmic process is therefore an infinite series of finite phases of alternate *diakosmēsis* and *ekpyrōsis*. What is surprising, perhaps, is that each newly generated universe was identical in every detail to the one(s) that had preceded it. I can see no compelling reasons within the cadre of Stoic cosmology as to why this should have been so: perhaps simply that the Stoics conceived of the cosmic process as cyclical (rather than as [say] an infinite spiral); but it seems to imply that the chain of fate as the Stoics conceived it was circular and continuous. Given this, the universal process would repeat itself infinitely. And if they had conceived of the chain of fate as circular, they would have been left with the logical necessity—but patent absurdity—that all universes must be identical in every minute detail: in every universe the same Socrates would marry the same Xanthippē, instruct the same Plato, and so on (SVF 2. 625-6). (Needless to say, perhaps, this obstinate adherence to logic provided the Stoics' Christian detractors with endless amusement).

It is not immediately clear why Zeno should have wished to posit an *ekpyrōsis* in the first place, nor is it clear whence he derived the notion. He conceived the universe as a *zōon*, and like all other living things the universe must inevitably die. But must it go up in flames? Some ancient commentators (e.g., Simplicius

[SVF 2. 617]) suggested Heraclitus as the source of the Stoic theory of universal conflagration; but recent scholarship has shown that it is extremely doubtful that Heraclitus taught anything resembling the Stoic *ekpyrōsis*. As I mentioned earlier, there seems to be no reason within Stoic doctrine which would require a periodic purification and regeneration of the universe. This may be why the causes of *ekpyrōsis* which are given in Stoic sources seem so unconvincing. In effect, three causes are given (none of which is mutually exclusive of the others): first, that god within the universe keeps on increasing until he absorbs himself into himself (SVF 2. 604-605). But why should god keep increasing? This question is perhaps answered by the second and usual explanation of the cause of *ekpyrōsis:* namely, that the *aithēr*—that is, the sun and stars—gradually consumes the moisture in the universe until, when all water has been exhausted, the universe catches fire (SVF 2. 593). But there are also problems with this explanation. On the one hand, the Stoics undoubtedly taught a theory of elemental *anathymiasis* ("exhalation") whereby the sun and stars were "nourished" by the sea (SVF 2. 650, etc.). But the sun and stars are explicitly said by Zeno to consist in creative fire that, unlike terrestrial/destructive fire, does not consume and convert its nourriture into itself, but rather is productive and preservative (*tērētikon*) (SVF 1. 120; cf. 1. 504). In what sense, then, may the sun and stars be said to "consume" the moisture in the universe? No resolution of this patent contradiction seems ever to have been proposed, nor can I propose one. And the third explanation of *ekpyrōsis*—namely, that when the planets return after a certain fixed period of time to the same relative positions that they had when the universe was first created, the conflagration will occur (SVF 2. 625)—may well be a signal of that conflagration, but I do not see how it could be its cause. Here as elsewhere, the fragmentary nature of surviving Stoic testimony raises more problems than it can solve.

In spite of these problems, the general outline of Zeno's and Cleanthes' theory of *ekpyrōsis* is clear: a universe turns into creative fire, whence a subsequent universe is generated from this same creative fire. But if, as I suggested earlier, Chrysippus inclined to supplant the earlier Stoic creative fire with his conception of a cosmic *pneuma*, it is worth asking how he squared this theory of a

cosmic *pneuma* with the traditional conflagration. One would reasonably expect that, for Chrysippus, the conflagration would involve a conversion into *pneuma;* but no Stoic fragment makes
such a statement. Perhaps the nearest statement is that preserved
by Arius Didymus, whereby all things are said to resolve into
ethereal (*aitherōdes*) fire (SVF 2. 596); the *aithēr,* it will be recalled,
was for Chrysippus the command center of his cosmic *pneuma.*
Another problem that Chrysippus must have posed: the stability
and coherence of the universe derived from the tension created by
the pervasion of *pneuma;* conflagration must therefore involve
somehow the release of this cosmic tension. This release is implied
in the term that is most often used to describe the conflagration:
analysis, that is, "loosening" or "dissolution" (SVF 2. 602, 609-610,
618-620). Here again the cosmic phenomenon is explained by analogy with a medical theory: Chrysippus described death as a
"loosening" (*anesis*) of the sensory *pneuma* within the body (SVF
2. 767); thus the universe "dies" when its pneumatic tension is released. But if tension is released at *ekpyrōsis,* what then prevents
the fiery mass from dissolving into the surrounding void (if such it
be)? To put the question another way, what shape does the cosmic
substance assume during *ekpyrōsis*? The question is answered by a
comment of Chrysippus on the shape of souls: after souls have left
the body, he argued, they assume a spherical shape (SVF 2. 815).
This must imply that soul or *pneuma* of its own accord will naturally assume a spherical shape. By extension, the cosmic substance
at *ekpyrōsis,* when it becomes pure *aithēr* or *pneuma,* will retain
its sphericity. In fact it would appear that the natural tendency of
pneuma to sphericity will account for the spherical shape of the
universe during periods of *diakosmēsis* when it is pervaded by
cosmic *pneuma.*

There is one final problem inherent in the Stoic theory of *ekpyrōsis.* It is this: at *ekpyrōsis* the universe is said to resolve itself
into creative fire; but cosmic regeneration or palingenesis requires,
as we have seen, the interaction of this creative fire with precosmic
moisture. If the universe dissolves into fire alone, whence comes
the moisture? The Stoics clearly conceived of an intermediary
stage when, somehow or other, the fire was quenched so that
palingenesis could get under way. Thus Diogenes Laertius, speaking of the destructibility of the universe (*phthartos:* presumably a

reference to *ekpyrōsis*), states that "it is first dried up completely (*exauchmoutai:* a very rare word whose precise meaning here is uncertain) and then made watery" (SVF 2.589). Similarly, Plutarch reports the teaching of Chrysippus:

When *ekpyrōsis* takes place, [Chrysippus] says that the universe is totally alive and is a living being, but thereafter, as it is quenched and becomes concentrated, it turns into water and earth and things substantial. [SVF 2.605]

That is to say, after *ekpyrōsis* the fire is at length contained by moisture; the fire and moisture then set about creating the next universe. But no Stoic provides any explanation as to why the fire should be quenched; and here as elsewhere we are left to conjecture. It would seem consistent with Stoic theory that *ekpyrōsis* would imply not merely the dissolution of the created universe, but also the dissolution of the four created elements back into primal substance (*ousia*) that, as we saw, had two aspects: active/fiery and passive/watery. Thus, although no Stoic source says as much, both fiery *theos* and watery *hylē* would have been extant at *ekpyrōsis*. This at least is how Alexander of Aphrodisias understood the theory:

But especially at *ekpyrōsis* god appears according to them [*scil.* the Stoics] to be the shape of matter, if indeed in the fire, which is all that exists at that time according to them, matter and god alone are preserved. [SVF 2.1047]

It may be that, in the initial phase of *ekpyrōsis*, the fiery *theos* aspect of the primal substance predominated—this would be the *katharsis*—but that a balance was eventually restored wherein the watery *hylē* aspect regained some equality (which process the Stoics allusively described as "quenching"). From this point a cosmic regeneration in accord with biological principles could take place. And at this point, we are back where our investigation of Stoic cosmology began.

The Stoics' theory of *ekpyrōsis* was perhaps the most notorious of all their cosmological theories. The notion of palingenesis was attacked and ridiculed by generations of Christian dogmatists. Even given the Stoics' persistent logic, there are still many logical difficulties with the *ekpyrōsis* theory. Not surprisingly, perhaps, the *ekpyrōsis* theory was one of the first cosmological theories to be abandoned by later Stoics. Already Boethus of Sidon, in the second century B.C., had rejected *ekpyrōsis*, because, as he explained, God would be left with nothing to do while the universe was burning (SVF 3. 7). Apparently Boethus had neglected to learn that, for his Stoic predecessors, God *was identical with* the fire that consumed the universe. Somewhat later Panaetius, too, denied the Stoic theory of *ekpyrōsis*, apparently because he wished to believe with Aristotle that the universe was eternal and indestructible (fr. 64-66, 68 Van Straaten).

The rejection of a cardinal doctrine of Stoic cosmology by Boethus and Panaetius is symptomatic of what happened to Stoic cosmology at large when Stoicism was transplanted to Rome during the course of the second and first centuries B.C. The Romans, as everyone (who has read at least one textbook on Roman civilization) will know, were a down-to-earth, practical people concerned with the problems of morality in daily life, not with the niceties of cosmological speculation about a mentally constructed universe. The result was that, at the hands of Roman Stoics, speculative cosmology fell into desuetude and was effectively abandoned. Not that the theoretical justification for cosmology was forgotten: Epictetus exhorts us to learn from Chrysippus the "orderly arrangement" (*dioikēsis*) of the universe (1. 10. 10; 2. 14. 25-26); Musonius Rufus instructs us as to the meaning of "living in accord with nature" (fr. 17 Hense); Seneca frequently admonishes Lucilius to live in accord with the nature of things (e.g., *Ep.* 107. 7-10); and Marcus Aurelius aspires to live "in accord with the physical law of the universal community" (3. 11. 3). But with the exception of Seneca, not one of these philosophers gave more than a passing nod to the structure of the universal order they were hoping to emulate, and we feel that Marcus Aurelius speaks for the others when he thanks the gods that he did not waste his time studying celestial phenomena (1. 17. 8). Even Seneca, who occasionally in his *Letters to Lucilius* adverts to cosmological matters and who in his *Natural Questions* attempts to describe a variety of celestial and terrestrial phenomena, was content to rehash the views of his Stoic predecessors. At no point does he venture into independent speculation concerning the order of the universe. Stoic cosmology was by then a dead letter. It passed from the domain of philosophers to the domain of poets where, with its copious and intriguing

metaphors, it was enthusiastically received and nurtured for centuries to come. And it so happens that the most fitting tribute to
Stoic cosmology paid by a Roman is that paid by the poet Mani-
lius, who in his *Astronomica* claims to be setting out on poetic seas
never before charted:

> For I shall sing of God, mighty through the silent mind of nature
> And infused in the heavens, in earth and the seas,
> Governing the immense mass with a measured bond;
> (And I shall sing) that the entire universe
> Through its alternating sympathy is alive,
> And is driven by the movement of reason,
> Since one *pneuma* inhabits all its parts,
> And, pervading all things, strengthens the spherical world
> And assumes the likeness of an animate body.
>   [*Astronomica* 2. 60-66]

8

Necessity and Fate in Stoic Philosphy

Margaret E. Reesor

Perhaps the most crucial problem for a reconstruction of the Stoic concept of fate is the interpretation of the following statement in Alexander of Aphrodisias's *Concerning Fate:* "The Stoics, although removing the possibility that man has the power of choosing and performing one of the contradictories, say that that which happens through us is attributable to us" (SVF 2. 979).[1] What are the contradictories to which Alexander is referring and why is "that which happens through us" attributable to us? A second problem is the Stoic interpretation of true propositions that refer to the future. The Stoics believed that every proposition was true or false, but at the same time argued that events in the future were contingent. Their views were directly opposed to the position adopted by Aristotle in the *De Interpretatione.* My purpose in this paper is to offer a solution for these two problems and to provide a general discussion of the relationship that exists between the *logos* of the individual and the *logos* of the universe.

The Stoics argued that, if every proposition was true or false, there could not be a movement without a cause and that consequently there are antecedent causes for everything that happens. Pseudo-Plutarch places first in his list of the topics that were discussed by Chrysippus in his *Concerning Fate* "That nothing happens without a cause but according to antecedent causes" but he seems to have been guilty of an oversight for he adds at the end of the list, as if it were a separate topic, "This much discussed point, that every proposition is either true or false" (SVF 2. 912).[2] In *Concerning Fate* Alexander of Aphrodisias begins his refutation of the Stoic interpretation of fate with a discussion of antecedent causes. The fullest statement that we have of the Stoic position, however, is found in Cicero's *De Fato*:

If any motion is without a cause, not every proposition that the logicians call an *axiōma* will be either true or false, for that which will not have efficient causes will be neither true nor false. But every proposition is either true or false. Therefore, there is no movement without a cause. But if this is so, everything which happens happens because of antecedent causes. If this is so, everything happens by fate. Therefore, it follows that whatever happens happens by fate. [SVF 2. 952]

A proposition that was related to action received assent or failed to receive assent from the impulse (*hormē*). The impulse gives assent to the proposition (*axiōma*) and this is followed by a movement toward the predicate that is evidenced in some way in the proposition to which the assent is given (SVF 3. 171). For example, if the impulse should give assent to the proposition "To resist the enemy is good," the assent would be followed by a movement toward the predicate "resisting." The double role of the impulse, as assent and movement, is stated in a passage in Stobaeus: "All the impulses are assents but the practical impulses have within themselves the power of moving. Now assents are to some things; impulses to something different. Assents are to some propositions; but impulses are to predicates which are included in some way in the propositions to which the acts of assent are given" (SVF 3. 171). The assent to the proposition "To resist the enemy is good" is the principal cause of the action "resisting." We have to recognize also an initiating cause, the *phantasia hormētikē*, a presentation such that it arouses the impulse immediately for what is appropriate (SVF 3. 169), as, for example, "The enemy is attacking."[3]

What, then, is the antecedent cause? In order to answer this question we have to turn to the third function of the impulse (*hormē*) the exercise of desire (*orexis*) and reasonable desire (*boulēsis*). *Orexis* is defined as the rational impulse (*hormē logikē*)

directed toward something that causes pleasure so far as is necessary.[4] *Boulēsis* is reasonable desire (*eulogos orexis*, SVF 3. 432).[5]
In an important passage Cicero suggests that Chrysippus recognized natural and antecedent causes of our reasonable desire
(*voluntas* = *boulēsis*) and desire (*adpetitio* = *orexis*). This passage
reads as follows:

> But inasmuch as there are differences in the nature of men so that sweet things
> please some, and bitter things delight others; and some are licentious, quick to
> anger or cruel or proud, and others shrink from such vices—since, therefore, he
> [Chrysippus] says, one nature differs so much from another, why is it strange
> that these dissimilarities are due to different causes? *In this argument he fails to
> see the point at issue or in what a cause consists. For it does not follow that, if*
> different people have different inclinations because of natural and antecedent
> causes, as a consequence *there are natural and antecedent causes of* our reason-
> able desires (*voluntates*) and desires (*adpetitiones*). For if that were the case,
> nothing would be in our power at all. Now as a matter of fact, we admit that it is
> not in our power to be keen or dull, strong or weak. *But he who thinks that it fol-
> lows from this that it is not according to our own reasonable desire (voluntas)
> that we sit or walk does not understand the sequence of cause and effect.* For al-
> though clever and slow people are born like that because of antecedent causes
> and likewise the strong and the weak, *it does not follow that their sitting and
> walking and doing anything is defined and constituted by principal causes.* [SVF
> 2. 951]

It seems clear that the antecedent cause of the reasonable desire
(*boulēsis*) is the fixed disposition (*diathesis*) of the man himself.
The evidence is found in the following passage in Seneca:

> Action will not be right, unless the reasonable desire (*voluntas*) is right; for from
> this action arises. Again, reasonable desire will not be right unless the disposition
> (*habitus* = *diathesis*) of the mind is right; for from this the reasonable desire
> arises. The disposition (*habitus*) of the mind, therefore, will not be in the best
> state, unless it grasps the laws of life generally, and carries out what ought to be
> decided about each thing. [SVF 3. 517]

If the fixed disposition (*diathesis*) is the antecedent cause of the
impulse (*hormē*) functioning as reasonable desire (*boulēsis*), it is
also the antecedent cause of the impulse as assent (*synkatathesis*).

In his refutation of Chrysippus Cicero made the following statements (SVF 2. 951): (1) "It does not follow that their sitting and
walking and doing anything is defined and constituted by principal

causes"; and (2) "But he who thinks that it follows from this that it is not according to our own reasonable desire (*voluntas*) that we sit or walk does not understand the sequence of cause and effect." I have argued that an action requires a principal and an initiating cause. "Resisting," for example, had as its principal cause "To resist the enemy is good," and as its initiating cause the *phantasia hormētikē* "The enemy is attacking." The causes that are needed for "walking" are indicated by a passage in Seneca: "Every rational animal does nothing, unless he has first been roused by the appearance of something; then, he receives an impulse, and then assent confirms this impulse. I shall tell you what assent is. 'It is fitting for me to walk.' Then, at last I walk, when I have stated this to myself and approved this opinion of mine" (SVF 3. 169). What Seneca calls "the appearance of something" is the initiating cause. His words "It is fitting for me to walk" express the principal cause.

The assent (*synkatathesis*) to the proposition is attributable to us. Alexander of Aphrodisias in his *Concerning Fate* writes: "At this point you might wonder why they say that 'that which is attributable to us' is to be found in the impulse and assent because they observe this in all living creatures alike."[6] Just as we find the assent of the wise man giving assent to a proposition that is good, so the judgment (*krisis*) of the man who is not wise gives assent to a proposition that is wrong. If the wise man were to give assent to the proposition "To resist the enemy is good," the man who is not wise would give assent to the proposition "Not: to resist the enemy is good." The judgment of the man who is not wise is also an example of what the Stoics designated by the technical term "attributable to us" (3. 380). What is more, the action that follows from the assent to a proposition is also "attributable to us" (*eph'hēmin*). Alexander of Aphrodisias in another passage in *Concerning Fate* writes as follows: "The Stoics, although removing the possibility that man has the power of choosing and performing one of the contradictories, say that that which happens through us (*di'hēmōn*) is attributable to us" (*eph'hēmin*, 2. 979).[7] The Stoic assents to a proposition such as "To resist the enemy is good," and the act of resisting follows from his assent to this proposition. "That which happens through us," as, for example, "resisting," follows from the assent (*synkatathesis*) and is attributable to us.

The Stoics argued that a man does not have the power of choosing the contradictory of the proposition to which he gives assent. There is no doubt that the Stoics held that the assent was determined by the nature of the fixed disposition (*diathesis*). The wise man is prevented by his fixed disposition from giving assent to any proposition that is not compatible with his own virtue. A passage in Alexander's *Concerning Fate* states this as follows:

If, they say, these things are attributable to us, of which the contradictories are in our power, and praise, blame, encouragement and dissuasion, punishments and honors are attributable to such acts, the state of practical wisdom and the possession of virtues will not be attributable to those who have them, because they are not now capable of receiving the vices which are the contradictories of the virtues. In the same way, vices too are not attributable to the evil, for the state of not being evil is not attributable to these. But surely, to deny that virtues and vices are attributable to us and that praise and blame do not follow upon these [i.e., virtue and vice] is absurd. Therefore, that which is attributable to us is not of such a kind. [i.e., not of such a kind that the contradictories are in our power, SVF 2. 984][8]

Moreover, "that which is attributable to us" is according to fate. Alexander in his *Concerning Fate* writes:

That nothing is attributable to us is the contradictory of that something is attributable to us. [But that nothing is attributable to us] is impossible.[9] It is impossible, therefore, that anything should be the contradictory of that which is attributable to us. *But surely, that of which the contradictory is impossible is according to fate,* if indeed these things are according to fate whose contradictories cannot possibly exist or have existed. Therefore, that which is attributable to us is something according to fate. [SVF 2. 1007]

The assent to the proposition is determined by the fixed disposition (*diathesis*) of the individual. It cannot be other than it is. The individual, however, is responsible for the state of his fixed disposition. The change from an inferior *diathesis* to one which is ideal is instantaneous, but the gradual improvement or deterioration in the quality of the individual's *hexis* (disposition) took place over a period of time.[10] For the Stoics any improvement in the quality of the *hexis* was to be found in those areas of mental and psychological activity that preceded the change from vice to virtue. Virtues and vices were fixed dispositions (*diatheseis*) (SVF 2. 393). Such qualities as endurance and self-control, however, are dispositions (*hexeis*) (SVF 3.384). In differentiating between the *hexis* and the *diathesis* Stobaeus uses such terms as tightening and slackening. The *hexis* is that which can be tightened and slackened; the *diathesis* is that which cannot be tightened or slackened. A *diathesis*, as, for example, the straightness of the rod, cannot be slackened or tightened or admit of variation of degree. The virtues are *diatheseis* precisely because they do not admit of variation of degree (SVF 2.393).[11] Since Chrysippus argued that virtue could be lost through drunkenness and melancholy (SVF 3.237), which were, in fact, dispositions (*hexeis*), he must also have argued that by forming a good disposition (*hexis*) the man who was not virtuous could become virtuous.[12]

The definitions of the end of life given by Diogenes of Babylon and Antipater of Tarsus prescribe conduct that will contribute to the development of a good disposition. Diogenes defined it as "acting reasonably (*eulogistein*) in the selection and rejection of things according to nature" (SVF 3.44), and Antipater as: "To live selecting things according to nature and rejecting things contrary to nature" (SVF 3.57).[13] "Those things which are according to nature" include such things as health and wealth (SVF 3.127), and are the source of the appropriate act (*kathēkon*) (SVF 3.491). So far as I have been able to discover, the act of selecting that which is according to nature and rejecting its contrary was not designated by the technical term "attributable to us" (*eph'hēmin*). Acts that require the selection of that which is according to nature and the rejection of its contrary are of such a kind that their contradictories are in our power and that they might reasonably receive praise and blame. It is possible to use health and wealth well or badly (SVF 3.117, cf. 123), that is, in Diogenes' phrase, to act rationally or irrationally in the selection and rejection of things according to nature. For instance, the improper use of wealth may lead to the election of an inferior candidate and excessive attention to health may lead to neglect of one's responsibilities.[14] Decisions of this kind may be made in ignorance of the particular situation at hand. As Aristotle wrote: "Ignorance of particulars, that is, of the circumstances of the action and the objects with which it is concerned."[15] In most cases, however, the consequences that follow the exercise of choice are of no great significance. To use a modern example, when I am faced with the presentation "It is fitting to deposit this money in the bank today," I do not necessarily have to make a moral judgment. "Depositing this money" is in my power but the "depositing of this money" is not in the technical sense "attributable to us" because the act of depositing does not follow in ordinary circumstances from assent to an ethical proposition.

There are two other areas in which a man could participate in his own development: the forming of preconceptions and conceptions on the basis of experience and elementary reasoning, and the giving of assent to a presentation. The *logos* (reason) is an aggregate of conceptions (*ennoiai*) and preconceptions (*prolēpseis*) (SVF 2. 841), and comprises the knowledge that we have acquired through types of elementary reasoning on the basis of experience (SVF 2. 83, 87). Since the conceptions and preconceptions are inferences made on the basis of events that are part of the series of events directed and controlled by the *logos* in nature, the Stoics could reasonably regard the development of the *logos* of the individual as parallel to and influenced by the events that are controlled by the *logos* in the world at large.

The apprehension (*katalēpsis*) is not "attributable to us." Alexander of Aphrodisias writes in his *Concerning Fate:* "For they say that 'that which is attributable to us' does not apply in a situation in which we yield [*eixai*] when a presentation falls upon us, or when we yield to a presentation that is formed by us ourselves,[16] and direct our impulse toward that which is presented" (SVF 2. 981). The presentation is something that moves or puts pressure on the apprehension (*katalēpsis*). Sextus Empiricus illustrates the pressure applied by the cognitive presentation graphically when he writes: "For it [the apprehensive presentation], being clear and striking, seizes us almost by the hair, they say, dragging us into assent" (*Adv. math.* 7. 257). It is precisely because of this pressure that assent to the presentation is not "attributable to us." The giving or withholding of assent to the presentation, however, is in the power of the individual (SVF 2. 91). Because of our weakness we give assent to false presentations. This point is made clearly in a passage in Plutarch: "Again, Chrysippus says, 'God makes false presentations, and the wise man too, requiring us not to give assent or yield to them, but only to act and direct our impulse towards the phenomena, but we, being inferior, in weakness give our assent to such presentations'" (SVF 3. 177).

The treatise *Concerning Fate* written by Alexander of Aphrodisias contains a passage in which it is argued that the contradictory of "that which happens according to fate" is possible. It may be translated as follows:

> To say that, although all things happen according to fate, the possible and the contingent are not destroyed, because it is possible for that which is prevented by nothing from happening to happen, even if it does not happen. "Of those things which happen according to fate the contradictories have not been prevented from happening; therefore, even if they do not happen, nevertheless, they are possible." The fact that those things that would prevent them, of whatever kind they are, are unknown to us is a demonstrative argument for their not being prevented from happening. For those things which are responsible for their contradictories' happening according to fate are responsible for their not happening, if, as they say, it is impossible for the contradictories of the same events to happen. But as for the fact that they say that their happening is not prevented for the reason that we do not know what those things are [i.e., which would prevent them]—surely, to say this is child's play. [SVF 2. 959]

The last sentence is an inaccurate interpretation of the Stoic source on the part of Alexander. The passage states that the fact that those things that would prevent them are unknown to us is a demonstrative argument for their (i.e., the contradictories) not being prevented from happening. It does not say that they are not prevented from happening because that which would prevent them from happening is unknown to us.[17]

"Those things that happen according to fate" include presentations (*phantasiai*) specified by statements (*lekta*), as, for example, "The Athenians resist the attack of the enemy." We know that the event specified by this statement can be prevented from happening by something external to it, as, for example, the failure of the enemy to attack. That which prevents the contradictory "The Athenians do not resist the attack of the enemy" from happening is that which is responsible for the event specified by the statement "The Athenians resist the attack of the enemy." There is, therefore, no external circumstance that can prevent the contradictory from happening, and the contradictory is possible.

"Those things that happen according to fate" are events that have antecedent causes. They include events whose contradictories are impossible (SVF 2. 1007), as, for example, those events which are specified by both types of necessary propositions: (a) a proposition in which the predicate is derived from the principal cause inherent by fate in the subject, e.g., "Virtue benefits" and (b) a proposition about the past which is prevented from being false by external circumstances.[18] The contradictories of the proposition to which assent is given, as, for example, "Not: to resist the enemy is good," and of the action that follows from assent to the proposition, as, for example, "not resisting," are impossible because this type of proposition and this kind of action are determined by the fixed disposition (*diathesis*). They belong to the first type of necessary proposition. On the other hand, the phrase "those things that are according to fate" includes those events whose contradictories are possible, as, for example, "The Athenians resist the attack of the enemy."

In the ninth chapter of the *De Interpretatione* Aristotle argued that with regard to what is and what has been it is necessary for the affirmation or the negation to be true or false, but not with regard to particulars that are going to be. He concluded that it was not necessary that of every affirmation and negation one of the contradictories should be true and the other false, for what holds for things that are does not hold for things that are not but may possibly be or not be (19b1-4). Taylor summarizes Aristotle's position in the following passage: "Aristotle believed that any statement which asserts or denies, concerning a contingent event, that it is going to occur, is neither true nor false, the world being as yet indeterminate with regard to the existence or nonexistence of such things."[19]

To support his thesis that, if every affirmation or negation were true or false, everything that would happen would happen necessarily Aristotle argued as follows: "Further, if it is white now, it was always true to say earlier that it would be white so that it was always true to say of any of those things that have happened that it would be. But if it was always true to say that it was or would be, it could not not be so, or not going to be so. But if something cannot not happen, it is impossible for it not to happen; and if it is impossible for it not to happen, it is necessary for it to happen. Therefore, it is necessary for everything that will be to happen" (18b9-15).

The Stoics held that all propositions with regard to what is, what has been, and what will be were true or false (2. 198), and yet they believed that all events in the future were contingent. How, then, did Chrysippus answer Aristotle? Aristotle assumed that an event in the present specified by a statement such as, "It is white," necessarily is when it is (19a23-24), and that a statement that specifies that which necessarily is is true (*Met.* 1051b6-9). Chrysippus argued that an event in the present is contingent (i.e., of such a kind if external circumstances do not prevent it), and that a statement regarding the event is possible. He accepted the third proposition of the Master Argument of Diodorus Cronus: "That which neither is true nor will be true is possible" (SVF 1. 489). The proposition "Cypselus is reigning at Corinth" is possible even if it is not true or will not be true. We know, moreover, from the definitions of the possible stated by Boethius and Diogenes Laertius that this proposition, if true, is possible. Boethius: "The possible is that which is capable of receiving the predicate true if those things which, although they are external to it, happen to occur with it, do not prevent it"; and Diogenes Laertius: "The possible is that which admits of being true if the external circumstances do not prevent it from being true, as, for example, 'Diocles lives.'"[20] In what must be regarded as a direct response to Aristotle, Chrysippus asserted that it would not have been necessary for Cypselus to reign at Corinth although that had been predicted by the oracle of Apollo a thousand years earlier (SVF 2. 954). The proposition "There will be a naval battle tomorrow" was simply a possible proposition about a contingent event. Alexander's Stoic source argued that a proposition of this type should not be regarded as necessary. Alexander writes: "The proposition 'There will be a naval battle tomorrow' can be true and yet not be necessary. For the necessary is that which is always true. But this no longer remains true when the naval battle takes place" (2. 961).

The Stoics seem to have regarded true propositions concerning the future as propositions that are true at the present moment. For instance, Sextus Empiricus states that in the proposition, "If this man is wounded in the heart, he will die," the premise, "he will die," although spoken about the future, is true now (*Adv. math.* 8. 255-256).[21] "The gem is broken" and "The gem will be broken" are true propositions at the present moment, although one refers to an event in the present and the other to an event in the future.

There is evidence that Chrysippus introduced the notion of a hindrance or impediment to the individual into Stoic philosophy. A necessary proposition in Stoic philosophy was defined by Boethius as "That which, being true, in no way receives the predicate false," and in Diogenes Laertius as "That which, being true, does not admit of being false, or which does admit of it, but external circumstances prevent it from being false, as, for example, 'Virtue benefits.'"[22] The first part of Diogenes' definition agrees with that of Boethius and is illustrated by Diogenes' example. The second part of Diogenes' definition seems to refer to a true proposition about the past which is prevented from being false by external circumstances. Chrysippus, however, accepted the first proposition of the Master Argument of Diodorus Cronus: "Everything true about the past is necessary" (SVF 1. 489), and Cleanthes did not. It would follow, therefore, that, although Chrysippus would have accepted the second half of Diogenes' definition of the necessary proposition, Cleanthes would not have done so.

Chrysippus stated emphatically that there were many impediments to the particular natural entities but none to the nature of the whole. Plutarch writes: "In all his books on *Physics* he wrote that there were many impediments and hinderances to particular natural entities and their movements, but none to the nature of the whole" (SVF 2. 935). The individual may be hampered by necessary propositions, both those that indicate a relationship that cannot be otherwise, and those that are true propositions about the past. He may be hampered also by external events so that possible propositions will not be realized. The proposition "Cypselus will reign at Corinth" may be prevented by the death of Cypselus from being true or by a change of government, as, for example, the establishment of a democracy. He may also be hindered, as we shall see, by the *logos* in the universe in its role of oracle or prophecy.

In his interpretation of the *logos* of nature Chrysippus seems to have parted company with Cleanthes. Cleanthes wrote in his *Hymn to Zeus:* "Nor does any act take place on the earth apart from thee, lord, neither in the divine aethrial heavens nor on the sea except what evil men do in their folly" (SVF 1. 537. 11-13). Chrysippus, however, argued that even what men do in their folly was according to common nature and the *logos* (reason) (SVF 2. 937). Several definitions of the *logos* of nature are attributed to

Chrysippus. He is quoted as saying in the second book of his *Concerning Definitions* and in his *Concerning Fate:* "Fate is the *logos* of the cosmos"; "the *logos* of those things that are organized by forethought in the cosmos"; "the *logos* according to which the things that have happened have happened, the things that are happening are happening, and the things that will happen will happen" (SVF 2.913). Elsewhere, he wrote: "Since in this way the management (*oikonomia*) of the whole directs, it is necessary according to this for us to be as we are, whether we are sick contrary to our own particular nature, or maimed, or whether we are skilled in letters or trained in music"; and "According to this *logos* we shall make similar statements about our virtue and about our wrongdoing and generally about our proficiency and lack of proficiency in skills, as I said" (SVF 2.937).

Particularly puzzling, however, is a passage in Plutarch from the second book of Chrysippus's *Concerning Nature* which reads as follows: "Wrongdoing which results in terrible consequences has a certain *logos* peculiar to itself (*idios logos*); for this comes to pass in some way according to the *logos* of nature, and, if I may say so, it arises in a manner which is not useless with respect to the whole. For otherwise the good would not exist" (SVF 2.1181).[23] Does the sentence "Wrongdoing which results in terrible consequences has a certain *logos* peculiar to itself" mean simply that various causes, which are according to the *logos*, brought this wrongdoing to pass, or that the wrongdoing was brought to pass by the particular *logos* of the individual who committed the wrongdoing? The two interpretations are not far apart since the principal cause of the wrongdoing must be the assent of the man who perpetrated it. Chrysippus distinguished between the *pathos*, the excessive impulse that drives us forward into activities that are contrary to the *logos* (SVF 3.390) and the *logos* itself. He refers to "that which is turned aside with respect to the *logos*" (SVF 3.475 and 476). Chrysippus, however, did not recognize a dualism in the human psyche, or a force in opposition to the *logos*. The *logos* in the individual was both a body of experience and reason ordering the impulse to do what ought to be done. It is, therefore, necessary to see the wrongdoing of the individual in terms of the *logos* of the individual just as it is necessary in the world order to reconcile the actual event, for example, the murder of Laius by Oedipus, with forethought working through events to bring about that which is good.

It is possible to understand Plutarch's statement that wrongdoing is "not useless with respect to the whole." It is more difficult to understand how wrongdoing can come to pass in some way according to the *logos* of nature. The clue to the connection between the *logos* of the individual and the *logos* of nature is perhaps to be found in the fact that the *logos* of nature is a power working through events, and the *logos* of the individual is an aggregate of conceptions and preconceptions formed on the basis of experience gained from events. Perhaps the best way to explain Plutarch's statement is to examine the role of the *logos*, as represented by the oracle at Delphi, in the story of Oedipus. According to a passage in Alexander of Aphrodisias's *Concerning Fate* the oracle was given to Laius by the Pythian because without such an oracle the whole series of events that terminated in the murder of Laius would not have taken place. The oracle said: "If you beget a child, the one who is begotten will kill you." The Pythian gave the oracle in the knowledge that Laius would beget a child, and realizing that if he did not give such an oracle none of the events pertaining to the reversal in the fortunes of Laius and Oedipus would take place. Laius would not have exposed the child who was born to him, and the child would not have been taken up by the herdsman and given to Polybus of Corinth. Further, Oedipus would not have killed Laius in ignorance of his identity. For if he had been brought up with them as a son, Oedipus would not have been ignorant of the identity of his parents, and he would not have killed the one and married the other (SVF 2. 941).

We can go further in our interpretation of the story of Oedipus. When Oedipus received the oracle at Delphi—"You will murder your father and marry your mother"—he decided not to return to Corinth, where his supposed father and mother were living, and took the road to Thebes. He met a man on the road to Thebes, who refused to allow him to pass, and he gave assent to the proposition: "To kill this man is just." The assent and the murder that followed were attributable to Oedipus alone. Oedipus was faced later with the necessity of deciding whether he should marry an older woman, Jocasta, the wife of Laius. He was solely responsible for his decision to marry her. The oracle brought about the set of

circumstances in which Oedipus would make the decisions that
would fulfill the oracle. The *logos* in nature and the *logos* in Oedipus were progressing toward the same end—the murder of Laius
and the marriage of Jocasta. The fact that fate, as represented by
the oracle, had to intervene is sufficient proof that that which is
fated will not come to pass regardless of the decisions of the individual.

As we have seen, the Stoic source of Alexander of Aphrodisias
maintained that the Pythian gave the oracle to Laius because
without such an oracle none of those events that pertained to the
reversal of the fortunes of Laius and Oedipus would have have
come to pass (SVF 2. 941). Chrysippus, we are told, discussed the
futile attempts of the parents of Oedipus and Alexander to kill
their sons and avoid the fulfillment of the oracles (SVF 2. 939). We
should not conclude from these examples, however, that the oracle
would be fulfilled regardless of the attempts made by the individual to prevent it. Alexander's Stoic source stated that the Pythian
gave the oracle to Laius in the full knowledge that Laius would not
be persuaded not to beget a child (SVF 2. 941). The begetting of a
child was the responsibility of Laius.

The Greeks practiced divination to obtain answers to specific
questions, such as, "Should we attack the enemy today?" If the
omens were unfavorable, the attack would be postponed. Divination was a manifestation of the goodness of god. Pseudo-Plutarch
listed as the third topic in Chrysippus's *Concerning Fate:* "That
divination enjoys a good reputation among all men on the grounds
that it really comes to pass with god's help; and the satisfaction felt
by the wise with whatever befalls them, since all things happen
according to fate" (SVF 2. 912).

"The predictions of seers would not be true unless all things
were embraced by fate" (SVF 2. 939). This quotation from Chrysippus's *Concerning Fate* raises serious questions. What did the
Stoics mean when they said that a prediction was true, and that
the prediction would not be true unless all things were embraced
by fate? A true proposition was defined by Sextus Empiricus as a
proposition that is the case (*hyparchei*) and which has a contradictory (*Adv. math.* 8.85). Sextus defined the *hyparchon* as that
which arouses the cognitive presentation (*kataleptikē phantasia*,
SVF 2. 69, 97). If a prediction is true, the prediction is such that it

arouses the cognitive presentation. The cognitive presentation, on the other hand, receives assent from the apprehension (*katalēpsis*) and guarantees that that to which assent is given is true. At this point we should recall the statement from Cicero's *De Fato* which I quoted at the beginning of my paper: "Every proposition is either true or false. Therefore, there is no movement without a cause. But if this is so, everything which happens happens because of antecedent causes. If this is so, everything happens by fate" (SVF 2. 952). What is the antecedent cause of the prediction? This may be answered on the basis of a passage in Sextus Empiricus in which he gives the following example of a demonstrative argument: "If a god has said to you that this man will be rich, this man will be rich; but this god has said to you that this man will be rich; therefore, he will be rich" (*Adv. math.* 8. 308). Sextus adds that we accept this conclusion because we believe the statement of the god. The antecedent cause of the particular prediction, we may assume, is the authority of the oracle or the seer. That which has an antecedent cause, however, is according to fate. It is ultimately man who vouches for the truth of the connections he draws. When, for instance, Laius received the prediction: "If you beget a son, the one who is begotten will kill you," Laius himself decided whether he should accept the prediction. This conclusion is supported by a statement in Sextus Empiricus which reads as follows: "For the sign is of such a form: 'If this, then this,' Therefore, the fact that the sign is the case (*hyparchei*) is due to the nature and constitution of man" (SVF 2. 223).[24]

The Stoics took elaborate precautions to protect their system from rigid determinism. They were much maligned by the misinterpretations of their critics.

NOTES

1. I have adopted Long's translation of *eph'hēmin* as "attributable to us." For further discussion of the topics discussed in this paper, see particularly A. A. Long, "Freedom and Determinism in the Stoic Theory of Human Action," in *Problems in Stoicism* (London, 1971) 173-199; A. Graeser, *Zenon von Kitiòn* (Berlin, 1975) 125-135; J. M. Rist, *Stoic Philosophy* (Cambridge, 1969) 112-132.

2. On this passage see the commentary in Pseudo-Plutarco, *De Fato* ed. E. Valgiglio (Rome, 1964) 64-67.

3. For a discussion of principal and initiating causes, see my article "Fate and Possibility in early Stoic Philosophy," *Phoenix* 19 (1965), 285-297.

4. SVF 3.463, 464, 441.

5. Aristotle distinguished *epithymia* (mere appetite) from desire (*orexis*) and reasonable desire (*boulēsis, De An.* 3.433a23-26). He held that desire (*orexis*) was desire for the pleasant (*De An.* 2.414b5-6).

6. SVF 2.981 cf. 992, 974. 283. 27-28. The reference to living creatures is explained by a passage in Cicero: "Therefore, since the difference between the inanimate and the animate lies particularly in the fact that an animal does something—either sensation ought not to be attributed to it or that assent which is in our power ought to be assigned to it" (SVF 2.115).

7. On this passage see Long *Freedom and Determinism*, 180.

8. Ibid., 183-185.

9. The words in brackets are a conjecture by von Arnim.

10. On this point see G. E. L. Owen, "Tithenai ta phainomena," published in *Aristote et les problèmes de la méthode. Symposium Aristotelicum* (Louvain, 1961) 99-103, and Long *Freedom and Determinism*, 184-185.

11. On this point see S. Sambursky, *Physics of the Stoics* (London, 1959) 85.

12. See my article, "The 'Indifferents' in the Old and Middle Stoa," *Transactions of the American Philological Association* 82 (1951) 104-105.

13. The term *eulogistein* in Diogenes' definition may be significant, since Chrysippus defined endurance and self-control as dispositions disposed to follow the *logos* which exercises choice (SVF 3.384). According to Diogenes Laertius "appropriate acts" (*kathēkonta*) are those which the *logos* chooses to do, as, for example, to honor one's parents, borthers, and fatherland (SVF 3.495 cf. 459).

14. The examples are my own.

15. Aristotle, *E.N.* 1110b33-1111a1.

16. A presentation formed by us ourselves is a presentation grasped through the *dianoia* (SVF 2.61, 84).

17. For a different interpretation of this passage, see A. A. Long, "Stoic Determinism and Alexander of Aphrodisias's *De Fato*," *Arch. Gesch. Phil.* 52 (1970) 254-257.

18. See p. 197.

19. R. Taylor, "Aristotle's Doctrine of Future Contingencies," published in *Essays in Ancient Greek Philosophy* (Albany, 1971) 522.

20. Boethius, *Comm. in Arist. De Int.* 234.27-29 = SVF 2.201, and D.L. 7.75 = SVF 2.201.

21. On this point see A. C. Lloyd, "Activity and Description in Aristotle and the Stoa," *Proc. of the British Academy* 56 (1970) 9-10.

22. Boethius, *Comm. in Arist. De Int.* 235.3-4 = SVF 2.201, and D.L. 7.75 = SVF 2.201.

23. On this passage see also A. A. Long, "The Stoic Concept of Evil," *Philosophical Quarterly* 18 (1968) 331-334.

24. In spite of Sextus Empiricus's statement, the sign in Stoic Logic seems to denote the antecedent of a conditional rather than the whole conditional.

9

Stoic Determinisn and Moral Responsibility

Charlotte Stough

I want to take up an issue in Stoic philosophy which was particularly controversial in antiquity and has continued to be disquieting to commentators ever since then. It is the problem of understanding the relation between Stoic determinism and their stance in regard to moral responsibility. I propose to look into the matter of how the Early Stoics tried to accommodate their conception of a universal determinism to the normal practices of holding persons responsible for their actions, of praising and frequently rewarding them for behavior deemed commendable and of reproaching and punishing them for conduct base or unlawful. Most of the presentation will focus on a very narrow region of Stoic Nature, the relatively small domain that deals specifically with *human* nature and actions. I hope to be able to shed light on some interesting distinctions the Stoics drew in their efforts to clarify the issues involved when persons are held accountable for their actions. It will emerge that the Stoic position is considerably stronger than is generally acknowledged. My discussion ends by suggesting that the implications of the Stoic theory and their bearing on commonsense intuitions about responsibility, as well as social institutions that reflect these intuitions, have yet to receive the serious attention they merit.

REASON AND NATURE

The ideas of order and reason (*logos*) are central to the Stoic concept of Nature and therefore, as we shall see, to their doctrine of
fate. The cosmos of the Stoic philosophers was a vast dynamic
continuum. It was conceived as a unified whole in which "all
things are bound together with one another" through myriad relationships of cause and effect.[1] These causal connections were
thought to be pervasive and without exception, permeating
Nature at all levels from the lowest inorganic matter to the highest
forms of life. In the words of Alexander of Aphrodisias the Stoics
held that:[2]

There neither exists nor occurs anything uncaused in the cosmos, because there is
nothing in it that is set free or separated from all that has happened before. For
the cosmos would break apart and disintegrate and would no longer remain a
unity eternally administered by one order and plan if some uncaused motion
were introduced. . . . In view of the multiplicity of causes they say equally about
all of them that whenever all the same circumstances obtain in regard to both the
cause and that to which it is related, it is impossible that sometimes one thing
should result and sometimes another.

It is clear from this passage that the Stoics believed the intelligibility of the universe to be dependent on a universal and rigorous
determinism such that each event can be understood by reference
to the causes that precede it and the effects that follow from it. The
emphasis that the Stoics placed on the intelligibility of such a
deterministic scheme is brought out further in a passage from
Cicero in which the theoretical possibility of predicting future
events from antecedent causes is imagined.[3]

If there were a man whose soul could discern the links that join each cause with
every other cause, then surely he would never be mistaken in any prediction he
might make. For he who knows the causes of future events necessarily knows
what every future event will be. But since such knowledge is possibly only to a
god, it is left to man to presage the future by means of certain signs which indicate what will follow them. [W. A. Falconer]

The ordered universe is thus a rational "plan" (*oikonomia*),[4]
and the Stoics went so far as to identify it with divine *logos* itself. I
am stressing the connection between reason and the uninterrupted

succession of causes and effects, because it helps us to understand the uncompromising attitude that the Stoics adopted toward fate (*heimarmenē*). For fate is nothing more than the "ordered interweaving of causes," the divine and rational order of the cosmos by which all events past, present, and future are determined.[5] To insist, as the Stoics did, that all things in the universe are fated is merely to affirm that the cosmos is an intelligible system of interdependent parts in which all events, including human events, are linked causally to other occurrences that precede and follow them and hence could, in principle, be predicted from relevant conditions in Nature, were all those conditions known to us. Thus Chrysippus asserts that "no particular event, not even the smallest, can take place otherwise than in accordance with universal Nature and its *logos*."[6] His words proclaim the universality of fate, and that is tantamount to the claim that everything in the cosmos down to the smallest of its parts occurs necessarily in such a fashion as to invite rational explanation. When others, notably Epicureans and followers of Aristotle, sought to preserve chance and spontaneity in Nature, the Stoics postulated "hidden causes,"[7] arguing that to accept an uncaused event is like allowing that something comes into being from nothing. The one is no less impossible (presumably by virtue of its inconceivability) than the other.[8] The reasoning is a priori and is splendid evidence of the rigorous and consistent rationalism of the Stoics.

It is important to see how the Stoics applied their deterministic theory to the workings of Nature at all levels. They distinguished roughly two sorts of causal agency which combine to bring about a given natural occurrence: (1) the external causes acting on a body, which they attributed to the workings of fate, and (2) the "nature" of the body affected, which was regarded as an internal cause and may have been linked to necessity.[9] Stoic determinism implies that every event is an effect brought about jointly by these two types of cause. The manner in which the nature of the body and the antecedent causes combine to produce a certain effect is described by Alexander as follows:[10]

For, they say, since the natures of things and events are various and different ... what happens by the agency of any particular thing happens in accordance with its own specific nature. The behavior of a stone is in accordance with the nature of a stone, that of fire with the nature of fire, that of a living thing with the nature of the living thing. None of those things that happen by the agency of a particular thing according to its nature can happen otherwise, but they all happen so by necessity, though not from compulsion, since it is impossible for something whose nature it is to behave in one way, given that certain circumstances are invariant, to behave differently on some occasion. If a stone is released from a height, it cannot fail to fall down if nothing prevents it, because it contains weight in itself which is the cause of its natural movement. And when there are also external causes present which contribute to the stone's natural movement, the stone by necessity is moved according to its nature.... The same principle applies also to other things. What holds for inanimate things also holds for living things, as they say. For living things possess a natural movement, and this is a movement in accordance with impulse.

For a more detailed picture of the operation of these causes in living creatures, including human beings, I quote from a passage by Origen:[11]

> For sentient creatures are moved from themselves when a presentation arises in them and calls forth impulse; moreover in some living creatures this occurs when the presentational nature of the creature prompts the impulse according to a fixed pattern, as in a spider the presentation of spinning occurs and the impulse follows until spinning results—its presentational nature calls forth this behavior in a prescribed manner and nothing else beyond the presentational nature is believed to belong to the animal—and in the bee the same process results in the making of wax. The rational animal, however, in addition to a presentational nature has reason which judges the presentations, rejecting some and accepting others, in order that the animal may be guided in accordance with them.

Together these passages give us a fairly full account of the way in which fate and necessity operate throughout Nature according to the Stoic view. All bodies, inanimate and animate, including plants, animals, and the human animal are parts of Nature. Even though they differ in regard to the complexity of their natures, all behavior can be subsumed under the same sorts of causal laws. To say that everything in Nature is determined is to say that every phenomenon, or the behavior of every body, is a product of external causes operating jointly with causes intrinsic to the body and fixed by its nature. Just as the properties of a stone help to explain what happens when it is released from a height, so the more complex natures of living things must be taken into account in understanding their behavior. Sentient creatures move according to impulse. When they are affected by external causes, sensory presentations arise in them to which they react by an impulse to a certain sort of behavior. Some creatures, such as the spider and bee, react automatically to sensory stimulation, which is to say that in those animals the presentation of sense is automatically followed by an impulse to behavior of the appropriate sort. The transition from sensory presentation to impulse and behavior in human beings, however, is not automatic. The faculty of reason enables humans to judge critically the data of sense, to respond selectively, and therefore to act intelligently in consequence of sensory stimulation. The resultant action must be a product of external causes represented by sensory presentations, the critical faculty whose function it is to make judgments, and the impulse that ends in action.

Because the Stoics held that all Nature without exception is governed by causal law and in that respect human beings are no different from the rest of Nature, it is perhaps not surprising that a dispute arose between them and critics over the question of human responsibility. Although activities of reason, such as judging, deciding, choosing, and the like, seem to set humans apart from other animals and the more so from inanimate Nature, human events, including mental activities, are nevertheless natural events and so are subject to the same inviolable laws that govern the rest of Nature. Consequently, whatever does happen must happen in conformity with the laws of Nature and, given prevailing conditions, could not have happened otherwise. From there it is but a short step to the conclusion drawn by opponents of the Stoic theory that:[12]

If all things are set in motion and directed by fate, and the course of fate and its coils cannot be turned aside or evaded, then the sins and faults of men too ought not to cause anger or be attributed to themselves and their inclinations, but to a certain unavoidable impulse which arises from fate. [Rolfe]

To many Stoic determinism seemed incompatible with the practice of holding persons accountable for their actions and thus seemed to threaten the foundation of morality. The Stoics, however, without compromising their deterministic theory of Nature sought to show that it did not rule out culpability in matters of human conduct. We must now look into their efforts to establish this point.

HUMAN NATURE AND RESPONSIBILITY

It is difficult from the fragmentary (and often hostile) testimony of our sources to piece together the Stoic position(s) in regard to responsibility along with their supporting arguments. Yet the available evidence, incomplete as it is, indicates that the Stoics did attempt to meet criticism that their deterministic theory ruled out a legitimate use for such standard moral and juridical concepts as praise, blame, responsibility, and punishment. We can see this from a number of important distinctions they drew entirely within the context of a deterministic system. I wish to set forth some of this evidence and try to assess its significance in light of the Stoic theory of Nature and, in particular, their concept of human nature and action.

Perhaps the most crucial distinction from the standpoint of its significance for moral discourse is the contrast the Stoics drew between *ta eph'hēmin* and *ta ouk eph'hēmin* (things that are "attributable to us" and things "not attributable to us").[13] The distinction is Aristotelian but its meaning in Stoic philosophy is not. In fact the Stoics quite intentionally altered the sense of this pair of expressions from Aristotle's notion of things that are or are not "in our power" to one more harmonious with their own view of human nature and action. Their repudiation of the Aristotelian conception of *ta eph'hēmin* is reported by Alexander as follows:[14]

If, they say, those things are attributable to us (*eph'hēmin*) the opposites of which we are also capable, and in such cases praise and blame, encouragement and discouragement, rewards and punishments are given, then wisdom and virtue cannot be attributable to those (*epi tois*) who have them, because they are not (any longer) (*mēketi*)[15] capable of receiving the vices opposed to their virtues; similarly neither can vices be attributable to those (*epi tois*) who are vicious, since it is not attributable to them (*epi toutois*) not (any longer) to be vicious. But it is absurd to deny that virtue and vice are attributable to us (*eph'hēmin*) or that praise and blame are given for these. Therefore "that which is attributable to us" (*to eph'hēmin*) does not have this meaning.

Two things are striking about this passage: First, the very strong claim that virtue and vice are among the things that are attributable to us,[16] and second, the explicit detachment of this concept from the idea of capability or power. The argument looks like a *reductio ad absurdum,* and it proceeds according to certain rather curious but typical Stoic assumptions about the nature of virtue and vice. Among these is the complex proposition that virtue and vice are mutually exclusive traits of character which determine conduct. We can rough out the argument informally as follows:

(1) Suppose *ta eph'hēmin* means "those things the opposites of which we are capable."
(2) The virtuous cannot be vicious, and vice versa.
(3) For those who possess them virtue and vice are therefore not *eph'hēmin.*
(4) But it is absurd to deny that virtue and vice are *eph'hēmin.*
(5) Therefore *ta eph'hēmin* does not mean "those things the opposites of which we are capable."

Our understanding of the passage rests almost entirely on the meaning of the second premise, which is crucial to the argument and is quite obviously connected with the assumption mentioned above. Since Alexander's formulation is far from clear, I list the following three interpretations as compatible with the text:

(2a) Those who are virtuous cannot, inasmuch as they are virtuous, act viciously, and vice versa (logical "cannot").
(2b) Those who are virtuous cannot, because their moral character will not permit, act viciously, and vice versa (moral "cannot").
(2c) Those who are virtuous cannot become vicious, and vice versa (natural "cannot").

Each proposition contains the treacherous term *cannot (mēketi dektikoi, dynametha* in Alexander's text) occurring with a different force, and I have dubbed them "logical," "moral," and "natural," respectively. To understand the import of the passage for the argument and for Stoic ethics we must try to determine which among the above alternatives captures the meaning of premise (2). A necessary criterion of course is that the candidate be accepted as true by the Stoics; and, if true on independent grounds, the possibilities need not exclude one another.

All three interpretations are compatible with the Stoic doctrine that virtue and vice are mutually exclusive traits of character such that, although every mature person is either virtuous or vicious, no one simultaneously possesses both moral qualities. That a single individual should embody contrary moral dispositions at once is logically impossible on the Stoic view. This seems to be part of what is claimed by the proposition that is premise (2) above. Moreover, inasmuch as virtue or vice, as the case may be, is part of our makeup as individuals (the disjunction being intrinsic to our specific "nature" as human animals) and we act in accordance with our individual natures, a virtuous person cannot act viciously on occasion without displaying a character trait inconsistent with the one he possesses. Given the logical incompatibility of virtue and vice and Stoic determinism in the area of human action, then, there is a sense in which human behavior cannot contradict moral character. The second premise of the argument seems also to be making a claim along these lines. But it is just this "cannot" that needs to be unpacked and whose meaning is distributed differently over the three interpretations of premise (2). Let us look at each candidate separately.

(2a) affirms that action inconsistent with character is logically impossible. It claims that a vicious action is sufficient condition for denying possession of the opposite character trait by a moral agent. Therefore if a person alleged to be virtuous is believed to perform a vicious action, either the individual does not in reality possess a virtuous character or the action is mistakenly characterized as vicious. The implication that a virtuous person performs a vicious action is logically incoherent. This is the weakest reading of (2), because it puts the minimum burden on "cannot." That the logical claim would be accepted as true by the Stoics seems entirely uncontroversial.

(2b) makes a stronger claim. It says something about the consistency and reliability of virtuous and vicious persons. Given the kinds of persons they are, we can count on them to behave accordingly. In the case of virtue the matter is relatively straightforward. We can suppose that the virtuous are committed (however unconsciously) to principles that prohibit behavior of a kind judged by them to be vicious. They cannot (logically) act in certain ways without violating those principles and they cannot (morally) violate their principles. The second "cannot" is the relevant one for interpretation (2b). What is meant by saying that a virtuous person cannot violate his moral principles? Surely not that such an individual could not, if he chose to do so, act in ways that are inconsistent with his moral principles. Of course he could. Such a person could opt for the unjust course of action over the just alternative if he so desired, but being the kind of person he is he does not want to act unjustly. The impossibility in question is a moral one. It is impossible for some persons to act viciously because of profound moral disapproval on their part. If we ask whether someone with strong moral feelings could cease disapproving of vicious actions, we are asking whether such a person could experience a change in the relevant attitudes, and this raises the kind of question that comes up in (2c). But before proceeding to the third reading of (2) let us turn to the morally vicious person. (2b) claims that it is impossible for him too to act out of character. Again we may inquire what is meant by denying that the vicious person can act virtuously? Not (typically) in this case that he is prohibited from such action by a commitment to principle. Yet there is a sense in which he is, as it were, prevented from choosing the just course of action by a kind of commitment, or more accurately, an attachment to something. Given his aims in life, the goals he has set for himself and the unscrupulous manner in which he pursues them, he cannot act justly. Again that is not say that he could not do so if he wished, but merely that he does not want to perform certain actions which consistently are of the sort deemed just. The impossibility in this case too is predicated upon the choices, wants, and desires of a moral agent. In denying that the virtuous can be vicious and vice versa, (2b) affirms that virtue and vice are stable and relatively permanent dispositions to act morally or immorally. We have good reason to believe that this was in fact the Stoic view. For the Stoics identified moral dispositions with physical states of the soul, which they believed to be relatively constant.[17] In the case of those physical states that were moral dispositions, only one relevant change could occur, namely, one to a state identical with the opposite moral disposition. Since the physical state/disposition entailed behavior of a consistent moral quality, the agent acted accordingly unless he underwent the relevant sort of transformation.[18] (2b) is evidently compatible with Stoic ethical theory.

(2c) makes the very strong claim that a person's moral character, once it is established, is permanently fixed. That is to say, if we are virtuous we run no risk of moral backsliding, but if we are vicious there is no hope for improvement. It follows that moral dispositions will remain what they are in spite of our experiences in the world and our desires and efforts to change. Moral character is not only beyond a person's control but it is also quite impervious to external influences. The "cannot" in (2c) imports natural impossibility in regard to both persons and events. By this I mean, in the case of persons, that it implies a genuine lack of capacity in a moral agent, not the inability to act or to influence the course of one's life, but powerlessness to become a "different person" morally, either through one's own efforts or as a result of the kinds of experiences that might otherwise be expected to have a profound effect in altering character for better or worse. Notably (2c) does not say that in regard to character a person is at the mercy of external events, which toss him this way and that quite independently of his desires, choices, and purposes. That is precisely what it denies. External events are of no greater efficacy in altering character than are a person's idle hopes or wishes. What it does assert with respect to the powerlessness of persons is that a moral agent has no control over himself, over the kind of person he is or might wish to become. If virtuous, then regardless of his desires, he is incapable of acting viciously, and vice versa. (2c) affirms the helplessness of the individual in the iron grip of his own moral character.

Despite Alexander's assessment of the Stoic argument, which seems to rest on construing premise (2) along the general lines of our third interpretation,[19] there is reason to believe that (2c) is the only one of the three possibilities that would have been rejected by the Stoics. And of course if they thought it false, they could not have used it in a *reductio* proof against the Aristotelian notion of *ta eph'hēmin*. Textual evidence independent of this passage indicates that the Stoics thought that virtue and vice are acquired dispositions.[20] They are not innate nor are they determined exclusively by an inherited nature. An innate potential, however, develops into moral character, which is shaped by training or, in the case of vice, by corrupting influences or simple neglect. The Stoics pointed to the fact that some bad men become good as evidence that virtue can be taught and moral progress made. And we are told that Chrysippus also maintained (against some other Stoics) that a virtuous disposition can be temporarily lost through melancholy or drunkenness.

Moreover, the view that virtue and vice are permanently fixed traits of character does not harmonize well with Stoic determinism. That doctrine implies that a person's choices and actions *are* influenced by external causes as well as those internal to the agent himself. So determinism clearly does not rule out the possibility of moral improvement in a vicious person who wants to change and makes the appropriate efforts to do so. But what does seem incompatible with the Stoic position is that a person should suddenly and *for no reason* desire, let us say, to improve his character and thereupon commence to act virtuously. Given that his character is formed, a vicious person may not want to change. If so, there is little hope for him from the standpoint of the deterministic moralist. But even that is not to say that certain unforseen circumstances, certain life experiences, might not *give him reason* to want to change his life and that he might not therefore respond accordingly. That view of human nature is consistent with determinism, and it allows for (indeed accounts for) changes in moral character. Inasmuch as (2c) is contradicted by textual evidence and clashes with determinism in the area of character and action it should be ruled out as a plausible interpretation of premise (2) and of the Stoic position in regard to moral character.

What are the implications of the above analysis for the argument and, more generally, for Stoic moral philosophy? Our first conclusion must be that premise (2), as the Stoics understood it, does not rule out the possibility of moral responsibility. (2c) is the only interpretation of the three examined that constitutes a genuine denial of capacity on the part of a moral agent to act in accordance with choice. (2a) denies that a person can do what is logically impossible, and (2b) denies that he can do (is willing to do) what is incompatible with his moral principles or with his aims and purposes in acting. Neither of these negative propositions would count as a good reason for denying that a person can legitimately be held accountable for his actions. The argument concludes that *ta eph'hēmin* cannot mean "those things the opposites of which we are capable," because the virtuous are not capable, logically or morally, of being vicious, nor the vicious virtuous, but virtue and vice are *eph'hēmin*. The upshot is that the argument detaches the concept of *ta eph'hēmin* in definition from the notion of capacity for opposite behavior *without* at the same time implying that a moral agent is powerless to do the opposites of things that are *eph'hēmin* if he chooses.

What then do the Stoics mean by *ta eph'hēmin*? The translation "things attributable to us" comes very close to the idea intended. It is clear that by "to us" the Stoics mean "to us as human beings," so that an inquiry into this concept will deal with only a small part of Nature, namely, the domain of human nature and events, and will leave to one side the very large areas of inanimate nature as well as plant and other animal life.[21] But I want to suggest that the meaning of the concept is even more specific for the Stoics. To investigate the area of things that are "attributable to us" in Stoic philosophy is to confine our interest in human nature to human beings *considered as moral agents*. It is to focus attention on that dimension of human events that is the realm of moral discourse. Built into the Stoic notion of things "attributable to us" is an idea very like our concept of an *action*, which is a "doing" as contrasted with a mere happening or event. And an action, unlike a happening, presupposes an agent to whom as "doer" it can be ascribed. Happenings are not by their very nature "attributable to us" as human beings, whereas actions are of necessity *someone's actions*. I want to propose, then, that the Stoic concept of "things attributable to us" marks off something like a sphere of human actions, of things we *do* as contrasted with events that merely *happen* and perhaps happen *to* us. If that is so, the concept of "things attributable to us" functioning, as it does, entirely within a deterministic scheme of Nature will be highly relevant to the attack from Stoic opponents. For questions of moral responsibility, praise, and blame arise and can be intelligibly debated only within the context of human action. The Stoics would then be in a position to argue from the very nature of "things attributable to us" as they understood it that, other things being equal, we as moral agents are indeed responsible for our actions, for the things we do, whereas of course we cannot be held accountable for what befalls us. Since the Stoics held that virtue and vice are among the things attributable to us, they could argue that to escape responsibility in a given case a person would have to show that a vicious action had been *erroneously* attributed to him. That is, he would have to show that the alleged action was not *his doing*, perhaps because someone else did it or, he might argue, because what he actually did does not fall under the description of the action attributed to him or even, let us say, because what occurred was not really a doing at all but a kind of mishap—something that happened to him. Because these are just the kinds of considerations that do play an important part in determining responsibility and in allocating praise and blame in the conduct of everyday affairs, the distinction between things that are and are not attributable to us, on the interpretation I am suggesting, reflects the very insights embodied in the standard practice of holding persons accountable for their actions. Let us see whether or not the Stoic doctrines bear our this intepretation of the meaning of *ta eph'hēmin*.

A case can be made for the idea of a special class of events in Nature which are properly attributable to human beings from a passage in Cicero's *De Fato*.[22] There we are told that Chrysippus distinguished between two types of cause, in order to avoid the imputation of necessity to fated events. All events in Nature (including human actions) are fated, he maintained, but not necessitated by antecedent causes. Chrysippus called these antecedent conditions "auxiliary and proximate causes." In the case of human behavior, persons cannot act without sensory stimulation, for example, but sensory stimuli are auxiliary and proximate causes. He argued that although the auxiliary causes are not "in our power" (*in nostra potestate*),[23] not attributable to us, it does not follow that the impulse to action that results is not attributable to us. That conclusion would follow only if the antecedent determining conditions were "perfect and principal causes."

The import of Chrysippus's reasoning is unfortunately rather obscure. Particularly difficult, and most interesting to us, is the question of how his distinction between types of cause is supposed to undercut what he considered to be the undesirable consequence of the necessity of fate. We are not told, for instance, what "necessity" means in this passage or whether its meaning is equivalent to the sense of that term in which events following from internal causes (the specific natures of things) were, in other contexts, said to be necessitated (though not compelled).[24] Moreover, the passage seems to link the notion of antecedent causes to that of external causes, and hence both of those to "auxiliary and proximate causes." There is little doubt that Chrysippus had external causes in mind in most cases when he mentioned antecedent causes. So it is a tempting conjecture that he also thought of "perfect and principal causes" as corresponding (in fact if not necessarily) to internal causes, the natures of the entities in question.[25] Yet it would be premature to draw that conclusion if, as I shall indicate, there is reason to suppose that the two distinctions are not intended to be equivalent.

In spite of the above-mentioned difficulties of interpretation, we can be fairly sure that Chrysippus did believe that the doctrine of the necessity of fated events had disastrous implications for human action. At the very least, he seems to have thought (1) that if all events were determined by antecedent causes that were perfect and principal, human behavior would be necessitated by antecedent causes; and (2) that if human behavior were necessitated by antecedent causes, there would be no such thing as autonomous human action. Proceeding on that assumption, let us try to bring to light a rationale for Chrysippus's distinction between types of cause.

Some commentators have inferred from the passage that Chrysippus meant to convey that auxiliary causes are necessary but not sufficient conditions for an event to occur, while principal causes are sufficient (or necessary and sufficient) conditions.[26] I think that is a reasonable inference for reasons that will become clear from what follows. But I also believe that the distinction between types of cause provides a clue to the meaning Stoic philosophers attached to the concept of things "attributable to us." We can see this best from the context in which Cicero introduces the distinction in his account of those "ancients" who held that if human behavior is fated, it must be subject to the constraints of necessity as well.[27] The distinction between types of cause is designed to break the back of an argument, one that incorporates an important, if simplistic, assumption about things attributable to us: if the cause (C) of an event (E) is not attributable to us (in Cicero's text literally "in us" (*in nobis*), "in our power" (*in nostra potestate*)), then E, the effect of C, is not attributable to us. Chrysippus repudiates this assumption with his distinction between "auxiliary and proximate causes" and "perfect and principal causes." Because the distinction is intended to block the inference from "C is not attributable to us" to "E is not attributable to us," there is reason to suspect that the Stoic concept of things attributable to us may be different in meaning from *ta eph'hēmin* as it was employed by those philosophers whose views Cicero is reporting. We have already seen evidence that the Stoics detached the meaning of this expression from that of capacity or power. If instead it is more closely linked to the concept of human action and of things that are "ours," Chrysippus's distinction between types of cause may be more than just hairsplitting.

Let us suppose that auxiliary causes of human behavior *are* to be understood as necessary but not sufficient conditions of that behavior. In view of the equation of auxiliary causes and antecedent causes, the latter (whether external or internal) must also be understood as no more than necessary conditions of behavior. Now if that is indeed Chrysippus's meaning, the antecedent causes of human behavior will not detract from the status of that behavior as action, the type of natural event that is properly attributable to us as agents. The reason why this is so is that antecedent causes which are external causes of human behavior are not the sorts of things that *could be* attributable to us: they are not a part of human nature nor do they belong to the sphere of things we do.[28] But from the evident fact that external antecedent causes of human behavior are not in the category of things attributable to us, given that antecedent causes are merely necessary conditions of behavior, we can draw no conclusion about the effects of these causes and, in particular, about whether or not certain kinds of behavior can be attributed to us. On the other hand, if antecedent causes were not only necessary but also sufficient conditions of human behavior, such behavior could not in principle be attributed to us as agents. Because actions are partially constituted by mental acts internal to the agent, such as intentions, decisions, choices, and the like (terms that would fall under the Stoic concept of "assent"), human behavior conceived as determined by external antecedent causes both necessary and sufficient could not be considered "ours" at all. So on the correlative assumption that principal causes are to be understood as sufficient (or more likely necessary and sufficient) conditions of human behavior, Chrysippus would be justified in concluding that if the antecedent conditions determining such things as the impulse to behavior in human beings were "perfect and principal causes," there would be no such thing as human autonomy. Given the interpretation of "things attributable to us" that I am suggesting, Chrysippus's distinction between types of cause *can* undermine the damaging application to human actions of the doctrine of the necessity of fated events.

In the same passage Cicero goes on to mention the role of "assent" in Stoic theory. Events that are attributable to human beings are not an automatic consequence of sensory presentations. To issue in an impulse to action, as he explains, sensory presentations require the assent of the person experiencing them. And Chrysippus held that although assent cannot occur unless it is stimulated by a presentation, the sensory stimulus[29] is an auxiliary not a principal cause. Cicero continues:[30]

In the same way therefore, he says, as a person who has pushed a cylinder forward has given it a beginning of motion, but has not given it the capacity to roll, so a sense presentation when it impinges will it is true impress and as it were seal its appearance on the mind, but the act of assent will be in our power (*in nostra potestate*), and as we said in the case of the cylinder, though given a push from without, as to the rest will move by its own force and nature. [H. Rackham]

Human behavior, like the motion of a cylinder, requires a stimulus without which it cannot take place, and Chrysippus located this antecedent cause in sensory presentations. But the behavior of human beings like the motion of cylinders cannot be understood without looking beyond (external) antecedent causes to the respective "natures" of these things. Human nature, unlike that of a cylinder or anything else in Nature, is characterized by the faculty of intelligent assent,[31] so that the impulse to behavior that issues from assent in a human being will not be quite like that of any other part of Nature. It will be an impulse to behavior that is distinctively human, the sort of event that I have called an action. Because Chrysippus believed that the act of assent is atributable to us, we may say that the faculty of assent gives human beings the capacity *to act*, as opposed to the capacity merely *to move*, or perhaps *to be moved*, as is the case with the cylinder. Intelligent assent therefore is a necessary feature of an action and distinguishes it from an event or happening. What a person does will depend on which presentations he assents to, and the assent given to sensory presentations will be a function of his own individual "nature," his own personality and character. A human agent by virtue of giving *his* assent makes the event that follows *his* action.

If this analysis is correct, talk of cause and effect by itself will not be particularly illuminating in contexts of moral discourse, where it is often important to establish responsibility for actions. For that we need to do more than to look for causal explanations of behavior considered merely on the model of natural events. In matters of responsibility we are dealing with human behavior, with persons and their actions. To insist, as the Stoics did, that virtue and vice are attributable to us as persons is to say, in effect, that certain events in Nature are properly regarded as *our* actions, and to that extent they are events that fall into the domain of moral discourse—events for which we as agents *may* be held responsible. To determine responsibility we must look for an agent or doer, and that is not the same as looking for the customary causal explanation. There may be many causes of an occurrence, but if that occurrence is an action none of those causal explanations can cancel the fact that it is the action of some person or persons. A passage from the text of Clement of Alexandria makes a very similar point.[32] Many factors, he says, may combine to bring about a certain result; and although the end occurs *because of (dia)* all of them, not all are *responsible for (aitia)* what results. To be *aitia* the event because of which something occurs must also be *poiētikon*, that is, productive of it. The notion of a cause which is *poiētikon* comes very close to what I have called, in the case of persons, an agent. Clement's illustration with the case of Medea elegantly captures this distinction: Medea would not have killed her children if she had not been angry; she would not have been angry had she not been jealous; she would not have been jealous had she not been in love; she would not have been in love if Jason had not sailed to Colchis, and so forth (Clement continues the series of antecedent conditions even further). The end result of this chain, namely the slaughter of the children, can be said to have occurred *because of* all these events, but only Medea is *aitia*. In this example the multiple reasons for the slaughter of Medea's children do not constitute competing explanations because they are not commensurate. By this I mean they are different

sorts of explanation, answering different questions. We may ask:
(1) Why did it (the event) *happen*? or alternatively (2) Who *did* it?
(whose action was it?). Only if there is an answer to the second
question are we likely to be dealing with an event that falls into the
category of things attributable to us. Of course the existence of an
answer to the second question does not imply that the person
whose name is mentioned may *in fact* be held accountable but
merely that questions of responsibility may be legitimately raised.
The category of things attributable to us does not *establish* responsibility but rather distinguishes a domain of events within which
moral responsibility is *possible*.

The Stoic view of human nature and action is further elaborated
by Origen in a text from which I quoted earlier.[33] Origen's account
focuses on the capacity for movement of things in Nature. Although it differs significantly from Alexander's testimony in regard
to internal causes of motion (SVF 2. 979), these differences do not
detract from its importance as additional justification for drawing
a distinction between human action and events in our attempt to
understand and set forth the Stoic view. As Origen reports their
position, the Stoics carefully differentiated human beings from all
other natural things by a particular kind of movement unique to
them. He begins by distinguishing those things that have a certain
kind of cause (*aitia*) of motion in themselves from others that are
moved only from without. Things which have "nature" and "soul"
such as plants and animals have an internal cause of motion,
whereas inanimate objects such as stone and wood must be borne
along by the agency of something external. This contradicts Alexander's understanding of the Stoic use of "nature" as well as his
testimony that all events both animate and inanimate are the product jointly of internal and external causes. But even though his testimony may be suspect in that respect, Origen seems to be getting
at a distinction (not incompatible with Alexander's text, if absent
from it) between that which is as he terms it "self-moving" (*auto-
kineton*) and that which must be moved by something external to
it. Plants and animals in virtue of having soul (and nature?) are
capable of self-movement. (Origen adds that the Stoics also included in this group certain inanimate things, such as metals, fire,
and perhaps streams, which were held to move "out of themselves," but those things were nevertheless contrasted with living

things which move "from themselves,") In the case of animals sensory stimulation is a necessary condition of the impulse to self-movement, and those lacking intelligence move according to a prescribed pattern (*tetagmenōs*). Human beings, however, do not move in a set fashion, because the faculty of reason (*logos*) enables them to judge (*krinai*) their sensory presentations, to reject some and accept others, and to be guided accordingly. Origen calls this third kind of self-movement, of which only rational animals are capable, motion "through themselves."[34]

It is reasonable to say that on Origen's account the faculty of reason, which distinguishes the assent of human beings from that of other animals, gives rise to morality. For he goes on to say that our nature as human beings furnishes the tools for considering the noble and base and for judging between them. Even though we have no control over the fact that something external causes in us a presentation of this or that sort, "the decision (*to krinai*) to use this occurrence in one way or another is the function of nothing other than the reason within us."[35] So when we choose the noble and avoid the base we are deserving of praise, but when we follow the opposite course we are blameworthy.[36] As a consequence, Origen reasons (SVF 2. 990):

... it is neither true nor reasonable to lay the blame on external things and release ourselves from the accusation, making ourselves analogous to wood and stones inasmuch as they are drawn along by external things that move them; such is the argument of someone who wants to set up a counterfeit notion of autonomy (*autexousion*). For if we should ask him what autonomy is, he would say that it obtains "if there are no external causes, when I intend to do something in particular, that incite to the contrary."

Origen's testimony, in spite of its departure from Alexander's account, lends support to the distinction between human action and other natural events, which I have suggested is implicit in the moral philosophy of the Stoics. If the substance of his testimony is accurate, the Stoic believed that human beings and other living things are capable of self-movement without actually initiating their own motion. The beginning of motion is in the world of external objects, and self-movement consists in the response of a *sentient* creature to those external causes. Moreover, it is clear that the faculty of reason, which informs assent to sensory presentations, makes the self-movement of human beings different in kind from that of any other living thing. That difference, which is crucial to the Stoic position, can be captured by contrasting the notion of action with mere movement. If we apply the distinction between motions (events) and actions to Origen's text, we may understand him to say that it is the faculty of intelligent (*logikos*) assent that gives persons the capacity to act (autonomously) rather than merely move, or be moved, as wood and stones are moved.[37] That is, *logos* qualifies the self-movement of human beings as action. An important consequence of the Stoic position on Origen's (and Alexander's) account is that human action is not to be understood as a beginning of motion;[38] indeed the idea of an action seems to be logically independent of the notion of cause and effect. This is a significant departure from the view of those whose "counterfeit" definition of autonomy mistakenly makes reference to the concept of external causes.[39] For the Stoics it is *logos* that defines the notion of autonomous action, and which (unlike the idea of cause) has logical ties to the concept of responsibility. So there will be many forms of movement behavior in living things which on the Stoic view will not qualify as action and for which the question of moral responsibility will not therefore arise. It is an appropriate matter of concern only within the domain of behavior of living things capable of giving rational assent. And it is worth noting that not even all human behavior must count as action on the Stoic account. A person can *be moved* against his will if he is pushed, for example, and he can *move* involuntarily if he falls, but he cannot *act*, cannot (say) run, without giving his intelligent assent. To misplace the responsibility for human *actions* on external events is to "make ourselves analogous to wood and stones." It is to misconceive human nature on the model of inanimate objects, which are capable of nothing more than *being moved*.[40]

A famous simile attributed to Chrysippus and Zeno vividly illustrates the Stoic view of the relation between human action and fate.[41]

Just as a dog tied to a wagon, if it is willing to follow, follows as it is also being pulled, making its own autonomy coincide with necessity; whereas if it is unwilling to follow, it will in any event be compelled. So it is too with human beings.

This example incorporates the Stoic view of human action and mental events attributable to us into the deterministic framework of their philosophy. The special realm of human action is located by the Stoics *within* an all-encompassing Nature governed by causal laws. There is therefore an important sense in which our actions, the things we can do, are limited by Nature. We cannot change the laws of Nature, including those of our own human nature. There are no actions we can undertake that will alter the course of the seasons, for example, or the dimensions of space; none that will transform us into a species of plant or kind of rock. To believe otherwise and to attempt to act on such beliefs would betray not merely profound ignorance of Nature and of our place in it but irrationality to the extreme of madness. No sane person would attempt to accomplish the impossible. The madman, though he is "unwilling to follow," will be "compelled" by Nature in any case. But other limitations on what we can do are not so easy to discern. There are many actions that we *can* undertake which are nevertheless regulated by our own individual natures, and it is in this region that the above quotation is especially relevant. For human beings can set out to do many things that are impossible in fact for them to achieve, given their individual temperaments, talents, and capabilities. This sort of limitation, though rarely plain to the understanding, is no less binding for the Stoics.[42] So by our self-ignorance we may *show* ourselves "unwilling to follow" and end by being "compelled" by the boundaries of our own natural capacities. Notice, however, that the simile does not imply that our actions, whether undertaken out of wisdom or ignorance of Nature, and the consequent success or failure of these undertakings, are not attributable to us. The effort to bring ourselves into harmony with Nature as well as the effort to resist will result from mental acts that are attributable to us, and so they will qualify as actions for which we as agents may be held responsible. Far from doing violence to such mental acts as choosing, deciding, deliberating and the like,[43] the Stoic simile actually reinforces the importance of these acts in determining responsibility. Nevertheless, any attempt to exceed the limitations that Nature has imposed on us, though preeminently our own and for which we are in principle responsible, will be defeated by the necessities of Nature compelling us in spite of ourselves to yield to its power. The same subtle relation between fate and human responsibility is implicit in the following lines of Cleanthes:[44]

Guide me, Zeus, and you, Fate, wherever I have been appointed by you. For I
shall follow willingly; and if, become evil, I am unwilling I shall follow no less.

The supreme importance that the Stoics placed on *logos* and the
understanding of Nature can be most fully appreciated in this context. Understanding frees one from the compulsion of Nature. The
person who comprehends the laws of external Nature as well as
those of his own inner self will be able to approximate more closely
the ideal human condition that the Stoics called freedom (*eleu-
theria*) and contrasted with slavery. Because Nature is an intelligible system identified (as we have seen) with *logos* in Stoic
thought, the ideal is not in principle unattainable.[45] But it is essential to recognize that although the concept of freedom is of singular importance in Stoic moral philosophy, it cannot be equated
with their theory of action and responsibility. Both the ethical
ideal of freedom as well as its opposed state of enslavement *presuppose* the concept of autonomous action.[46] The man who is
ignorant and thus a slave to Nature and his passions is no less an
agent, a doer of actions, than the enlightened sage who is free.
That part of our behavior that is attributable to us as persons,
whether undertaken in a state of freedom or slavery, is just that
part for which we are morally responsible.

CONCLUSION

What are the implications for human responsibility of a view that
divorces action from the idea of a beginning of motion and connects it instead with the notion of intelligent assent and that which
is attributable to us? We have already noted that the Stoics felt justified in denying that the ground for ascriptions of responsibility
lay in the absence of external causes of human behavior. On their
view persons are responsible for actions that are their own doing,
actions attributable to them, independently of the matter of causal
explanation.[47] They consistently maintained that there are external causes that influence our actions, but they also insisted (and
they were surely right in doing so) that that fact by itself is not sufficient to invalidate moral responsibility. For it would take a good
deal more in the way of hard argument to show that the mere

presence of causal factors operative in human behavior under-
mines the Stoic claim that some (though not all) behavior is attributable to us. Intelligent assent defines that area of behavior as one
in which persons are appropriately thought of as agents responsible for what they do, in contrast to the realm of events in which
persons, along with such objects as wood and stones, are merely
acted upon by external causes to which they react without assenting, and are therefore not regarded as agents or doers of actions
but victims of circumstance or sufferers of occurrences that
happen to them. The Stoic view repudiates what is indeed on the
face of it an extravagant claim, namely, that there can be no external causes of autonomous human action; and that claim seems
consequent upon the no less dubious assumption that a person is
responsible for an action only if he is responsible for all the causes
of that action. The impetus for such an extreme position on the
part of critics may have been provided by the Stoic account of the
formation of character.

The Stoics, who maintained without qualification that a person
acts in accordance with his character, were apparently equally
bold in their views on the matter of character formation. According to ancient testimony, they held that the kind of person someone is, or will become, is a product of both his own individual
nature, which is inherited, and the environment external to him,
including the persons he encounters and with whom he associates
especially in early years.[48] It is obvious that neither of these sets of
conditions is of a sort to be within the range of choices that any individual can make. The Stoics could only affirm therefore that
human behavior is causally linked to many factors over which we
as persons have little or no control. Indeed they are reported to
have located the causes of human wrongdoing in particular in
painful childhood experiences and a corrupting environment.[49]
Many critics, following a line of reasoning that appears to have its
historical origins in the third book of the *Nicomachean Ethics*,
have argued that if we as individuals are not responsible for our
characters, we cannot justifiably be held responsible for actions
determined by our characters.

The assumption mentioned above is clearly at work in this reasoning, and I have tried to show how the Stoic account of human
action and responsibility, which differs markedly from the Aristo-

telian view, attempts to undermine it. But it is also worth pointing out that the above inference gains further plausibility from treating a person's "character," somewhat bizarrely, as if it were a causal determinant in behavior distinct from the person himself and operating independently of his purposes, wants, and desires. For, governed by such a picture, one might be led to inquire how, if someone's *character* causes him to behave in such and such manner, *he* can be held responsible, especially when it is remembered that he could not have had a *different* character, given the external conditions of his environment. Such reasoning conjures up the image of an individual as a prisoner of his character, itself fashioned independently of himself and his wishes by external forces to which he has fallen victim. Thus far we have seen nothing in the Stoic doctrine that would warrant such an extreme picture. What, then, can be made of the view apparently held by Stoics that a person is responsible for his actions but not his character?

Character on their account is shaped by inherited nature and environment and not by choice, with the implication presumably that human beings cannot be held accountable for that to which they have not given their assent. The position that we are responsible for what we do but not for what we are can be made intelligible on the supposition that character is something over and above the things an individual actually does—the actions he actually performs—perhaps a set of dispositions to behave in such and such ways conceived independently of the actions he does in fact perform on any given occasion. Such a position is compatible with Stoic materialism, according to which mental dispositions are identical with physical states of the human soul. Given that view of character, it might plausibly be argued that even though a dishonest person (for example) is surely blameworthy, it is for his dishonest dealings that we blame him and not because he has become a person of the sort to be inclined to act in those ways. For that he may very well be disliked, disapproved of, shunned, and perhaps even pitied, but not held accountable or blamed.

The common practice of holding persons accountable only for their actions is not, on the face of it, unreasonable even on the Stoic view of character formation. It clearly does not follow from the proposition that a person is not responsible for his character in the above (Stoic) sense that he cannot legitimately be held responsible for his actions. For that to follow it would have to be established that he cannot help acting as he does, because his "character compels" him to act in certain ways. But now we have come full circle. To be damaging to the Stoic position that proposition would have to be construed to mean something more than the (morally) innocuous Stoic doctrine that a person cannot act out of character. It is at just this point that much of the criticism of Stoicism seems to break down. For it is not enough merely to point to the causal determinants (whether "external" or "internal") of human behavior and hastily to conclude that given these conditions human behavior "cannot be otherwise." The Stoics can readily grant that point[50] without compromising their theory of action and responsibility, that is, of "things attributable to us." To be successful as a rebuttal of Stoicism the critic's argument would have to show that the "cannot" in question is a relevant one in contexts of moral discourse. If it could be demonstrated, for example, that (on the Stoic account) persons cannot act otherwise than they do in the sense of "cannot" which implies that they are compelled independently of their wills by forces external or internal to them, that would be sufficient to establish that, in just those cases, human beings cannot legitimately be held responsible for what they do because they are in fact *not* responsible. Or, alternatively, a critic might attempt to show that the causal determinants of human behavior operate in such a way as to render the Stoic notion of intelligent assent either meaningless or pointless in matters pertaining to moral responsibility, praise, and blame. Such an argument would amount to the claim that in the Stoic deterministic schema there is no place for the concept of a human action as distinguished from a mere happening or event. The import of that sort of criticism would be that persons cannot justifiably be held responsible for their behavior, not because they are *not* in fact responsible, but because the concept of responsibility has no application.[51]

NOTES

1. Alexander, SVF 2. 945.
2. *Ibid.;* Nemesius, SVF 2. 991.

3. Cicero, *De Div.*, I. 127-128.

4. The term *oikonomia* points to the teleological dimension in Stoic thought. However, it is not divine purpose to which I refer in calling attention to the "rational" character of the Stoic cosmos. Reason may be said to permeate Nature in the sense that the cosmos is not a "mindless" chaos of events but an intelligible nexus of causes.

5. Aetius, SVF 2.976. For other definitions of fate that stress order and *logos* see SVF 2.915, 916, 917, 1000.

6. Plutarch, SVF 2.937. See also SVF 2.912, 943, 945, 973.

7. Alexander, SVF 2.970; Aetius, SVF 2.966; Simplicius, SVF 2.965; Plutarch, SVF 2.973.

8. Alexander, SVF 2.945. Sambursky traces the supposition of determinism back to the Hippocratic writings of the fifth century B.C., where the notion of "spontaneous" recovery from illness was repudiated (*Physics of the Stoics*, London, 1959) 151 ff.

9. Alexander, SVF 2.979. Cf. also Cicero, SVF 2.974. A distinction between fate and necessity is not consistently observed in the ancient testimony on Stoicism. Cf. J. M. Rist, *Stoic Philosophy* (Cambridge, 1969) chap. 7. For a discussion of the distinction and its implications see A. A. Long, "Stoic Determinism and Alexander of Aphrodisias De Fato (i-xiv)," *Archiv für Geschichte der Philosophie* 52 (1970) 247-265. My own conjecture is that the notion of "necessity" (contrasted with "fate") was meant to apply to an event when conditions both necessary *and* sufficient for its occurrence were present. The texts of both Alexander and Cicero can be construed in this way.

10. SVF 2.979.

11. *Ibid.* 988.

12. Aulus Gellius, SVF 2.1000. Cf. Plutarch, SVF 2.937, 993; Nemesius, SVF 2.991.

13. Following A. A. Long's translation in "Freedom and Determinism in the Stoic Theory of Human Action" (*Problems in Stoicism*, ed. A. A. Long (London, 1971)).

14. SVF 2.984.

15. Long ("Freedom and Determinism," 185) notes that *mēketi dektikoi* need not have the force of "no longer capable" but can mean "not now capable." He claims that in the present context "it states a fact, not a prediction."

16. For reasons that will become clear later in the text I shall interpret the Stoic claim to mean: "Virtuous and vicious actions are attributable to us."

17. Alexander, SVF 2.786; SVF 2.'806; D.L., SVF 3.39; Sextus, *Adv. Math.* 11.23. For discussion of this point see A. A. Long, "The Stoic Concept of Evil," *Philosophical Quarterly*, 18 (1968) 341-342.

18. D.L., SVF 3.237; Simplicius, SVF 3.238; Plutarch, SVF 3.459; Stobaeus, SVF 3.560. Every morally relevant physical state/disposition that was not identical with virtue was termed "vicious" by the Stoics. Hence "vice" refers to multiple physical states of the soul, including those cases, not covered by (2b), in which the vicious person *wants* to improve his moral character. Cases of that sort would fall under (2c).

19. *De Fato* 27-28. Long ("Freedom and Determinism," 197 n. 35) conjectures that Alexander may be misapplying Aristotelian theory in this passage.

20. D.L., SVF 3.223, 237; Clement, SVF 3.224, 225; Simplicius, SVF 3.238; D.L. 7.89.

21. The concept of that which is *attributable to something* applies more generally in Stoic philosophy to all living things whose behavior is characterized by impulse and assent. But that which is *attributable to us* (as human beings) is more narrowly restricted by the addition of intelligence (*logos*) to impulse and assent. Cf. Stobaeus, SVF 3.169; Plutarch, SVF 3.175; D.L., SVF 3.178.

22. Cicero, SVF 2.974. Cf. also Plutarch, SVF 2.994, 997.

23. Cicero's translation misleadingly transmits the Aristotelian connotation of *eph'hēmin*.

24. Alexander, SVF 2.979 (quoted on pp. 205-206).

25. See, for example, M. E. Reesor, "Fate and Possibility in Early Stoic Philosophy," *Phoenix* 19 (1965) 285-297; Long, "Freedom and Determinism."

26. For various versions of this suggestion see Josiah Gould, "The Stoic Conception of Fate," *Journal of the History of Ideas* 35 (1974); Long, "Freedom and Determinism." Applying the distinction to human behavior, Long writes (p. 196 n. 32) that "the agent's assent is a necessary and sufficient condition [of action] since assent entails there being something, though not necessarily one particular thing, to which its response is given." This seems to me correct, so that in the case of action the principal cause does coincide with the internal cause of behavior. But the equation of principal and internal causes cannot be generalized to inanimate objects like the "cylinder" whose internal "nature" is not a sufficient condition of its motion.

27. Cicero, *De Fato* 40 (omitted from SVF 2.974).

28. Auxiliary causes of human behavior which are internal to the agent will also fall outside the domain of things attributable to us. Though a part of human nature, they do not belong to the class of things we do. See note 29.

29. Here is a case in which very likely an antecedent auxiliary cause is internal to the agent. If it is correct on the Stoic account to distinguish between the *external* sensory stimulus and the *internal* presentation of sense, then the latter is an internal auxiliary cause. The argument is not affected by this example, however, since sensory presentations would not be "attributable to us" in the sense of that expression which I have been urging. They are merely events or happenings internal to the agent. It is equally true of sensory presentations that if they, like other antecedent causes, were not only necessary but also sufficient to explain human behavior, such behavior could not be considered action.

30. SVF 2.974. Cf. Aulus Gellius, SVF 2.1000.

31. The faculty of reason (*logos*) distinguishes the assent and behavior of human beings from that of other animals (Origen, SVF 2.988; Clement, SVF 2.992; SVF 3.377; Plutarch, SVF 3.175). For a discussion of the relation between impulse and assent in human behavior see Long, "The Stoic Concept of Evil."

32. SVF 2.347.

33. See note 11.

34. In another context at SVF 2.989. This terminology does conform to Alex-

ander's usage in his account of the Stoic view (SVF 2. 979).

35. Cf. Clement, SVF 2. 992, where assent is called a *krisis*.

36. Alexander again (SVF 2. 979) seems to contradict Origen's account when he says that the Stoics denied humans autonomy (*to exousian*) of choice and action between contrary alternatives. But that is very likely a hasty inference from the Stoic denial that the concept of what is attributable to us can be defined as the capacity for opposite behavior. The context in which he makes the remark indicates as much.

37. Hence the following criticism is undercut: If (as the Stoics say) human beings are capable of autonomous action inasmuch as what happens *through* human nature (impulse and assent) cannot happen without it, then fire (and other inanimate things) should be credited with autonomy too, since heating occurs *through* the nature of fire and cannot occur without it. (Nemesius, SVF 2. 991; Alexander, *De Fato* 14. 183).

38. Compare Aristotle, *E.N.* 1113b20, 1114a19, whose views are in sharp contrast to the Stoic position on this score.

39. For views equating autonomy with the absence of causes cf. Plutarch, SVF 2. 973; Alexander, *De Fato* 4. 169.

40. A similar argument against those who would deny that anything is *attributable to us* is also recorded by Origen (SVF 2. 989): Anyone who claims that nothing is attributable to us is foolishly committed to the view that we are neither animals nor rational. Alexander (SVF 2. 979) reports that movements that take place "through us" are "attributable to us" on the Stoic view.

41. Hippolytus, SVF 2. 975.

42. At least not so for Chrysippus. Cf. D.L. 7. 89.

43. Cf. Gould, "Stoic Conception of Fate," 31.

44. Epictetus, SVF 1. 527.

45. Consider the following paradox: A person makes the effort to act virtuously but because of his own limitations does not succeed. The limitations of his "nature" would be defined in this case by a vicious moral disposition (physical state of the soul). Such a person might seem to be in a condition of ignorance of his "nature." Is he therefore in a state of slavery on the Stoic view? If, on the other hand, he does not make an effort to improve morally, he will remain enslaved to the passions that govern his life. And his state in that case would surely be thought of as a condition of ignorance of (human) "nature." This sort of paradox seems to be generated by an ambiguity in the term *physis*, which can have descriptive or normative force. The ambiguity permeates Stoic doctrine at all levels. For a good example see D.L. 7. 87-89.

The Stoics, however, might attempt a reply along the following lines: Since the *fact* of moral improvement in human beings implies the capacity to change, a person's "nature₁" (descriptive) must include this capacity. Hence, "nature₁," when it comprises a vicious moral disposition, does not entail that a person *cannot* succeed in improving (full stop) but merely that he *does not* succeed (that he cannot as long as he retains his vicious disposition). The Stoics might conclude therefore that such a person is insufficiently conscientious, that his efforts are not of the right sort, etc. "Nature₂" (normative) comprises the virtuous moral disposition and is coextensive with the ideal of "freedom" for the Stoics. Hence failure in one's efforts to improve morally need not imply ignorance of "nature" or bondage. For a discussion of some of the difficulties connected with the Stoic use of *physis*, see I. G. Kidd, "Stoic Intermediates and the End for Man," in *Problems in Stoicism*.

46. The Stoic ideal of freedom is often confused with the quite different concept of "freedom of the will." The early Stoics did not conflate the notion of what is attributable to us with that of freedom, but this important distinction does become blurred later in the writings of Epictetus (*Ench.* 1; *Disc.* 4. 1).

47. This means that the term *aitios* is no longer adequate to express the complexities involved in problems of moral responsibility. On the Stoic account I may be *responsible for* an action that, even though I am not the *cause* of it (something having prompted me to do it), I (having given my assent) have a *reason* for doing.

48. Cicero, SVF 2. 951; Aulus Gellius, SVF 2. 1000; Plutarch, SVF 2. 937; Clement, SVF 3. 225.

49. D.L., SVF 3. 228; Chalcidius, SVF 3. 229.

50. It is compatible with their theory of "co-fated" events. Cf. Cicero, SVF 2. 956.

51. I am indebted to Maria T. Celo Cruz for beneficial criticism of a draft of this paper.

10

Emotion and Decision in Stoic Psychology

A. C. Lloyd

The Stoics' treatment of emotions is interesting for a number of reasons. It presents a puzzle, which is as much philosophical as it is historical and philological, about the original definition of emotions. It raises problems that are fundamental in Stoic psychology, in particular the ambiguity of "reason" or *logos* and the anti-Platonic and anti-Aristotelian principle of the unity of the soul. But, as is well known, emotions had also an ethical significance: they were what caused wrong choices or decisions. So it was natural to consider them in connection with action. The Stoics' psychology of action raises equally important problems and has affinities with certain thoroughly twentieth-century notions, in particular the rejection of a conventional sequence of desire, deliberation, choice, action. It has tended to be neglected, or rather to be kept out of focus, through attention to moral philosophy. Here I wish to look at it in conjunction with the treatment of emotions, believing that each helps to solve the other's problems. In each case these arise, more directly than has perhaps been recognized, from Aristotle. I shall mostly be concerned with early and "orthodox" Stoicism and try not to be indiscriminate about testimony that applies to different periods. It is not known when the three genera of "right feelings," joy, wishing, and caution, came into

233

Stoicism, and they will be ignored here. Since they were presumably rational states they would not alter my arguments.[1]

Aristotle introduces emotions to his audience by examples, anger, pity, fear, and their opposites in the *Rhetoric* (1378a20), desire, anger, and fear in the *Nicomachean Ethics* (1105b19-28); and he characterizes them in general, and obviously inadequately, by saying that they are what are followed by pleasure or pain (1105b19-28). His only term for them, however, covers more than we should call "emotions." The Stoa offered definitions of emotions: the most popular were, or for our purposes were synonymous with, "an irrational movement of the soul" and "an impulse which is excessive" (or "has got out of hand"). Both are well attested for Zeno. According to Galen, Zeno also described emotions as the irrational contractions, elations, depressions, and the like that are the effects of certain intellectual judgments, while his successor Chrysippus said that they were the judgments themselves. More about this startling divergence later. In the second place the Stoa offered a classification of them under four genera, pleasure, pain, fear, and desire. (This does not mean that they cannot also be followed by pleasure and pain [Cf. SVF 2. 378].) Pity, for example, becomes a species of pain, anger a species of desire. And, presumably by degrees as time went on, more and more supposed distinctions were added, so that there were anything up to half a dozen species of joy or of anger (SVF 3. 394 ff.). Pain was defined by Zeno and Chrysippus as a fresh opinion that something bad is present (Galen *De placit. Hippocr. et Plat.* 391 Mü, [SVF 1. 212]), pleasure the corresponding opinion about the presence of something good, fear the corresponding expectation of something bad in the future (ibid. 336 [SVF 1. 463]). Desire had normally to be defined as an (irrational) urge for something good in the future. Chrysippus however was also willing to define pain as some kind of depression (or contraction) in the face of something which it seems proper to avoid and pleasure as elation at something which seems desirable, or right to choose (ibid. 337 [SVF 1. 463]). Irrational elation and depression of the soul appear to have become textbook definitions by Imperial times.

If we examine the accounts of specific emotions we find that according to Aristotle certain features are involved in both anger and fear. These are that,

(1) they include desire, which entails (1a) hope and (1b) pleasure;

(2) they include pain;

(3) they include physiological and sometimes overt bodily conditions;

(4) they occur for a reason, which is found in a presentation of the senses or a representation (mental image), and this entails a belief about a past or future evil;

(5) they are directed toward an object (or person).

The same features can be discovered in early Stoic description of these emotions. The definition of anger, desire to punish an undeserved injury, given as Stoic by Diogenes Laertius (7. 113) and Stobaeus (*Ecl.* 2. 91W) is evidently taken for granted in Chrysippus's illustrations, such as Medea's anger at her betrayal by Jason. (3) was used to argue about the location of the ruling principle (e.g. SVF 2. 886) as well as to explain the character called "heartlessness" (SVF 2. 899). (4) is implied by the generic definition of each emotion.

But so far from explaining the major difficulties of the Stoic account Aristotle's account only brings them to the front. According to his psychology, emotions must combine elements from the so-called rational and the so-called nonrational parts of the soul. According to Zeno, Chrysippus, and so far as we know all Stoics before Posidonius, the soul had no nonrational part; the self, let alone the soul, was identical with the capacity to think, reason, and use language; other activities or faculties were really special conditions or dispositions of this rational capacity, the ruling principle or *hēgemonikon*. That includes the emotions, as is attested for Zeno as well as for Chrysippus (SVF 1. 202). So we have a problem how the Stoics' inclusion of apparently nonrational elements in emotions is compatible with their conception of the singleness of soul. We have secondly a problem, which must not be confused with the first, how emotions can belong to a ruling principle that is supposed to be reason when their irrationality is included in their definition. Thirdly we have a problem that is to a greater degree historical: what exactly was the difference between Zeno and Chrysippus that was put to polemical use by Posidonius and Galen?

Emotions are or involve beliefs and they pervert action. As Aristotle presented them, the process of coming to believe something and the process of coming to do something are symmetrical. *De anima* 3.7 says that if some x is seen/heard etc. to be ϕ it is as though our senses asserted that it was ϕ: but when ϕ has the value pleasant/painful, having made the assertion, so to speak, they pursue/avoid x, pleasant and painful corresponding to good and bad. The same holds for nonpractical thinking that x is good/bad, except that it is images that take the place of sensa.

De motu animalium 7 presents a schema of this form: (1) desire to drink, (2) discrimination by perception, imagination or thought, of something as drinkable [i.e., good or possible to drink, 701a32-33], (3) desire (*orexis*) [which is the proximate cause (701a35) of], (4) the immediate act of drinking.

The Stoic psychology of action does not seem to have been very dissimilar from Aristotle's. For Aristotle desire is essential, and it appears at the first as well as the penultimate stage of the *De motu* 7 schema; in the Stoa the corresponding fact is the presence throughout of desire or impulse (*hormē*). Second there is for Aristotle an essential distinction between predicates like "pleasant" and "painful," "good" and "bad," "drinkable" or "to be drunk," which produce action, and others which just for abbreviation we might call purely descriptive. Third this production of action is automatic unless something prevents it: "one thinks that one must walk, and one walks" (*De motu* 701a17; see further *Met.* 9.5). That is why "pleasant" or "sweet" can fall in the same class as the gerundives; for nature has universally adapted pleasure and pain to pursuit or choice and avoidance or refusal. The distinction of what may be called the practical predicates and the purely descriptive was, I believe, equally essential for the Stoics; and the inevitability of action certainly was. In the fourth place it is a physiological fact for Aristotle that images cause bodily changes, which can be called *pathē*, of the same kind as those caused by actual cases of what they are images of—he instances hot, cold, pleasant, terrible. This is not without problems. But it seems that Zeus and Chrysippus assumed something similar: only, what is not always noticed, the contractions, elations, effusions were states (or motions) of the *soul*; moreover, although the evidence for this is slight and indirect, they probably restricted the assumption to properties connoted by our "practical" predicates.

Lastly Aristotle emphasizes the speed and virtual simultaneity of the process; the action that terminates it is repeatedly described as immediate. For the Stoics the corresponding fact is probably that the apparent stages of the process are really simultaneous and aspects of it rather than stages. Or rather, what one thought of as stages in fact sufficiently coincide as to have none that does not overlap or share a part with every other, like the leaf springs of a cart; and the overlapping is not merely simultaneity but referential identity, in the sense that where they overlap there are not two or more events but only different descriptions of one event. A number of modern writers perhaps following Pohlenz seem to imply something like this.[2] But what exactly the implication amounts to has been left too vague. I want to do something toward clarifying it and, while repeating that it is only probable because nothing like a statement of it has survived from the Stoa, I shall in effect suggest a set of arguments to support it.

This hypothesis of aspects instead of chronological stages would commit one to supposing that the act, say of drinking, had started as soon as the thought that I must drink, or some such thought or perhaps even the original desire had occurred in me. This can provisionally be made sense of by considering the action *from the point of view of the agent* and so including from the start a hitherto unmentioned feature, namely *trying* (e.g., to drink). But this is only a provisional remark; and the picture will need retouching.

Nor is this the only development of the Aristotelian schema. The Stoa gave a place to images earlier in the epistemic process: they were to be involved in sense perception itself. Moreover, neither process could proceed from a mere "judgment" to belief or to action without an act of assent. (This is familiar from Augustine to Descartes and Malebranche, none of whom learned it from Plato or Aristotle.) Stoics were willing to treat images themselves as objects of assent, so that the distinction of image (representation) and judgment tended to dissolve.

Chrysippus said that emotions were judgments. What judgments? They are fresh (i.e., very recent), false, bad, and contrary to reason (see, e.g., SVF 3. 459, 481). But what kind of predicates do they contain? The evidence is, as one would expect, that they are "practical" predicates, including "pleasant," "painful," "good," and "bad," but more typically or more immediately those predicates that derive their names from the names of the emotions, e.g., "shameful," "fearful" (in the sense of "terrible"). These, which we can perhaps call "affective," are by their meaning both descriptive and practical in a way that it is hardly necessary to spell out. But it would misrepresent Stoic psychology, and in my opinion the facts as well, to define their meanings as mere truth-functional conjunctions of a description and a prescription. This affects the logic of their falsity of course: but that cannot be pursued here. What is now crucial is the Stoic classification of the emotions: it connects by definition affective words with action. For since these words are defined in terms of emotions it makes them fall under genera each of which is defined in terms of something that seems good or seems bad; and these last are the triggers of action—not of action that ought to take place but of action that will take place. The seeming lies in the image, the automatic operation of which is implied also by Chrysippus's claim that the belief that an action is right is a function of the mere size of an apparent good or ill.

It is not perhaps difficult at this point to accept a telescoping of several of the supposed stages in the process leading to action, so that they will be at least in part one and the same fact. These are the imagination, the judgment, the assent, and even the action if we count the impulse that often combines intending and trying. More directly the impulse can be identified with the judgment that contains an affective and therefore practical predicate, for according to Chrysippus impulse was "the *logos* in a man which prescribes his action" (SVF 3. 175).

We can speak of the affective side of emotions. We need to operate with three notions—not just the physical or somatic conditions and the judgments but the feelings or psychic conditions—in order to explain the fourth notion, the emotion itself, which seems to be some kind of combination of the other three. For although it goes without saying that for a Stoic psychic conditions are somatic— though of a special kind—it is not the somatic conditions but the psychic ones that Platonizing critics like Posidonius and Galen wanted to identify with the emotion in opposition to Stoics who identified the *judgment* with the emotion. The names of the "feelings"—e.g., *systolē* ("contraction") and *diachysis* ("diffusion")— were in fact current names of the emotions for ordinary Greek speakers who did not think (or declined to think) of them as *literal* contractions and expansions. We too have inherited expressions such as "elation," "depression," "in an expansive mood," whose linguistic behavior distinguishes them as descriptions of feelings or sensations not physical states, but does not commit us, let us suppose, to the corresponding distinction—that is, a Cartesian irreducibility—in their reference. In Stoic psychology the feelings are just as necessarily triggered as is action by the images, or rather by the assent to the images, when affective predicates are involved. Though rather than seeing in this a simple causal power of mental representations to produce the effects of what they represent, as Aristotle did, we shall now be inclined to see the feelings as more like symptoms if not parts of the representing. We have of course no warrant to *identify* stages that we have only telescoped by making continuous and overlapping. There is however a fact of the Stoic theory which requires the feelings to involve and probably to be judgments; and this is the fact that they are psychic not somatic conditions. For this implies that they carry as it were their own consciousness with them, and this in turn implies a *lekton* and a proposition or judgment. Epictetus tells us that the difference between men and animals is that animals have no awareness of what they are doing (*parakolouthēsis*) because they have no need to be conscious of or follow with understanding (*parakolouthein*) and to discriminate among, representations, while "God has introduced man in order to be a spectator of God and his works, and not merely a spectator but an interpreter" (*Disc.* 1. 6. 13-22).

On the other hand the awareness or recognition of the feeling would be some such judgment as "here is a contraction of the soul," while the erroneous judgment that the fear—the emotion itself that is more than the feeling—was said to be would be the recognition or judgment about something external, "here is something fearful." For this reason I do not think that the feelings are to be *reduced* to the erroneous judgments. In other words they are identifiable as independent events in a way in which, for example, the presentations or sense impressions, the representations, the judgments, and the assents are not. The upshot is that if Chrysippus said that emotions were erroneous judgments he meant erroneous judgments that led to irrational feelings. It is quite likely that he said, as J. B. Gould supposes, that they were erroneous judgments that led to an excessive impulse;[3] for he may have thought that the feelings were symptoms or in some way counter-

parts of the "impulse." Stoics are reported to have said that the
essence of anger was a kind of boiling of the cardiac heat (SVF 2.
878). But this does not advance us; we knew already that there is
always a material basis for psychological phenomena; and exactly
the same problem whether they are to be included in a definition
of emotions in terms of erroneous judgment arises over such
bodily conditions as has arisen over the psychic feelings. The difficulty that faces us is that we do not know just what *function* the
feelings were supposed to have in the emotion, what part they
play in a process leading to an irrational act, say of revenge. At
the points where we might guess such a function, it is significant
that Galen reports nothing relevant from Chrysippus. This is the
case when he discusses the irrational impulse, but it is equally
striking when he quotes Chrysippus's explanation (or part of it)
how pain can cease while the erroneous judgment remains. Chrysippus seems to have thought that there was no scientific explanation, but that the "contraction" had probably the "impulse" to it
just stopped or weakened for reasons that cannot be discovered, as
people laugh, stop crying, or cry without wanting to (Gal. *Plac.*
394-95 Mü [SVF 3. 466]). Anyway we learn also from Galen that
he defined pain as "a contraction at something which seems to call
for avoidance" and in parallel terms pleasure. Pain and pleasure
are two of the genera of emotions, and each definition names in
the first half the feeling and in the second half implies the judgment.

What must be emphasized is that this only half concedes the
independence of the erroneous judgment and the feeling. It does
not mean that an emotion is an erroneous practical judgment
accompanied by an irrational feeling. That could be a conjunction
of the form "measles is a disease accompanied by spots." It means
that it is one leading to an irrational feeling; and this is not a conjunction. One important consequence of this, which has not I
think been noticed, is that Chrysippus's definition will be logically
equivalent, that is truth-conditionally, to Zeno's "feelings resulting from erroneous judgments." (The word translated "resulting
from" does not imply something "epiphenominal": it is a Stoic
technical term for a causal relation.) A formal parallel would be "a
cure is a treatment that results in the patient's health" which is
equivalent to "a cure is the patient's health which results from

treatment." But in such transpositions the intensional, or at least pragmatic, as opposed to extensional meaning may not be the same; and it is easy to envisage Chrysippus wishing to emphasize some priority or greater importance of the judgments. "All [our pains] hang on opinion. . . . Opinion is what we are sad for. Each of us is as wretched as he believes," writes Seneca (*Ep.* 78. 13).

We noticed at the start three problems that were in effect caused by the Stoic unity of the soul. The first was how apparently non-rational elements could be included in a soul that has no non-rational faculties. With the exception of desire, the dubious elements have been covered by the suggestions I have been making—in particular the suggestion that the psychic motions called feelings involve a *lekton*. Desire, so far as it is *orexis*, is equally rational, being defined by Chrysippus as "rational impulse toward what is, to the extent that it ought to be, pleasing" (Gal. *Plac.* 337 M. [SVF 3. 115, 39]). What has been translated as "rational" is *logikē*, so a *lekton* is involved. I should presume again that this is or has to do with the fact that a human being is conscious of his desires. For a similar reason we must not be disturbed by the falsity of the judgments on which emotions depend. It is only because one is inclined to translate the relevant adjectives by "rational" that one is inclined to associate it with some Platonic-Aristotelian notion of pure reason from which only truth can emerge. For the Stoics the ruling principle (*hēgemonikon*) is what makes propositions; Galen commonly refers to it as the faculty of thought. But there is a connection with truth, as we shall see.

This brings us to the second problem, how what is by definition contrary to reason can be included. For emotions are described not merely as "nonrational," or "without *logos*," but as "disobedient to the *logos* choosing," and the like (e.g., Stob., *Ecl.* 2. 88, 9W [SVF 3. 378]). What is the *"logos* choosing"? Fundamentally it is, as Stoic principles of translation would suggest, "the description that is making the choice." This is not removed from, or incompatible with, understanding it also as "reason involved in choice," which would imply the right choice whether or not actual. "Description" means both the act and the product, which is an abstraction: but each implies the other. For a Stoic the describing is how the agent's reason manifests itself. If Medea *described* the facts as she did—because she imagined—that her husband had done her an injury, where "injury" is an effective word, that act of description or imagination made her angry and it made her *choose* retaliation. Conversely, to take a pleasing example from Roman Stoicism: "if Menelaus had represented to himself that it was an advantage [trigger word for action] to have been deprived of a wife like Helen, what would have happened? Gone would have been not only the *Iliad* but the *Odyssey* as well" (Epictet., *Disc.* 1. 28. 13). Vice is not (in Bentham's phrase) miscalculation, but misdescription. In the case of affective predicates it should now be clear that such misdescription is likely to be, among other things, an emotion.

What will have been missed so far is the cause of the error of the description or of the image. Pohlenz followed an argument of Posidonius to which we have already referred, to point out that there were two parts to the explanation of the error.[4] There is first the magnitude of the apparent good or harm which is the subject matter of the judgment and the content of the image. The second factor is a weakness of the reason on the part of the person who makes the emotional judgment. This was a correct account, but it could mislead. Let us ignore the conceptual difficulties raised by the first factor, which are due to the fact that the magnitude is not the magnitude of an image but an imagined magnitude, for these are difficulties that belong to a theory of belief and can be found equally in Hume. The image is still erroneous, is not an "apprehending" one; it cannot, therefore, be used to explain its own error, and it will explain only tautologically the error of the judgment that it turns into. The weight of the explanation must lie on weakness of reason. This is identical with, or at least a symptom of, insufficient tension in the soul, as Galen testifies clearly for Chrysippus (*Plac.* 377 ff. M. [SVF 3. 473]). It is a fault of the ruling principle: but Platonizing critics like Galen do not understand that there is no room in Stoic psychology for a dilemma between categorizing it as weakness of intellect or of some other faculty such as will. In this context it is equally one-sided to speak as is common today, of the Stoics' intellectualism: as much as they made will or the passions intellectual they could here be said to have made the intellect volitional and passionate. The obviously Stoic—though just as much Cynic—virtue of endurance, which is not at all obviously intellectual, was in fact the simple opposite, according to their theory, of the lax psychic tension whose overt appearance was false judgment and emotional reaction. (Cf. D.L. 7. 158 [SVF 2. 766] for lack of tension and *Cic. Tusc.*, 4. 9. 22 for *intemperantia* as cause of all emotions.) The notion has still survived in the expression "poor tone," used for instance of some English public school thought to be temporarily marked by vices and a lack of esprit de corps. The same theory made Stoics regularly describe emotions as being, or being brought about by, "opinion." What they meant by "opinion" is not without problems. It probably had to be false: but it was certainly the form of nonknowledge whose defining characteristic was to be a *weak* assent, or weak judgment —the difference being unimportant for the present purpose. (SVF 1. 18. 25-27; 2. 90; 3. 548 and especially 3. 92. 21-22).

The same explanation holds when we see the *logos* that fails to control an emotional response in the more familiar and equally correct way as reason. Galen and some modern critics believe that the Stoics were landed with a passionate element or faculty of the soul which is expressly denied by their general psychology. They have not grasped that the reason in question is not the reason that people attain according to Stoics at fourteen. That could be said to perform the functions of a faculty of reasoning: but it is not that which is perverted by emotion as it might be in an Aristotelian model of action. It is, I think, the more universal and less developed form, which is little more than *the natural tendency of the rational animal to adapt himself to his environment by recognizing the properties connoted by practical predicates.* If "tendency" suggests *hormē* that will not be misleading. One has only to recall the "first *hormē*" according to Diogenes Laertius 7. 85, which (though Diogenes does not say this there) could as well be called the first manifestation of reason or *logos*. As Chrysippus said about it, it is nature making the living creature belong to itself (7. 85); and Zeno seems to have the label "contrary to nature" interchangeable for emotions with "contrary to reason" (cf. SVF 1. 205). In my formula "recognizing the properties" must of course mean recognizing them correctly. In fact Stoics thought—there are independent arguments for this—that to recognize truth and assent to it when recognized was the natural behavior of human beings. It is this that removes the equivocation in this context between a descriptive and a normative sense of "rational." "Natural" means here "normal and healthy," which insofar as it admits degrees does not suggest an unqualified opposite. A failure in this respect is a failure of tension, which is manifested by a weakness in the construction of the correct representations.

Although in the last analysis the error of emotional judgments is due to a lack of tension in the *pneuma*, we have at no point been examining the psychology of the Stoics, who were materialists, on what might be called the reductionist level. It must be appreciated that the surviving ancient discussions do not do so either. Error, whether it is vice or emotion, is considered as misdescription or failure to recognize. This puts us in mind of modern parallels— Kant's "maxims" and perhaps still more of recent English speaking discussions about "redescribing." Both of these have to face charges of arbitrariness. Roman Stoics tried to avoid that pitfall, while holding on to naturalism, by what is really an extension of the notion of affective predicates to relationships such as father— not good or bad father. These according to Epictetus determine most of our duties (*Ench.* 30; cf. *Disc.* 3.2.4; 1.2; 3.22). It is in effect the concept of *rôle*, which is again a special case of practical predicates. Anyone who desired to combine naturalistic ethics with either a collection of objets d'art or a successful marriage might care to consider the following example of redescribing. "If you have a favorite piece of china don't think of it as that: think of it as a jug. You will not be upset then if it gets broken. If you have a wife, don't think of her as that: think of her as a human. You won't be upset then if she dies" (Epictet, *Ench.* 3).

We have been suggesting that what appeared in the Aristotelian schema for the emotions as stages of the process were replaced in the Stoic schema by aspects, though with the proviso that the psychic feelings were probably independently identifiable. A mental representation (image) *is* a sense impression remolded. Making a judgment that Helen is lovable is the same act or event as having, meaning being aware of, a lovable mental representation of her. Choosing or deciding to love Helen is the same act as assenting to the judgment that she is lovable. Choosing or deciding to do something is usually the same or partially the same act or event as trying to do it. We must bear in mind too that all this, except for the sense impression, is voluntary in Stoic terms because, although it is determined, it is the work of our own ruling principle.

What has happened to deliberation? Well, of course the process can be interrupted. We can wonder about a representation, so that the stretch called imagining will no longer be the same stretch as assenting. But normally—though my evidence is from Roman Stoicism—to interrupt with deliberation is a sign of incompetence in the art of living. When Florus was wondering whether to risk his neck by abstaining from a festival of Nero's Agrippinus advised him not to. But asked why he did not go in himself, Agrippinus replied, "I don't have to calculate" (Epictet., *Disc.* 1. 2. 12-14).

If it is the case that we have aspects, not stages, choice or the decision to act have in no way become less important. But if we wish to describe the process as assenting and acting, the deciding will be adverbial, so to speak, or in Ryle's sense not episodic. In any case the whole process, except perhaps for the feelings, can if we wish be called a deciding to act. That suggests rather than the *Concept of Mind* another modern philosopher, Sartre. Aristotle said that we can think of something fearful without telling ourselves to be afraid, even though the heart beat is automatically affected (*De. an.* 432b7-8). Sartre and the Stoics would suppose that in that case we should not be thinking of it as fearful. . . . The workers did not revolt in 1830 because they suddenly found their poverty intolerable, they found it intolerable because they had already revolted. (See *L'être et le néant* Part IV, chap. 1.) Or rather Sartre rejects the notion of an ordinary *causal* connection altogether; but even when Zeno said that in emotion the judgment causes the excessive impulse the term that we should expect and which we find is "moves," and this is consistent with their being both part of one and the same movement. One difference however is that the affective predicates, which are all-important for both, stand in Sartre for real properties—this is the meaning of his phenomenology or antidualism. In Stoicism they can be only predicates or *lekta*. Indeed what we choose to do is a predicate according to Stoics, for we choose to walk and *to walk* is a propositional entity. (Stob., *Ecl.* 1. 138W = SVF 1. 89; Simpl., *In Cat.* 388. [SVF 2. 49, 36]; Sen., *Ep.* 117. 13.) This is at a technical level that reflects metaphysics and does not need to enter psychological theory. But even so it helps to confirm the telescoping of psychological stages by presenting an obstacle to supposing that we decide to act after we have chosen a course of action. For the supposition implies a distinction between choosing some x and deciding to ϕ : but in Stoic theory the object of choice takes the form, "to ϕ." (Stob., Ecl. 2. 78. 9W [SVF 3. 89]).

NOTES

1. See for instance J. M. Rist *Stoic Philosophy*, 25-26.

2. M. Pohlenz, "Zenon und Chrysipp," *Nachrichten zu Göttingen* (1938) 173-210 (repr. in *Kleine Schriften* [Hildesheim, 1965]); Joseph Moreau, *Epictète, ou de la liberté* (Paris, 1964); Rist, *Stoic Philosophy*; A.-J. Voelke, *L'idée de volonté dans le stoicisme* (Paris, 1973).

3. J. B. Gould, *The Philosophy of Chrysippus* (Leiden, 1970) 182, 185, 189, 192, 193.

4. E.g., *Die Stoa* II 2 (Göttingen, 1959) 80.

11

Moral Actions and Rules in Stoic Ethics

I. G. Kidd

(This study is based on a paper delivered at the third International Colloquium on Ancient Philosophy held at Toledo, Spain, in August 1974.)

I want to raise certain questions relating to three aspects of Stoic ethics which have commonly been held to be both characteristic of Stoic moral philosophy and of some importance in themselves in the history of Greek thought. The three aspects to which I refer are: (1) that Stoics stressed more than other Greek philosophers the overriding importance for moral behavior and human happiness of intention and motive rather than the content of the act as the ultimate criterion of moral action; (2) most, and possibly all Stoics were committed to a theory of moral progression whereby any human being might develop from infant or indeed adult turpitude or moral imperfection to perfect goodness; (3) Stoicism was regarded not only as a theoretical construct or system but also as a practical philosophy by which an individual could be guided to happiness. The first two have roused more interest than the third, but I want to keep all three in mind, because I wish to consider whether some arguments advanced for the three sections by Stoics, or rather perhaps, since the evidence is fragmentary, by modern interpreters of their statements, are consistent.

The key to all three sections lies in a theory distinctive to the Stoa, and for which they coined a series of technical terms which it will be convenient to bring into play, the theory of appropriate

acts (*kathēkonta*, or in Latin, *officia*) and their relation to morally
perfect actions (*katorthōmata*). Stoics held that appropriate acts
were derived initially from early natural impulses to which human
beings were said to have a natural affiliation. These developed in
adult life to comprehend the mature personality of the individual
and his social relationships, and as "the things according to
nature" (i.e., human nature), they were thought to form the field
where morality is displayed, or, more loosely, the material (*hylē*)
or content of moral action. Within this sphere a value system was
drawn up from the criterion of human "nature," whereby some
items were given general precedence, "promoted" or "preferred"
(*proēgmena*), such as, for example, preserving one's health,
acquiring wealth, honoring parents, sitting by the bedside of a
dying friend, keeping one's promises; their opposites, which had
"disvalue," were "relegated" or "demoted" (*apoproēgmena*). But
at once a problem arose, for these were only of relative value within their class, because in certain circumstances such "preferred"
material could be the wrong thing to do, or done for an inadequate
or vicious reason, or for no reason at all. Therefore Stoics argued
that a "perfect" act or morally right action (*katorthōma*) depended
not on the content of the act or on what was done, at least in the
sense of the objective value classification of "the things according
to nature," but only on "virtue" (*aretē*) which related to how or
why it was done ("rightly," "morally," "wisely," *dikaiōs, iuste,
phronimōs*), and this in turn seemed to depend on the agent, his
attitude, intention, and disposition.[1]

Now the Stoics, by apparently removing any criterion whatsoever of the rightness of an act from content to place it solely in
moral virtue were hotly criticized in antiquity. More recently,[2] the
switch of *emphasis* from objective content to aim has been regarded as a culmination of a painful development traceable in
Greek legal and ethical theory and a turning point in the history of
ethical thought. And a number of eminent scholars have described
this as the distinction between the "what" and "how" (or "why") in
moral action.[3] But the relationship between content and motive in
moral action in the Stoa remains unclear, as can be seen from reflection on the three aspects of Stoic ethics listed above: on the one
hand, in the theoretical analysis of the criterion of moral action,
the emphasis on *katorthōmata* and virtue and the demotion of

kathēkonta, the "natural things" and "the preferred" among them, stressed the separation of morally right actions and appropriate acts, the attitude of mind of the agent and the material of the act; on the other hand, the concept of progression to moral virtue emphasized a relationship, because at least in some accounts,[4] one progressed from *kathēkon* to *katorthōma* by doing the appropriate act morally (*dikaiōs, iuste*), as if this were an additional factor, even if to Stoics the exclusively important additional factor, which by its supervention rendered the act "perfect." And for a Stoic, although not every *kathēkon* was a *katorthōma*, yet every *katorthōma* was *kathēkon* or "appropriate." And thirdly, in passages relating to practical ethics there is much preoccupation with appropriate acts, involving a whole admonitory section of ethics, as if by this pedagogic training we may learn what to do, before proceeding to the higher education of perfect moral action and knowing why we do it, or ought to do it. Again at first sight there seems to be a horizontal division between *kathēkon* and *katorthōma*, although progression assumes a developed relationship between the two.

Let us return for a moment to what it is that makes an act appropriate, as distinct from right, and what is the relationship between the two. For a right action is also an appropriate act. So is the appropriateness, as distinct from the rightness, the same in each case? This seems to raise puzzles. Plutarch tells us (*Comm. not.*, 1069E) that the *archē* or governing source of appropriate acts lies in "the things according to nature," which are only the material (*hylē*) of *katorthōmata*. So it seems that the criterion of the appropriateness of appropriate acts must lie in the valuation of "the things according to nature," that is, would depend on the valuation of the content, the "what" of the act, the material deployed by moral choice. Then will an act be appropriate if from within the range of these "natural" things we choose one of the "promoted" goals, *proēgmena*, and reject *apoproēgmena*? But that would be odd; because there will be times when it is wrong to choose wealth, for example, or health, which although *proēgmena* are only of relative value; on some particular occasions we should choose rather their opposites. When this was so, if the progressor chose health because it was *proēgmenon*, i.e., "preferred" on the "natural" value system, would his act be "appropriate," although it now differs from the *katorthōma* which would have been done if he had been a morally good man, not only in motive but also in its content, in its object of choice? Surely not. But then if the action on this occasion to be "appropriate" (*kathēkon*), must have content appropriate to the occasion (in this particular case the opposite of health), then on what grounds would one in a kathekontic act choose an *apoproēgmenon*, which on kathekontic scales has "disvalue"?

It would appear to be a crude mistake to assume a direct correlation between appropriate acts and the preferred natural things, and Cicero in *De finibus* indicates as much when he says that appropriate acts aim at anything that is in accordance with nature, including things that are productive of natural things, and which have value. But in any particular case there may be conflict of value; for example, acquiring wealth might involve something unnatural, which would be *contra officium*, the opposite of appropriate. Then, it is not that one chooses an *apoproēgmenon*, but that in any given situation the progressor goes for what he thinks has the greatest value. But where do the rules for *that* come from? We had been led to believe that the progressor had been operating with general rules (*proēgmena*) tied to a value system grounded on the natural things, the material of the moral act, in themselves regarded solely by themselves. But there is no indication of how one arrives at comparative valuation among *proēgmena* from within the class itself. Again, the man who does an appropriate act is judged for appropriateness on what he did,[5] and his defense could only relate to his valuation of the natural things that are what he achieved, or at least tried to. Not only will the progressor act for the wrong reason, as the Stoics argue, but he will inevitably at times, although acting "appropriately," in the sense of following the rules operative in *kathēkonta*, namely *proēgmena*, choose the wrong thing; *what* he does will be wrong, although the process of training here appeared to be directed to getting the "what" right. There remains a gap between what is appropriate in general and appropriate in particular situations, and no obvious guidance about how the two may be reconciled; and one of the problems is how the progressor deals with the particular situation, as he must, operating with *proēgmena*. Some have seen a related problem with *katorthōmata*, where the emphasis is put on aiming, and not much of a story on what you aim at. I want to say that this is over-simplification.

There are clearly a number of different ways of approaching these difficulties, but I should like to investigate tentatively one that has received little attention.[6] It appears that both the progressor and the good man operate with what might very loosely be called rules. The most extended evidence of how these differ and relate is discussed in two of Seneca's Letters, 94 and 95, on which I now wish to concentrate. These Letters deal with the relative importance of what Seneca calls *praecepta* (precepts) and *decreta* (principles), and are complementary. In the first (94), Seneca puts the case and argues against it that *praecepta* are useless for ethical training and that only *decreta* are necessary; in the second (95), he puts the case and argues against it that *praecepta* are sufficient to make a man good. The Greek equivalent for *decreta* is *dogmata*,[7] and refers to the ultimate philosophical principles that the "wise" man knows and operates in right action. The exact Greek technical equivalent of *praecepta* is not so apparent, but Seneca refers the term to the paraenetic department of ethics,[8] that concerned with advice, admonition, exhortation, and the like. In a recent article[9] Professor Dihle has argued that Seneca was simply following innovations of Posidonius, but even apart from the Posidonian evidence which I cannot examine here, I do not think that this can be so. *Praecepta* and *admonitio* are frequently linked without comment by Cicero in *De officiis* with appropriate acts and the progressor.[10] *Praecepta* are mostly based in Seneca and Cicero on *proēgmena*, the "preferred" goals of relative value among the "natural things." Above all, Seneca presents the case against *praecepta* from Ariston of Chios, the pupil of Zeno, the founder of Stoicism. This fits, because we know that Ariston denied even relative value to "the things according to nature," and hence did not recognize a classification of *proēgmena*, and so any base for such maxims.[11] Ariston came rightly to be regarded as unorthodox, but at least the evidence shows the existence of the debate already in the early Stoa, a debate that appears to have continued at least on problems of emphasis until Seneca's day. So I now turn to Seneca with the assumption that he reflects a general Stoic problem, limited no doubt by Seneca's own quirks and restricted philosophical capacity.

Praecepta are usually illustrated by *proēgmena;* they operate with rules directed toward type situations.[12] And Seneca says that *praecepta* may warrant that a man does what he ought to do (*quod oportet*), but not how (*quemadmodum*) (*Ep.* 95. 40). But already there is confusion, and a rather crucial confusion of which we have no warning from Seneca; sometimes Seneca switches suddenly to *praecepta* which are not rules at all, but a specific command to a particular action: do this; don't do that (*Ep.* 94. 50). This is not a rule at all, but an instruction. Seneca remains rather unclear and ambiguous between the two.[13] But the ambiguity is important, because particular commands or injunctions when issued from a man who knows to an obedient subject will insure that an appropriate act will be done. But the educative value of telling the recipient nothing but merely instructing him to do a particular act is negligible, a fact well known to Stoics, put tartly by Epictetus (2. 2. 21-24) and recognized by Seneca himself (*Ep.* 95. 44). On the other hand *proēgmena* type rules cannot ensure a correct result; as Ariston pointed out,[14] they cannot take all cases into account, and therefore cannot hold good for all. *Proēgmena* precepts in other words are more like maxims or guides, and so inaccurate, and their inherent vagueness brings uncertainty of result. If an errant and dangerous politician is told to resign by a man whose knowledge and judgment he respects, he will resign, and so act "appropriately"; but if he is advised to act for the good of the country, there is no saying what he might do. So one can understand the attraction of the muddled conflation in Seneca between instructions with their greater certainty of result but educational deficiency, and the more illuminating but vaguer *proēgmena* rules. Also, there seem to be no grounds within the class for preferring one "preferred" *proēgmenon* to another. And further, although in a sense *proēgmena* are summary descriptive rules of the human condition, they do not carry authority in themselves; they are no more than hypothetical imperatives implying "may" not "must." It is true that Seneca relates *praecepta* to *decreta:*[15] *decreta* are the "cause" or reference point of *praecepta;* they are organically related; *praecepta* are the ally or supplement of *decreta;*[16] but it is not clear how all this is so, although clearly the relationship would be important. Finally, apart from the fact that no specific *proēgmenon* rule can be binding, one can even opt out and refuse to play the game governed by them altogether. This is most clearly put for the progressor by Epictetus,[17] and rather drastically illustrated by the Stoic doctrine of suicide.

Decreta on the other hand are more like rules of practice: they are definite and fixed, the "cause" of everything, and as such they "bind everything together" so that our conduct of life is constituted by them.[18] Whereas in *kathēkonta* or appropriate acts, what is justified is the particular act, which cannot ultimately be justified by its "rules," in *kathorthōmata* or moral action the justification *is* the practice or rule. *Decreta* are also like principles or general truths in being strongly allied to truth values: they infer truth by demonstration and proofs; they are required to demonstrate what is good and evil by rigorous proof; they involve judgment of good and evil, and are connected with understanding and teaching.[19] They cannot be controverted, superseded, or ignored. One cannot opt out of *decreta* rules. They are more like categorical imperatives. Also it begins to seem that *only decreta* supply the equipment not only for acting rightly but also for getting the "what" of action correct too. A hint of the reason for this arises from Seneca connecting *decreta* with the valuation of everything (*Ep.* 95. 58 f.). Now one of my earlier problems was concerned not with settling among the "natural things," which are "preferred" and which are not, but with the difficulty of comparative preference among "the preferred" themselves on any occasion; it now looks as if that problem would have to be approached from the direction of *decreta*. For example, *decreta* are strongly related to particular actions, but in the sense of providing knowledge of "when one ought to act and how far and with whom and how and why" (*Ep.* 95. 5). So Seneca maintains that no one will correctly perform what ought to be done who has not been handed down "a rational means of assessment (*ratio*) whereby whatever the particular situation he can fulfill the whole gamut of appropriate acts."[20] That, says Seneca, will not be achieved by someone who receives *praecepta* for a particular situation instead of for all. This is reminiscent of Plato tackling the problem of practical skills in the *Phaedrus* (271d-272a); and indeed the analogy of practical skills is not infrequent in Stoicism.[21] Knowing how to act in any given situation is clearly different both from that class of *praecepta* which were instructions, and from *proēgmena* rules. But Seneca remains ambiguous between *quid* and *quemadmodum*, "what" and "how" in these two Letters, and does not say, for instance, that knowing how to act involves knowing what to do, and so his relationship between *decreta* and *praecepta* remains puzzling. Part of the difficulty arises from the evidence persisting in seeing *decreta* and *praecepta* not as different in kind but solely as a difference between more general and more specific, or as more certain and complete against what is more indefinite;[22] as if Stoics were simply looking for a more general rule or rules, the most general ultimately having authority (Sen., *Ep.* 95. 47-55). And yet this is a puzzling line for them to take, because it would be basically different from their view that moral goods were different in kind from other so-called goods.

For Stoic theories of progression, it begins to seem as if the *quid* and the *quemadmodum*, the "what" and "how," are getting in each other's way, and that we should not be setting them against each other. In fact, the evidence, apart from the unorthodox Ariston, suggests that Stoics regarded *praecepta* as being complementary in some way to *decreta*. Seneca, however unclear he may be on the relationship, is positive enough on the area where this happens; it is when or where theory turns into practice, when disposition is operative (*in rebus agendis*) (*Ep.* 94. 50) that *praecepta* can assist in leading the contemplative aspect to performance, when the rules are being applied. *Praecepta* cannot teach, but they turn one's attention, stimulate one to action as maxims and reminders (*Ep.* 94. 25-26). But "to action" is important, for to Stoics right action is necessary for virtue (*Ep.* 94. 45). As it is not enough merely to do what is appropriate (*kathēkon*), neither is it enough to contemplate the laws of the universe without acting. Indeed, an appropriate act may be defended as something that could have been done at the bidding of reason.[23] *Praecepta* are bound up with practice by pulling one's emotions up short (Sen., *Ep.* 94. 47), for example, or keeping guidelines before us by their classification; a prop especially for inexperience, they point the way to performance of appropriate acts (*Ep.* 94. 32), and in this way it is claimed that judgment itself is strengthened (*Ep.* 94. 34), indeed that there is a reciprocal benefit between precepts and disposition in progression (*Ep.* 94. 49). Yet *praecepta* can do no more than point the way; as such they are an ally (94. 29) of right action, but can no more ensure that the content, the "what" of the act is right, than they can produce a good disposition.

As for good disposition, which is the real basis of right action, Seneca lays down interesting conditions (*Ep.* 95. 57). A good disposition will not be perfect unless: (1) "the mind grasps the laws of life as a whole" (*totius vitae leges perceperit*), i.e., theoretical understanding; (2) "unless it weighs the judgment that must be made in any particular situation" (*quid de quoque iudicandum sit exegerit*), i.e., diagnostic judgment; (3) "unless it reduces (or refers) the facts of a given situation to truth (or reality)" (*res ad verum redegerit*), i.e., the relation and corresponsion of particular act with general principle, truth, and reality. *Praecepta* and *kathē-konta* are presumably involved in (2) and (3), but cannot be solely involved, because clearly diagnostic judgment ultimately requires *decreta* on Seneca's scheme; and while *res* will refer to the facts of the situation, the "material" of the action, *veritas* must refer to the fundamental laws of nature or principles which the wise man knows through the *logos* philosophy, and presupposes an essential link between the "content" of an action and morality.

Now evidence such as this may make one chary of being too schematic. The Stoics themselves encouraged this by driving paradoxes to extremes. As some have been misled into thinking that Stoics entertained a stark "black and white" moral theory, by remarks like "only virtue is good, and all else bad," or "all moral mistakes are equal," and fail to take into account Stoic theories of progression and the philosophy of intermediate relative values, so the sharp dichotomy between content and motive, "what" and "why," while fruitful and illuminating, and in some contexts necessary, may in other respects be inadequate and deceptive. Thus it is attractive to assume[24] that with regard to Stoic practical teaching that underlay their theories of progression, Stoics entertained a horizontal division between two philosophies, that of kathekontic *praecepta* to train the progressor in what to do, and the *logos* philosophy for the morally right action of the good man. But a closer inspection of Seneca's Letters seems to suggest that the two should be complementary for the progressor. More stress is laid on the educative interplay between learning and doing (*Ep.* 94. 47),

instruction and training, on the katorthomic and kathekontic systems progressing together and influencing each other concurrently
(*Ep.* 94.49). "The progressor needs control while he is beginning to
control himself" (*Ep.* 94.51). Real progress is marked precisely by
the awareness of the inadequacy of kathekontic *praecepta*, even
their inability to prescribe the appropriate act in the circumstances
without some understanding of the fundamental principles of
moral action.

We should beware of confusing and conflating Stoic answers to
different kinds of questions. One set of answers might come from
asking what practical guides there are for performing appropriate
acts, a pedagogic question. A different approach may be suitable
for a question of theoretical analysis, such as what is the criterion
of morally perfect action, or, what criteria distinguish an act that
is appropriate from one that is right. But at least they should be
consistent.[25] If in tackling the former question I should now wish
to avoid a polar dichotomy between kathekontic and katorthomic
training, and to limit the importance in therapeutic training of the
kathekontic system, I should still wish to maintain for the latter
two questions that the Stoic exposition of *kathēkon*, and the clear
distinction between appropriate acts and morally perfect acts and
of "the preferred" and "the good," is of prime importance for the
understanding of their theoretical explanation of what they mean
by morally good action. But is this inconsistent?

Let me finally return to the "what" and "why," the relation between objective content and motive in the Stoic *katorthōma*, as
distinct from progressive training. The Stoics do appear to have
distinguished moral choice, as characterized by "rightly," "justly,"
"morally," etc., from the material or field in which moral choice is
exercised, the "things according to nature" with their relative class
valuation of *proēgmena*. They hold that we do not choose the latter—health, wealth, honoring parents, and so forth—*for themselves*, but rather because the particular choice of one in certain
circumstances is right in relation to a whole theory of human and
universal nature; that is, the criterion of morality does not lie in
the content of the act per se, despite the relative value of the objective content as drawn up in "promotion" and "relegation" rules.
But on the other hand, "motive" is too restrictive a term for Stoic

"virtue" (*aretē*), their criterion of moral good, which not only involved the disposition of the agent and his intention, but also the knowledge of what was the right thing to do.[26] The moral motive of the agent includes what he ought to do. I cannot see any justification in Stoic sources for the interpretation of the archer simile, where Stoics stressed aiming rather than hitting the target, that correctness of aim merely involved aiming straight regardless of what you were aiming at. The concept of aiming implies the target, and it would have been ludicrous of Stoics to maintain that it did not matter in a moral action what one intended, although the simile could, and did, illustrate that responsibility for one's moral action was not affected by the result of the intention being diverted outside one's control. The target involved a preliminary set of considerations derived from natural human goals, engendering their own inadequate general maxims; these considerations of possible "appropriate" acts could also be checked downward, as Cicero suggested in *De officiis* (e.g., 1. 152), from concepts of the virtues. All this, lying within the Stoic kathekontic department, was still inadequate. The choice between *proēgmena* (or indeed *apoproēgmena*) in any particular set of circumstances could not be so decided. It is not the status of "the preferred natural things" which determines the target of the particular aim, although they are material factors in the judgment, but the informed moral judgment of the good man which determines the relative status of the "preferred" data. But this is not a subjective criterion because the good man could only define his target by "reducing (or referring) the circumstances of the case to truth (or reality)." That could only be done with certainty and infallibility, if at all, through complete knowledge of the rational laws and principles of the universe and man's relation to them, that is, by what Stoics called philosophy of nature. Or, as the Stoic Hierocles put it:[27] "Nature gave us reason (*logos*) . . . above all for it to see nature itself distinctly, so that aiming at that as at a bright and fixed mark, and choosing all that is in harmony with it, it may make us live our lives appropriately (*kathekontōs*)." The good man's action will then indeed not only be morally good, a *katorthōma*, but what he does will be "appropriate" (*kathēkon*). That presumably is what the Stoics meant by "virtue" and by saying that virtue was the only good.

NOTES

1. For a fuller account of this paragraph, with the evidence that supports it, see Kidd, *Problems in Stoicism*, ed. A. A. Long, chap. 7 = *CQ* n.s. 5 (1955) 181-194.

2. E.g., G. B. Kerferd, "Cicero and Stoic Ethics" in *Studies in Honour of Harold Hunt*, 74.

3. E.g., M. Pohlenz, *Die Stoa* I. 131; E. Bréhier, *Chrysippe* 231; G. Nebel, "Der Begriff des *kathēkon* in der alten Stoa," *Hermes* 70 (1935) 442 f.

4. Cf. e.g., Cic. *De fin.* 3. 20-22.

5. D.L. 7. 107; Cicero, *De fin.* 3. 58; Stobaeus, *Ecl.* 2. 85, 13 ff. (SVF 3. 493, 498, 494).

6. Although I raised the suggestion in *CQ* n.s. 5 (1955) 192 f.

7. Seneca, *Ep.* 95. 10.

8. Ibid., 95. 1.

9. A. Dihle, "Posidonius' system of Moral Philosophy," *JHS* 93 (1973) 50 ff.

10. E.g., *De off.* 1. 1; 1. 7; 2. 7; 3. 5; 3. 121.

11. Cf. Sext. Emp., *Adv. math.* 7. 12; 11. 64 ff.

12. Sen., *Ep.* 94. 1, 15 f., 35; 95. 45.

13. E.g., ibid., 94. 23; 94. 44; 95. 44; 94. 32.

14. Ibid., 94. 15 f.

15. Ibid., 94. 4; 95. 12.

16. Ibid., 95. 12; 95. 45; 95. 7-12; 94. 29; 94. 21, 25; 95. 34.

17. Epictetus, 4. 7. 30 f; 24. 20; 1. 25. 7 ff.

18. Sen., *Ep.* 94. 16; 95. 12; 94. 15; 95. 58; 95. 44.

19. Ibid., 95. 61; 94. 10; 94. 33-34; 94. 2; 95. 35.

20. Ibid., 95. 12; and cf. Cic., *De off.* 1. 59 that we must become good calculators (*ratiocinatores*) of *officia*.

21. E.g., Cicero, *De fin.* 3. 24; Sext. Emp., *Adv. math.* 11. 170; 200 f; Sen., *Ep.* 94. 51; 95. 7 ff.

22. Sen., *Ep.* 94. 1; 94. 31; 94. 35; 95. 12.

23. D.L. 7. 1088; Cic., *De fin.* 3. 58.

24. As I tended to do in *CQ* n.s. 5 (1955) 191-193.

25. So indeed Seneca, *Ep.* 89. 13.

26. E.g., Stobaeus, *Ecl.* 2. 59 4W.

27. von Arnim, *Hierokles Ethische Elementarlehre* 53. 8 ff.

12

The Stoic Concept of Detachment

John M. Rist

I

The picture-book Stoic wise man is devoid of passions, emotionless, and unfeeling. In some respects this picture is accurate, but in a number of others it is an influential caricature. The key to the problem is the Greek word *apatheia* (meaning "without pathē"), which is a characteristic excellence of the sage. Hence we need to know what a *pathos* is; and that the Stoics tell us without much ambiguity. A *pathos* is a special kind of "disturbance" (*Cic., de Fin.* 3. 35), or better "disease" which affects basic human impulses (SVF 1. 213). It was defined by Zeno as an excessive impulse or an unnatural movement of the soul which is contrary to reason (SVF 2. 205, 206), or as a violent fluttering of the soul (SVF 1. 206). All such diseased impulses should be extirpated, and replaced by others that are totally subordinate and obedient to reason.

What this implies is not that the Stoic wise man has no emotions, but that all his emotions are rationally controlled. Whether or not Zeno actually used the technical term *eupatheia* for such rationally controlled emotions is unimportant. The doctrine that he taught and enshrined in the word *apatheia* is clear; and it does not depart substantially from a regular earlier use of the term. In

259

the *Eudemian Ethics* (1222A3) Aristotle observed that the man who is *apathēs* does not act in order to avoid pain or to secure pleasure. He certainly feels pains and pleasures, but his actions are not determined by them. In a related but slightly different section of the *Physics* (246B19-20) Aristotle observes that virtue either makes a man *apathēs*, that is, not sensitive to pain and pleasure at all (this seems to resemble the Cynic sense of the word), or else he becomes sensitive to them in the way that he ought to be, which is what the *Stoics* mean by *apatheia*.

Thus much by way of preliminaries: the Stoic wise man is a man of feeling, but his feelings do not control, or even influence, his decisions and his actions. In their terminology he is passionless (*apathēs*), but not without rational feelings. In fact Zeno was apparently even willing to say that when a man has learned wisdom, the scars of his earlier vicious and irrational emotions still remain in his soul. (Sen., *de Ira* 1. 16. 7 = SVF 1. 215).

The judgments of the wise man are in accordance with "right reason." Morally he does not make mistakes. We need not spend time, however, on the fact that he is therefore not carried away by anger or sexual lust. Most people would approve of his conduct on these matters. A standard criticism of his stance, however, offered in both ancient and modern times, is that he is harsh and severe: he has no pity, gives no pardon for offenses committed and is not "equitable" (for the equitable man is supposed to look for the remission of punishment due under the law). I should therefore like to consider two questions, one that goes beyond the concept of detachment, but is closely related to it, the other that is related to the particular question of pity and mercy. For the first question is the wide one of the general Stoic attitude to the value of an individual human life, and the second may show the Stoic theory to be more sophisticated and philosophically interesting than it has sometimes appeared.

II

At all stages of Stoicism a great deal of weight was put on the doctrine that men have a sense of "affection" or "endearment" for themselves and their own bodies. This sense of affection, originally associated with the infant's instinct for self-preservation, may be expanded into some kind of feeling of "belonging" to a cosmic city, to its human and divine members, in the mature and unperverted adult. The universe is the dear city of Zeus, and we are citizens of it. According to Porphyry the Stoics held that the sense of justice can be defended as an extension of the feeling of affection for ourselves (*De. Abst.* 3.19 = SVF 1.197). And the Emperor Marcus Aurelius speaks of an affection for mankind (3.9).

The Stoics may have attempted to modify and improve on Plato in the *Republic*. Plato clearly attempts to transfer the natural affection felt within a family for its own members into a love for the whole community. In Plato's state there is no jealousy, no envy among the governing group. All those of the same age regard one another as brothers and sisters. Aristotle was unimpressed: better a real cousin than a Platonic son. And it may be readily admitted that Plato might have found it easier to enlarge a sense of *obligation* to all one's coevals than to produce a strong feeling of personal love or devotion.

Even Plato limited his band of brothers to a small group, the Guardian class of his *Republic*. When the Stoic Zeno drew up a "Republic" of his own, he too imagined that all the wise can be citizens under an ideal constitution; no one but the wise can be a free man. We have only a little evidence about this for the early Stoics, but the attitude persisted and can be clearly recognized again at the end of antiquity in Marcus Aurelius. What does Zeno's limitation of citizenship to the wise tell us? Almost certainly that only the wise have value, and that their value depends not on their mere existence as human beings but on their possession of wisdom. If the rest are "fools," it is easy to think of a fool as a worthless object.

Some comments of Marcus are of great interest here, for he tells us quite explicitly that what is of value in a man is what he calls his moral character (*prohairesis*). This moral character is in fact a purified reason; hence Marcus can tell us to value our own reason: "To reverence and value your own understanding (*dianoia*) will make you acceptable to yourself, harmonious with your fellows and in concord with the gods" (6.16.5, trans. Farquharson). Clearly reason is the source of value in the Stoic cosmos, for reason is ultimately identical with God. Accordingly, Marcus tells us that each man is worth as much as what he is concerned with (7.3). The implication is clear: those whose character is preoccupied with right reason and virtue are of value; those whose tastes are lower can be graded accordingly. Some people are presumably worth nothing at all; and these should be treated accordingly: "Nature has made rational creatures for the sake of one another, to benefit one another according to desert but to harm no one" (9.1.1). Perhaps the latter clause looks like a safeguard for the "less valuable" members of the human race, particularly as Marcus has observed earlier that the man who commits injustice commits sin, but we should be careful of reading the text that way. For justice is clearly to be equated for the Stoics with the awarding to each man of what is appropriate to him.

We must suspend judgment for the time being about what might constitute not injuring someone, but the possibility certainly remains open that it is to be interpreted as not injuring them (i.e., administering punishment) more than is deserved, either in that it is not injuring their moral character or that it injures them in some other way for a valid reason. And for dessert we may quote a much earlier Stoic source, probably Chrysippus: "Therefore the man without a share in virtue is said to be justly without honour" (SVF 3.563). There is a certain ambiguity in this passage, for the Greek word *timē* means both "honor" and "value," but the thought is basically clear enough, that those who are to be accorded no honor are clearly so treated because they are valueless.

Let it not be supposed that Marcus's attitude to value is determined by his social status. The ex-slave Epictetus preaches a similar theme: if a man does not realize that he cannot be made unfortunate by anyone but himself, he is "really" a carcass, a pint of blood and nothing more (1.9.34). Thus although he is called a man (in the broad sense), he is not really a man in the narrow sense of "real man" or "free man." Such language is not to be dismissed as metaphor or hyperbole. Men are indeed to be valued by what they make of themselves. Just as a good T.V. is good insofar as it does what a T.V. is designed to do, and otherwise is of no value, so men are valued insofar as they live up to what they ought to do.

There is no reason to think that Marcus and Epictetus differ substantively about value from the earlier members of the school. So the problem remains: how can it be that the Stoics, while valuing human beings in proportion to their particular moral excellence, can still talk of the cosmic city and argue to a sense of affinity between the wise man and the human race as a whole? To examine this apparent paradox, let us consider the "benevolent" side of Stoicism a little further. Even though the citizens of Zeno's ideal state are probably all wise men, the Stoic does feel obligated to extend his version of justice to cover the human race as a whole. He thus feels to a degree responsible for the whole, while at the same time only valuing the individual members insofar as they are virtuous.

From this situation arises the popular notion of the Stoic wise man as an unfeeling purveyor of impersonal justice, the agent of reason in a vicious society. Yet our texts tell us not only that the Stoic feels the obligation of justice, but also that he is a social being (*koinōnikos*): there is a natural law of community according to Marcus (3. 11, cf. 8. 59); and Epictetus comments (oddly) that even Epicurus understands that we are naturally social (1. 23. 1). This "sociability" is to be associated with the "early stages" of *oikeiōsis*, of the feeling of "endearment," that is, in particular, with concern for one's family and later with one's children—a virtue extolled by Epictetus and Marcus under the title of *philostorgia*. Yet along with their emphasis on *philostorgia*, these writers are inclined to point out that the wise man is not concerned over the loss of a child (Epict., 3. 3. 15; 3. 8. 2; 3. 26. 4, etc.). Marcus expressly points out both that the wise man is benevolent (*philostorgos*) and that he is the most devoid of passions contrary to reason (1. 9. 3). Hence we have to conclude that *philostorgia* neither confers nor recognizes value in its objects, nor does it think of its objects as unique or irreplaceable, nor does it demand any overwhelming emotional commitment in those who exhibit it. *Philostorgia* is more than a sense of duty, in that like all the Stoic states of right reason it has an emotional coloring, but the emotional detachment, the sense of community, is controlled by the knowledge that there is only one thing that one man can do for another which has any real value, namely, teaching, and only one feature of other people that has any value, namely their moral state; and that moral state depends and must depend only on the individuals themselves. But how do we know that it is not of irreplaceable value? Because its loss is a cause for contempt, not for sorrow. Do not allow your sympathy free rein, says Epictetus (3. 24. 8); and Marcus tersely comments on his fellows: "Men have been born for the sake of one another: either teach them or endure them" (8. 59). For ultimately we are to understand our "broad" and "narrow" sense of "man" as follows: (Epict., 4. 5. 20-21): "Neither the nose nor the eyes are sufficient to make a man, but he is a man who makes properly human judgments. Here is someone who does not listen to reason—he is an ass. Here is one whose sense of self-respect has become numbed: he is useless, a sheep, anything rather than a man."

Those who are unteachable have no value and need not be treated as human beings. Our *philostorgia* arises particularly for our children, because preeminently they *are* teachable, and it may presumably be extended so far as "people" are accessible to reason. But when they have passed beyond these limits, let us listen to Marcus again, this time on the Christians in the amphitheater: they perish not after reflection nor with dignity, and not without a histrionic display, but out of sheer stubbornness (11. 3). Amphitheatrical performances bore by their repetitiousness (6. 46); Marcus does not suggest that the wretched victims deserved any better treatment (10. 8. 3). He has no notion of any inherent dignity of man. Only "free" men have dignity.

We see then the limits of Stoic concern for others and the basis for their belief that each "man" is able to make himself valuable if he wishes. (We may contrast this belief with another common thesis in antiquity, namely that value is conferred by society or by particular members of the society, such as the father in the case of a newborn infant). His "value" in this sense cannot be affected by anything he suffers, though if it is "genuine" it will be recognized as such by the wise, and so far as he remains teachable at all he is assumed to have recognized his own value to some degree. This being so, it is clearly encumbent on each man to be emotionally committed to one human being, or rather one human phenomenon alone, namely one's own moral character and moral dignity. The later Stoics resurrected the archaic noun *aidōs* with its adjective *aidēmōn* to refer to this notion of moral innocence which the wise man cherishes in himself and honors in others.

Anything the Stoics have to say about a man's responsibilities to himself will forward our understanding of the detachment of the wise man. And we may start by looking at a particularly striking passage of Epictetus which deals with the notion of self-love (1. 19. 11 ff.). Epictetus begins by distinguishing man as animal and man as rational animal. Qua animal man does everything for himself directly; qua rational animal man does everything for himself, but in a different sense and indirectly. Zeus could not be called "Rain-bringer" unless he brought rain; similarly man can achieve none of his own goods (that is his moral well-being or virtue) unless he contributes to the general good. Hence there is no necessary conflict between "higher" self-interest and benefiting other people and, as Epictetus points out, it is not "unsocial" to do everything in this special way for one's own sake. But this passage is particularly illuminating in that it helps us to understand why the wise man is not emotionally committed to those whom he serves. He is by nature only able to be committed to himself. When he works for others in the right way, he is merely appropriating (or attaching) the needs of others for his own "higher" needs.

We may conclude this section of the discussion as follows. Each man has one and only one object of value to be cherished, namely his own higher self. By a law of nature he is not able to love others as he loves himself. Only another individual can love *himself*, just as only I can love myself. There is only one canon by which the wise man is able to judge his own behavior: is it conducive to my own virtue, or does it risk compromising the valuable self which it is my unique prerogative to preserve?

Some at least of the Stoics used to say that souls are parts or fragments of God (Epictetus, 1. 14. 6, 2. 8. 11, Marcus, 5. 27, cf. D.L. 7. 143). The term "fragments" suggests bits broken off and hence separate from one another; and this suggestion seems to convey Stoic doctrine very accurately. We are related to our fellow men, but only rather remotely via the whole of which we are all fragments, not by direct connection. Our direct relationships with human beings are to be strictly subordinated to the making of our own isolated moral excellence. We are different fragments of the whole, and hence only able to "appropriate" others to ourselves, not treat them as ourselves. This latter notion is simply an impossibility in Stoic terms, for the only virtue or moral excellence one can command is one's own. The most the Stoic wise men can feel for one another is mutual respect for virtue achieved. Marcus remarks (6. 30. 1), "Respect the gods, save mankind." The gods are to be respected as perfect; mankind is to be helped (so far as virtue allows) as imperfect. The ethical theory depends on the metaphysical claim that ultimately concern for one's own virtue is the only way in which we rational fragments can attain a state of harmony with external nature and with God. If everyone attained such harmony, everyone would be happy. If they do not, and they will not, what is that to us? If others do not create themselves as valuable, why should I regard them as possessors of value?

There is a single passage of Marcus which to some commentators seems to offer a less arid thesis.[1] Here (7. 13) Marcus compares the relation between individuals in the world not merely to parts of the universe, but to that subsisting between the various parts of the human body. In a way this is an appropriate variant for a Stoic, for the Stoics regarded the cosmos as a whole as a living organism. But Marcus's remarks in this section in fact shed no new light on Stoic theory. It is good to regard oneself as a "limb" of the cosmos, for then you will be able to love men "from the heart." You will rejoice in doing good not merely because you are performing a merely fitting act, but because you are, as it were, doing good to yourself. Now perhaps the biological relationship between the "limbs" of the cosmos could be developed further in a less "arid" direction. But that is not what Marcus does. His move is rather to suggest that doing good will be more pleasing if done "as though benefiting yourself." For that, by implication, is what you can really appreciate—if you do it "the Stoic way."

III

We have now considered the wider context in which the Stoic notion of detachment must be placed. That completed, we can turn back to the more specific problem of justice. As we have already observed, at least some of the Stoics attempted to derive justice from their notion of attachment to the self. Whether they were successful in this or not, there is no doubt that justice is a concern of the wise man, and that he alone is just. How does the Stoic account of the role of the emotions and of the sources of value of human beings relate to the virtue of justice? We shall probably be able to shed a certain amount of light on these questions if we consider in some detail the relationship between justice, pity, and mercy. Let us begin with the definition of justice, which, as will appear, will quickly bring us back to questions of value.

Justice is regularly defined as a science distributive of dessert (or of what is deserved) to each man (SVF 3. 262. 27; 263. 8, etc.). Now clearly the wise man is perfectly just and will therefore "distribute" the appropriate goods, rewards, and penalties perfectly. Hence, in the case of the wise man there will be no distinction (such as is made by Aristotle) between justice and equity (*epieikeia*). Indeed the Greek word, which in texts of Aristotle is translated as "equity," is denounced by the Stoics as the mark of a weak mind (along with indulgence and pity) which affects kindness instead of punishing (D.L. 7. 123 = SVF 3. 641). The Stoic sage, who for both Zeno and Chrysippus is responsible only to himself (D.L. 7. 122), thus has no need of "equity," which is elsewhere defined as concerned with relaxing a man's deserts. The "equitable" man is thus seen as wishing to treat the guilty with less severity than is laid down by the laws (SVF 3. 643 = Stob., *Ecl.* 2. 7. 95. 24W). This doctrine is consistently condemned as harsh and unfeeling by ancient opponents of Stoicism, but properly understood it has more to be said for it than is sometimes supposed. The Stoic claim is that "equity" and pity, or indulgence, or pardoning, involve treating relevantly similarly circumstances in dissimilar ways, thus laying the wise man open to the charge of partiality or unfairness, or, in a word, of injustice.

Problems immediately arise. First of all the Stoic sage is rare, and it is only he who is certain to be able to formulate the perfectly correct law and thus to dispense with all considerations of equity. The dispensing with such considerations by non-sages would therefore seem to be vicious. But again, only the sage, it would seem, could know that a sentence that is appealed and provokes a call for mercy is in fact perfectly just. Nevertheless in practice any lawgiver who is not the Stoic sage must allow for the possibility of his own error and for those of others, thus leaving room for consideration of equity and of the possible effects of particular punishments on the guilty person's character. Yet to this the Stoic could reply that although these considerations may be valid, such an appeal is not strictly on grounds of equity; it is merely a request that the possible fallibility of ordinary human beings be taken into account.

Furthermore, it is certainly the case that many so-called appeals for mercy are not really appeals for equitable treatment, as defined by Aristotle, at all. Often, as, for example, in the case of an appeal not to suffer the death penalty for stealing a sheep, they are concealed appeals against unjust laws, being in effect, appeals for a better system of social justice.[2] But if these cases are not genuine appeals for equity or even for mercy, are there any genuine appeals for mercy at all? It is probably correct that a genuine appeal for mercy is, as has recently been argued,[3] based on the view that mercy "reflects justice solely as a virtue of persons. It complements the justice of the institution of punishment." But, of course, it is exactly such a complementing that Aristotle thought of as "equity" and which is, by definition, unnecessary in the case of the Stoic wise man. If mercy is a genuine virtue, it would follow necessarily that there are cases where one *ought* to be merciful (Mercy is not merely a matter of benevolence; if it were, it might too easily be confused with partiality). And if there are such cases, it necessarily follows that the sentence that is being appealed *ought* not to be carried out strictly in this particular case. That being so, we can see why the Stoics might reject the notion of "equity" or of mercy so defined (and there seems to be another available variety) in the case of the wise man.

At this point the question of the value of the individual comes in again. If a man has acted viciously, and indeed to the degree that a man has acted viciously, he may be said to have become (for the Stoics) devalued. Hence an appeal to the sage for mercy could also be construed as an appeal to treat some *better* than they deserve, and would thus conflict with justice itself, as the Stoics define it.

There is a further problem as follows: the wise man, according to the Stoics, never treats anyone unjustly and never does harm to anyone even when he punishes him. Therefore it follows that, although justice involves the distribution of the appropriate penalties according to dessert, it cannot be defined merely as retributive. Although justice "pays back" what is due, it is not designed to injure but, if possible, to improve the moral character of the man punished. Hence when the wise man distributes his penalties, an appeal for mercy must either be dismissed as an inappropriate appeal for a better system of justice, or it is a request that the wise man do less good to the culprit's moral character than is in his power to achieve. In Stoic terms it then becomes nothing more than an unjust request to act viciously.

It is thus readily understandable why there can be no legitimate appeal on grounds of mercy against the rulings of the wise man. For such an appeal must be either an appeal to his emotions contrary to his reason, or an appeal against his understanding of justice designed to prevent a man being treated as he deserves. Such appeals will naturally be rejected. But treatment of a man as he deserves requires a further comment. Modern humanitarian legislation restricts or forbids the use of "cruel and unusual" punishments, such as torture. Reasons for this restriction may be that such punishments contribute unacceptable treatment for any human being qua human being or, more sophisticatedly, that they corrupt and debase those who carry them out. We should note that the former of these arguments does not occur in Stoic sources. Torture was an accepted "way of life" in the ancient world—the only question was when it was appropriate—and from a Stoic point of view certain types of criminal offense would so debase the perpetrator and lower his value that there would be no theoretical defense possible on the grounds of human dignity.

So far we have considered mercy and the wise man and have only noted in passing that there are very few wise men. Opponents of Stoicism in antiquity were quick to make this point too, being eager to observe that the Stoic attitude seemed oversevere and harsh. Seneca, as adviser to the Emperor Nero, is particularly aware of this charge in his treatise *De Clementia*, addressed to the emperor himself, a treatise in which he attempts to rehabilitate the term *clementia* (Greek *epieikeia*, equity). Those interested in these matters, he says (2. 5. 2 ff.), dislike the Stoic school on the grounds of its excessive harshness, claiming that it is least likely to give good advice to princes and kings. Seneca's report of this objection may well be precise in that since absence of pity and absence of a desire to pardon are characteristics of the wise man, it is certain that they were being held up as ideals and/or as guidelines even for those who were not wise in the Stoic sense. As it stands, says Seneca, this teaching seems obnoxious, since it makes no allowances for human weaknesses. In fact, he counters, the Stoic school is benevolent and serves the public; it concerns itself not only with self-interest but with the interest of each and every man. Now we have already discussed the nature of that concern and need not spend further time on it here, but Seneca then proceeds to offer objections to pity (*misericordia*) which he distinguishes from "mercy" on the following grounds:

1. that it blunts and hampers the mind;
2. that it indicates too great a disturbance over the suffering of others. The man who pities is like the man who bewails at the funeral of a stranger!

As for "pardoning," Seneca finds it too is objectionable in that it involves the remission of a *deserved* penalty, and is therefore unfair. But whatever might be supposed to be achieved by pardoning, he claims, is properly achieved by "mercy" which he then analyzes in some detail. Now at this point Seneca makes a distinction which we have earlier found that the Stoics seemed to reject. Mercy (*clementia*) is appropriate to the wise man in that it is arrived at in accordance with the free choice of the wise man. He is not trammeled by the letter of the law, but acts according to what is fair and good, and in doing so is in accord with the strictest justice. In other words Seneca seems to have gone back to the Aristotelian distinction between justice and equity, and speaks of "mercy" as both fitting to the wise man and, of course, just. The implication of this seems to be that even the wise man cannot draw up laws in such a form that the most just solution will always be reached in any particular case—a point that the earlier Stoics, with their apparent emphasis on carrying out the law, seem to have played down. But although Seneca rehabilitates "mercy," as distinct from pity and pardoning, as a just and rational activity, his actual thought is in essentials identical with traditional Stoicism insofar as in the case of the wise man his acts of mercy are perfectly just, and therefore ought to be performed.

The wise man, says Seneca (2. 7. 4) will remit punishment when the guilty man's character is not entirely corrupt or unsound. That sums the matter up well; only the wise man can (for a Stoic) show mercy in the good sense, a mercy that is genuine in that it is in accordance with justice, for he alone will understand the motivations and character of those whom he judges. Again mercy has nothing to do with the emotions; it is not an un-Stoic feeling of benevolence. It is strictly rational and depends on the dessert, visible only to the wise man, of the guilty party. It is not, therefore, to be impugned as the awarding of dissimilar treatment in relevantly similar cases, for although the acts might perhaps be formally similar, there is always room for a dissimilarity of intention.

Clementia (mercy) is not merely the Latin name for the suspect (to Stoics) Greek concept *epieikeia*. It is a Roman virtue, and particularly from the time of Julius Caesar, an imperial virtue. Both Augustus's *Res Gestae* (18) and Plutarch's *Life of Caesar* (57, cf. Dio 44. 6. 4) refer to the notorious "imperial" *clementia* under the name *epieikeia*. And Seneca, in praising *clementia* in a political context, has no option but to accept the term, un-Stoic though it may have originally been. But though he is obliged to accept the language, he is not obliged to accept much novelty of content. The "mercy" that Seneca preaches is not mere leniency, not good nature, partiality, pity, or political prudence. It is a genuinely Stoic virtue in that it is bestowed, for him, according to the judgment by the wise man of the worth (or its converse) of the recipient.

But is there another respect in which Seneca's account of the "mercy" of the wise man is heretical Stoicism? Seneca, as we have seen, operates with what amounts to an Aristotelian distinction between justice and equity; and with it he brings the theory that perfect justice, that is justice as witnessed by individual cases, cannot be institutionalized. We may wonder whether this affects the theory of natural law, as it is held in Stoic philosophy. For that seems to suggest that there are at least a number of immutable rules of justice which cannot be varied or waived. At least one interpretation of such a position is that in these cases at least there are no extenuating circumstances if the agent consents to do what he does. Or, as Aristotle would have it, there are certain things that the good man simply will not do. All that is no doubt correct from a Stoic point of view, but it does not affect the issue of mercy in Seneca. When we are dealing with mercy we are dealing with circumstances in which an admittedly unjust act has been committed, and when the agent is therefore vicious, but when his intention or character are said to be deserving of something less than the most severe penalty. Of course, from the point of view of Stoicism all acts of this kind are strictly vicious, but since some of them may have more or less "worth" from the standpoint of the possible moral improvement of the agent, these presumably are the cases where mercy should be shown. Since it is the function of the wise man to promote the rule of reason, he is obliged to encourage those who may still have the greater possibility of virtue in the future, or, in terms of value, those human beings who are not totally worthless. Again we are back to the value of the character of the agent. In proportion as such value remains, there is *rational* ground for mercy and such mercy is, even for orthodox Stoics, perfectly just. In these circumstances we see once again that mercy is not grounded on any value in "human nature" as such, but on a calm estimate of whether a particular seeming human being retains sufficient potential for moral excellence to be worth a less degree of severity than would be appropriate and desirable in the case of the wholly corrupt and unteachable. For the wise man it is necessary not only to weigh the axiom that relevantly similar acts be treated similarly but also to note that relevantly dissimilar characters should be treated dissimilarly. And, after all, in allowing a judge a certain discretion in sentencing, we pay a certain amount of tribute to this sort of principle.

Mercy then is a species of justice, but in defending that proposition Seneca would have no more time than any other Stoic for the dictum: "The heart has its reasons..." But Stoic justice is a detached evaluation of the value of the man judged and of his character, motives, and intentions rather than an assignment of rewards and penalties for specific acts committed. It is a moral rather than a legal virtue and depends on a set of moral theses about human nature. Within such moral theses the Stoic concept of detachment should be located, and we should not be surprised if these theses differ sharply from those of what may be vaguely labeled "liberal humanitarianism."

NOTES

1. E.g., C. J. de Vogel, "Personality in Greek and Christian Thought," *Studies in Philosophy and the history of Philosophy 2* (Washington, 1963) 49.

2. Cf. Mrs. A. Smart, "Mercy," *Philosophy* 43 (1968) 345-349.

3. Claudia Card, "Mercy," *Phil. Rev.* 81 (1972) 195.

13

Zeno on Art: Anatomy of a Definition

F. E. Sparshott

One thinks of Socrates and Aristotle as the ancient philosophers in whose thought definitions played the greatest part. But this may be misleading. The Socratic quest for definitions produced none: the philosophy lay in the search and in its inevitable failure. Aristotle's definitions tend to be inert, serving to sum up discussions or phases of discussions to which they add little. It seems to have been the Stoics who made the most strategic use of definitions. Our fragmentary tradition of the early Stoa sometimes reads as if their theory on any subject consisted for the most part of a series of linked definitions of terms used in novel senses, the definitions themselves being couched in terms that were freshly coined or used in new ways, in such a way that the unpacking of the full meaning of the definitions would suffice to establish the key points of the theory in which they figured. It may be that this impression is in part the incidental result of the fragmentary nature of the tradition. Despite the abundance of the evidence, we know very little of the real quality of Stoic thinking: the definitions and aphorisms survive, the arguments are mostly lost. But this can hardly be the whole truth of the matter. The definitory fragments have a strikingly pregnant character that cannot be accidental, and what has survived may well be an index to what was felt worth quoting and keeping.

273

This paper presents one such Stoic definition, that of art. It was a famous one, and is preserved with slight variations in several sources, but none of its contexts shed any light on its significance and we do not know what use Stoic thinkers made of it. We are reduced to divining its likely meaning by looking at the words in it, and by relating it to problems that had already been felt and are still felt in saying just what art is and what arts are. A large part of this study is therefore devoted to remarks on what use Plato and Aristotle made of the concept of art, and on the problems raised by that use. The significance of the Stoic definition then almost speaks for itself. And the process of exposition should bring out something of interest and value in the style of Stoic thinking generally which at least some commentaries seem to have missed.

The concept of an art, which has nothing especially to do with what we nowadays call the fine arts, is basically that of a body of expert knowledge, statable in general terms and teachable, which, by applying, the wielder of the art succeeds in producing results and artifacts of a certain desired kind. By the art of medicine, the physician produces health in his patients; by the shoemaking art, the shoemaker produces shoes from leather and thread. In the philosophies of Plato and Aristotle this concept plays a strategic role, one that modern metaphysics and epistemology no longer assign it. It is easy to see why in a prescientific and preacademic age such bodies of knowledge should have been assigned such theoretical importance: except for mathematics, they were the only evident successes of organized thought. Examining their procedures and contents, therefore, offered the best chances of inferring something about the conditions of success in organizing thought generally, and thus about the nature of the world in which such methods could succeed. But Plato and Aristotle each had a more specific interest in the concept. In the way in which the shoemaker's knowledge of what a shoe is enables him to produce pair after pair of them, Plato found the exemplar for the way in which likenesses among natural things might be explained by reference to a single formal entity after which they are in some sense patterned (*Rep.* 596B, *Crat.* 389A-B). He also used the idea of an art as a tool of social and moral criticism. When we wish to evaluate the performance of someone performing a complex task, such as a doctor treating a patient, a consideration of the different arts, the different bodies of practical expertise, to which his action is integral may lead us to conclude that it would be more accurate to think of him as doing two things at once (healing the sick and making a living, perhaps), and that the criteria of success in one are by no means the criteria of success in the other (*Rep.* 346 A-D). Again, the ways in which a user's art and the art of the manufacturer who supplies his tools complement each other serve to articulate not only the economic structure of society but also the very nature of the objects on which those separate interests converge (*Rep.* 601D-602A).

Aristotle takes these themes and develops them. The ways in which the complementary arts of navigator and carpenter combine in the design of a ship's rudder yield an important insight into the dynamics of natural processes (*Phys.* 194a36-b7), and an analysis of the sequence of operations by which the practitioner of an art proceeds from initial problem to achieved solution is in fact the main support of Aristotle's metaphysical analysis of substance (*Met.* Z. 7-9). In ethics, the possibility of learning through sheer practice to play a musical instrument well provides the paradigm for that very puzzling process, moral learning through "habituation" (*E.N.* 1098a9-12, 1103a32-b2, 1105a17-b5); and the ways in which means and ends are interrelated in professional skills provides the key to the articulation of moral reasoning and, beyond that, to the unfolding of the nature of the good as a system of ends (*E.N.* 1094a6-18). But above all, Aristotle assigns to art the crucial role in that development of autonomous abstract thought the capacity for which he takes to be the distinguishing characteristic of man as such (*Met.* A. 1). At a primitive stage of development, he says, people go by unreflective experience, simply doing what they remember as having worked well in a case they recall as similar. An art is born when they begin to formulate general propositions: in all cases of X, do Y. In order to do this they must decide what constitutes a case of X, must fasten on universal characteristics; and in doing that they are inevitably led away from merely observing what happens to figuring out how and why it happens—what it is about foxglove that makes it good for certain ailments, and what it is about those ailments that makes foxglove good for them. But the most significant fact is that their reason for pursuing inquiries in this direction is not purely practical, for experience is perfectly satisfactory in its own sphere, and the universal knowledge of art without the ability (obtainable only in experience) to recognize when and how to apply it is no use at all. Once the level of generalization has been reached, the intellect simply takes off, and universal inquiries into the why and how of things are carried on for their own inherent interest without regard for any practical application, and even in areas where no practical application is thinkable. So philosophy is born. But without that initial step from blind experience to reasoned generalization, none of this intellectual superstructure could have been erected.

That is the sort of use Plato and Aristotle made of the concept of art. The concept is beset with difficulties, of some but not all of which the authors were aware. Some of the difficulties have to do with general values. Plato conceived of an art as definable by what benefit it rendered to what (*Rep.* 332C, 341D), what lack it supplied in what. That is, the idea of an art depends on the possibility of isolating an end to be attained. But to be worth attaining, such an end must be really good; so until we know what *the* good is, we cannot know what an art is. And what *the* good is we cannot say. The paradigmatic value of the arts as uniquely successful organizations of knowledge, and successful just because their aims are limited (a point Plato makes in the *Apology*, 22D), is thereby lost. And at the same time we encounter the paradox that the complete shoemaker must be a philosopher—a paradox that the division of labor in the *Republic* suggests would be no more palatable to Plato than it is to us, although elsewhere he insinuates a similar argument about the perfect politician (*Phaedr.* 277B-C, *Pol.* 304B-D and passim). In effect, the arts lose their autonomy.

To avoid this unwelcome conclusion, Aristotle insists that practice of an art must be judged only in terms of its own end, the desirability of which is simply assumed (*E.N.* 1139b1-3). A poet is a bad poet if he lacks poetic skill, not if he makes historical errors —or, presumably, moral errors (*Poet.* 25). A critique of the ends of arts, and thus of artistic practices as organized wholes, belongs not to the internal structure of the art but to morals and statecraft (*E.N.* 1094a26-b10). Well and good; but as Plato had pointed out before, it is odd to say that the best doctor is the best poisoner, the best banker the best embezzler (*Rep.* 334A-B); and we might add that it is odder to say that there is an art of embezzling as there is an art of banking, or that one might go to poisoning school as one goes to medical school. Arts are in fact organized bodies of knowledge directed to ends conceived as really good, not merely to ends to the securing of which skill might conceivably be devoted; and Aristotle's actual treatment supposes this without being able to account for it. How are the arts to retain their autonomy without being relegated to irresponsibility? The problem is not effectively faced by either thinker.

Related difficulties are raised by a famous passage in the *Gorgias*, in which a mere knack such as cooking, which aims only at gratifying whims, is contrasted with an art like medicine, which aims to supply the real good of health (*Gorg.* 462B-466A). Why is cooking not an art? A good cook's knowledge of his techniques is surely secure, generalizable, and teachable. However fickle the taste buds, there is enough agreement about food to make cookery something one can learn and in which skill can be evaluated and rewarded. Even if we accept, as the argument seems to imply, that the quality of life is not in itself a real good, we might wonder how far the fallibility of cookery was due to the arbitrariness of taste and how far it was due to the necessary variability of practical situations. The word we translate as "knack" here is indeed the word we elsewhere render as "experience"—that experience of which Aristotle maintained that it is practically preferable to art if one has to have one without the other.

Plato conceives of an art as a system of general principles, and Aristotle ascribes to this universal character its epistemological significance as well as its teachability and its heuristic value. As Plotinus was to make yet more explicit later (*Enn.* 5. 8. 1), the way in which the form of a statue preexists in the sculptor's mind is not as an image of just that statue but as the art of sculpting as the sculptor has mastered it—"The art of building is the form of a house" (*Met.* 1032b13-14). But how are we to reconcile this universal character of artistic knowledge, in virtue of which an art differs from a theoretical science only in its having a practical application, with the basic idea of an art as essentially practical, whose mode of existence is as a "reasoned state of capacity to make" in the mind of the practitioner (*E.N.* 1140a7-10)? From the latter point of view, art is treated as analogous to practical wisdom (*E.N.* 1140b4-6), and as thus embodied it should accordingly be a set of universal propositions or imperatives, plus a capacity to reason about means and ends, plus the ability to recognize appropriate occasions for the exercise of the art (*E.N.* VI, 7-11). In all this, the reference to the universalized and verbalized knowledge seems essential. But when we nowadays think of an art what comes first to mind is that aspect of a practice that must be learned as skills are learned, not reduced or referred to verbal formulas: the "wisdom" of the trained eye, ear, and hand. It is true that one of the reasons for this emphasis is that we take as paradigms of art those "fine arts" in which such nonverbalizable skills play a preeminent part, but it is in fact applicable to those arts of shoebuilding, medicine, and the like, that Plato and Aristotle took as their prime examples. The general applicability of a skill does not demand verbal mediation. Neither Plato nor Aristotle ever quite takes account of this fact, and the passage in the *Gorgias* partly suggests why and partly points up the problem. Plato envisages "knacks" (or "experience") not as complementing art, much less as integral to art, but as inferior alternatives to art. When Aristotle redresses the balance by saying that an art without the related practice is useless he does not go on to say what the relation between them is: whether experience is a complement to art, or an integral part of it, and if the latter how it is integrated. In general terms this unanswered question might be posed thus: if the test of art is success in the work, what is the precise epistemological status of the general principles through which an art is taught? Or, if an art is a system of general truths, does it follow that practice cannot itself be amenable to any sort of systematization without recourse to such truths?

Another problem is raised by a thesis mooted by Plato to the effect that an art as such is perfect (*Rep.* 342 A-B). In its context it is a debating point, but there are good reasons for saying it. A textbook, after all, aims to contain all and only the truth in which an art could be codified. If it is incomplete or contains falsehoods that is not because the art is inherently defective but because the professional community has not yet eliminated all the errors from its conceptualization and practice of that art. Indeed it is obvious that if an art is a system of universal truths it must be, in a way, perfect. But how does this perfection relate to that "reasoned state of capacity to make" that is the only form in which the art is realized, in this or that fallible being, and which in its diffusion among a whole professional community we refer to as "the state of the art"? It seems that the concept of an art is the concept of an infinitely removed ideal; and this again works against our initial contention that it was in the arts (along with mathematics) that the organization of intellectual activity had achieved its most evident triumphs.

Further difficulties arise from the proposal that an art be defined in terms of a subject matter and a type of improvement thereof. Already in the *Republic* Socrates and Thrasymachus differ as to what the relevant "subject matter" and "improvement" are in the art of statecraft, and it is hard to see on what basis the issue should be decided, or whether indeed they are not describing two different arts to either of which the name of "statecraft" would be equally applicable. And in the *Sophist* the difficulty of hunting the sophist by definitions is that any number of descriptions of his skill seem equally apt (*Soph.* 218B-232A). True, this ambiguity might reflect a confusion in the very notion of sophistry, and hence the impossibility of making an art of it, but it might equally reflect a many-sidedness in what sophists legitimately do. That such ambiguities are there to be exploited shows at least that organized practice does not in reality conform to any such schematism as the concept of an art suggests, and it would be rash to suppose that this discrepancy reveals practical confusion rather than conceptual error.

It might be suggested, though neither Aristotle nor Plato suggests it, that the organization of practical knowledge has a threefold basis, the ground of which may be found in the distinction between makers' and users' arts and in the insistence that arts are inherently teachable. In the first place, the existence of a coherent practical goal may generate an art of reaching that goal, the art then being definable as whatever knowledge and skills may be found necessary to that end. But in the second place, such practical knowledge and skills may be hard to acquire and are likely to have their own mutual affinities. There is no reason to suppose a priori that such an internally cohesive body of practical knowledge will answer precisely to any similarly unified set of objectives; and one who has acquired such knowledge is likely to be called on, and to be willing, to apply it wherever it is applicable, as an orator's talents may be enlisted in any cause. And in the third place, the teachability of practical skills makes it likely that there will be institutions for teaching them: polytechnics, academies, conservatories. Such institutions necessarily have and impose their own organizations and generate their own inclusions and exclusions, and they are likely to develop their own objectives, not necessarily in step with those of society at large or humanity in general. There is a very real sense in which the medical art is all and only that which medical schools teach and practitioners are licensed to perform. Thus social goods, the transferability of skills and the inertia of institutions, provide a threefold organization of practical knowledge and thus a threefold articulation of the arts.

There are other aspects of the way skilled practice is carried on that might lead us to say that the organization of knowledge in the arts is not so much threefold as altogether indeterminate, and the concept of an ideally perfect organization fundamentally misleading. Whether in humble trades or in advanced specialisms, each master has his own mix of expertise, unlikely to answer to any generally accepted subdivision of an art, or even to be confined within any accepted art, but reflecting rather his own practical taste, his own specialism, his own local market, or the vagaries of his own training. Practice of an art in real life conforms to no such stereotyping as Plato and Aristotle suggest. Denis Diderot made this flexibility of art a key point in his article on "Art" for the *Encyclopédie* of 1751-1765, which seems to be the only serious treatment of the general concept of an art in modern times. He argued that technical thought should not be thought of as subdivided into separate specialisms so much as focused around certain nuclei of interest. An art is not a determinate system of universal propositions, but learned and organized skill *insofar as* it pertains to some one of these focuses. There is accordingly nothing specific that is necessary or sufficient for a person to know to contribute to such an end, nor is his contribution to it necessarily the whole of his technical skill or the organizing principle of that part of it that does pertain to the art. It would of course follow from this that an art as such could not be taught, although one could be taught to practice an art by being equipped with a repertoire of knowledge pertaining to a practical end. One who successfully completed such a training would not know everything, but he could do something. But now, how can we do justice to what is true in this account of art without giving up all that seemed of value in the Platonic and Aristotelian view?

It is against this background, and in the light of this problematic, that the Stoic definition of art is to be construed and its success—for it is quoted by a variety of sources in a number of variants, and Quintilian tells us that it was pretty well universally accepted (2. 17, 41)—is to be explained. Its author was Zeno himself, according to Olympiodorus (*In Gorg.* 53-54 = SVF 1. 73); and that in itself gives rise to a problem to which we now turn. A scholiast on Dionysius Thrax assigns to Zeno a definition quite different from the one that interests us (SVF 1. 72); but Olympiodorus and Quintilian both refer this other definition (or a slight variant on it) to Cleanthes, Quintilian supporting his attribution by insisting that Zeno could not possibly have defined the same term in two different ways. Despite this, von Arnim gives Zeno both definitions, and indeed there is no conflict between them. This other definition defines "art," a kind of human thinking or capacity; and the one that chiefly concerns us defines *an* art, a specific body of knowledge or skill that can be learned and put into practice. It is an important fact about the concept of art that it has this double aspect. On the one hand the arts are specialisms, accomplishments, achieved bodies of knowledge whether actual or (as with Plato) ideal. On the other hand, these bodies of knowledge testify to a general capacity or propensity of man, *homo faber.* This is first the ability, then the will, and lastly the actual propensity to do things systematically and not haphazardly: to organize and codify production and practice. And that is why even the virtues were said by Chrysippus to be manifestations of art (Sextus Empiricus, *P.H.* 3. 188 = SVF 2. 96): we apply the same systematization and specialization to our moral life as we do to our productive activities.

The Zenonian version of the subsidiary definition of art (the technological drive) as opposed to *an* art goes as follows: *Technē estin* (art is) *hexis hodopoiētikē* (a habit of roadbuilding). It is a fixed disposition to work out and construct ways that oneself and others can then follow: in a word, a habit of constructing *methods* (*methodous*—the scholiast who quotes the definition offers this word in explanation), for a *methodos* is etymologically a road, a *hodos,* that leads somewhere (*meta-*). That, then, is Zeno's version. But, because there was this question about who said what, it might be as well to cite the version ascribed to Cleanthes. Olympiodorus gives it as *hexis hodōi panta anuousa:* a fixed tendency (*hexis*) bringing to completion (*anuousa*) all things (*panta*) by a path or track (*hodōi*)—or, again, by a method (SVF 1. 490); and Quintilian, incorporating his own commentary into his version, gives it as *potestas viam id est ordinem efficiens,* a power affecting a road, i.e., an order (2. 17. 41). There seems to be no real difference between these versions, but close inspection presents us with a problem. For Quintilian is translating the Greek *hexis,* which we rendered by "a fixed disposition," by Latin *potestas,* or "power." That changes the meaning. And surely Quintilian, an erudite man though no philosopher, would not have been mistaken about a thing like that! Yet it looks as if he must be. A diligent search of the passages indexed by von Arnim under *hexis* makes it clear that the Stoics consistently and deliberately used that term in a way like that spelled out by Aristotle in his ethical theory (and usually Latinized as *habitus*). And surely if a virtue is to be an art it must certainly go beyond the mere ability to which Quintilian apparently assigns it to actual tendency. However, though the Stoic usage of *hexis* is like Aristotle's, it is not exactly the same. We have to distinguish between *hexis,* a fixed disposition to act, and *diathesis,* a state or condition—in our context, of the soul or person. Aristotle had said that a virtue was a *hexis* and relegated *diathesis* to a secondary position, for the important thing about virtue is that it makes a person ready actually to act in a certain way, and his "state" or "condition," if it is not such as to have that practical outcome, is of no independent moral significance. But Chrysippus went out of his way to redefine the parts played by these terms in the moral economy. A virtue is indeed a *hexis,* but it is more than a *hexis:* it is a *diathesis* as well. A *hexis* that was not also a *diathesis* would be something like a tendency to lose one's temper or drink too much, or second sight: a tendency not amounting to virtue or vice, though it might constitute a strength or a weakness in the character (SVF 3. 104-105). A tendency is after all only a tendency, a behavioral regularity. A virtue or vice must go deeper than that: it is the actual condition in which a man's ruling part really is. One is tempted to say that Chrysippus has done no more here than chop some logic and redefine some terms. But in fact there is a real difference of opinion. Aristotle deems virtues important only for the actions that issue from them, because ethics is not metaphysics but a purely practical study. For the Stoics, actions are of no moral consequence in themselves; all that really matters is the state of the universe's rational tension at this or that moment, and the condition of the wise man's ruling part is itself the locus of value. A wise man's actions are part of the causal web that is the fated divine plan of the world: all that is in his power is the condition of his mind, by which his virtue stands or falls.

It might be objected that all this, even if true or interesting, was irrelevant to the concept of art. But actually it has a very important bearing on it. Cleanthes and/or Zeno define art as *hexis* and not as *diathesis;* in fact, Simplicius tells us that the Stoics go out of their way to emphasize that arts are *not diatheseis* (SVF 2. 393). An art is a propensity to act. As such it is neither virtuous nor vicious, but not a mere potentiality either, and is of a sort that might constitute a strength or a weakness. In fact, art as we have described it in relation to ancient thought is one of the strengths of the mind. And a virtue, defined sometimes as an art, is a special sort of manifestation of this strength: it is a *hexis*, for every *diathesis* is a *hexis*, but though as art it is mere *hexis* as virtue it is *diathesis* too.

And now, how did Quintilian come to translate either of these words as *potestas*?—always assuming that he was not translating some lost version of the definition or representing some heretical tradition. It is possible he thought it really was a better translation of *hexis* in this context, because with the different slant Chrysippus has introduced it seems reasonable to say that clairvoyance (*mantikē*—Chrysippus's example of a *hexis*, which surely must mean in this context the gift of second sight rather than the professional practice of the skilled interpreter of omens) is a gift or a capacity rather than a tendency, and the same might go for Chrysippus's other examples, a hot temper and a weak head for alcohol. These can indeed be seen as temperamental weaknesses, deficiencies in normal powers, rather than as dispositions to act. But it seems more likely that Quintilian, at home in a language devoid of definite or indefinite articles, has not perceived the difference between defining art, the general human propensity to build highways for the mind, and defining *an* art, a specific body of practical knowledge. For he does as we have seen treat the definitions as alternatives; and it is reasonable to think of an individual's technical knowledge as constituting his *ability* to act in an expert fashion, whereas the concept of ability remains of rather slight relevance to the strength of the human mind that is art in general.

What, finally, is an art, in Zeno's standard definition? The ancient sources offer us virtually no help in our exegesis, and we have no recourse but to examine the plain meaning of the words it contains, at their face value and in the light of the problematic we deployed earlier. It will be convenient to introduce and expound it one word at a time.

Techne estin, art is: *systema*...a system. The word is one of wide application: it stands for any whole made up of any parts. One of its peculiarities is that it is never followed, as one might have expected, by a partitive genitive of the noun standing for whatever the parts are: it is always followed by *ek*, "out of," a fact to which it would be only slightly extravagant to attribute a double significance. In the first place, the parts are conceived as prior to the system made or developed "out of" them; and in the second place the (passive-perfect) verbal noun form of *systēma* keeps some of its verbal force. A system is something that has been systematized out of something that was already there. An art, then, is conceived dynamically and piecemeal. Unlike the Platonic ideal totality of perfect practical knowledge, art as envisioned by the Stoics takes its form from the actual systematization of items. But there is perhaps one further implication. On the Platonic-Aristotelian view it almost seemed that the art functioned as a sort of axiom set from which practical solutions could be derived in the light of experience, the axioms themselves being mutually independent items of abstract knowledge. But a system is a whole formed from its parts, as a literary composition (which is one of the special meanings of *systēma*) is an integrated whole formed from words that are interrelated within it. But this cannot be pushed too far: the word *systēma* could in fact be used of a mere congeries, so long as it did somehow or other (as its etymology suggests) "stand together" and not fall apart.

An art, then, is a system...*ek katalēpseōn*, constituted from graspings. *Katalēpsis* is a fundamental term in Stoic epistemology, and it means coming to be sure of something. A perception that has this quality of assuredness, answering to the "clear and distinct ideas" of Descartes, was for the Stoics the ultimate criterion of truth. The term is defined dynamically, as what is secured by and for the mind, rather than formally: it means the fact of grasping rather than what is grasped, and what is grasped could be a concept or it could be a proposition, and nothing in fact prevents it from being an item of unverbalized skill if such there should be. The Stoics were nominalists—or, perhaps we should say, concretists. Like man, the universe is a psychosomatic whole, rational in its processes rather than in its principles; the view of reason appropriate to such a philosophy is more Hegelian than Aristotelian. But what is actually implied, by way of degree of certitude and manner of comprehension, by this word *katalēpsis*? *Comprehensio* is the Latin equivalent, and the metaphor of "grasping" is not accidental: it was in fact for the sake of the metaphor that the word was introduced into philosophy (Cicero, *Ac. Pr.* 2. 144 = SVF 1. 66; cf. *Ac. Post.* 1. 41 = SVF 1. 60). Outside of philosophy, the word means the act of seizing and holding, most commonly the military occupation of a town; a *katalēptēr*, a device for seizing and holding, is a clamp. Zeno, notoriously, explained the term by a series of gestures: perception is illustrated by the outstretched hand, assent by a hooking of the fingers, *katalēpsis* by a closing of the fist, and true knowledge, which only the wise attain, by enfolding that closed fist in the firm grip of the other hand. This resort to ostension has its merits. No likely verbal method could preserve so well the unique emphasis on the degree to which an item is drawn into and incorporated in a body of knowledge and related to the knower, as opposed to its status as percept, concept, proposition, or whatever else, which it seems to have been the especial genius of Stoic epistemology to achieve. At the lowest level, then, we have bare awareness without reflection; then comes the assigning of the object to the world in which we live and whose reality we accept as answering to and incorporating our real selves; and then comes comprehension, *katalēpsis*, the taking of the item into our system of beliefs, and lastly its incorporation into a thoroughly confirmed and indubitable body of truth.[1] At the level of *grasping*, to which the arts are referred, this interlocking objectivity (which in fact only the infallible sage attains) is not yet presumed to be reached. The system to which the grasped item belongs is that of the grasper's convictions, and it is his own ruling aspect that sets its own characterizing and appropriating stamp upon it.

If we follow the guidance of this Ciceronian text, then, and we have no more authoritative or explicit guide to follow, the constituent insights of an art are not characterized as universal judgments, as by Aristotle, nor as certain truths, as Plato required; they are insights functioning within the belief system of an actual individual, and no doubt within that of any group of individuals thinking and working together.

What sort of insights enter into the system of an art? An art is a *systēma ek katalēpseōn*, a system of graspings, *syngegymnasmenōn. . . .* This is a passive perfect participle of a verb meaning *to exercise together*, and the participle agrees grammatically with the insights and not with the system. The insights are in a condition that they have reached by being trained or exercised together. Surviving quotations of and references to the definition are such as mildly to suggest that this was felt to be the key word in it. What constitutes an art is primarily the way the particular bits of knowledge, wrinkles, skills, or whatever do not merely lie side by side but are put into practice in relation to one another. We might say that an insight belongs to an artisan's art *to the extent that* it forms a regular and integrated part of his intelligent practice. The relation among insights is not one of subordination of application to principle, as the Platonic tradition had it, but of mutual interaction. And the implication of the perfect tense is that when we speak of an artist's art we do not refer to his ongoing use of the system (as Lucian pretends for satirical purposes, in defiance of the language [*Parasite* 6]), but to his having at his disposal an organized repertoire. The metaphor in the verb is that of a sports team or a musical ensemble or a military outfit who have rehearsed or trained together so that they are now ready to function as a team. And the appropriateness of training to military contexts reminds us, perhaps, that another of the special uses of the word *systēma* is to denote a military unit.

It seems at least possible that the basic idea underlying this account of how arts are constituted and function was derived from Plato's successor Speusippus, who for a rather different purpose made a similar use of the idea of a practice. He wanted to say that human powers of sensible discrimination, though exercised spontaneously, are not autonomous but developed in subservience to a rational world view. To make his position clear he used the parallel of musical skill. A musician's ear immediately recognizes whether his instrument is in tune or not, yet this immediate recognition is strictly relative to an artificial musical scale that in the first instance was stabilized and established by musical theory. Similarly, the musician's fingers, when he plays his oboe or guitar, have an "artistic activity" that seems spontaneous. But this activity is not brought to perfection by the fingers on their own: it is imparted by their practicing together in the interests of (the Greek preposition is *pros*) "reasoning," in this case the musician's project of mastering an instrument and performing on it in a musical fashion (Sextus Empiricus, *Adv. Math.* 7. 145-146).[2] It is altogether likely that Zeno, himself much concerned with the then vexed question of the "criterion" of objectivity in perceptual knowledge, would have been familiar with Speusippus's observation, and perhaps equally likely that he would have been struck by the contribution it could make to a general account of technical knowledge.

"In the interests of" (*pros*—Zeno uses the same preposition that Speusippus used, though it is more clearly called for by Speusippus's context than by his own)—in the interests of what are the insights of an art practiced together? Speusippus's general word "reasoning" gives the wrong sort of answer, one calculated not to differentiate among arts but to insinuate just that hierarchy of intellectual levels that the Zenonian definition eradicates. So the immediate answer is simply *pros ti telos*, "in the interests of some objective or other." An art is individuated primarily by an identifiable aim and by the mutual interconnections of what serves this aim, and only secondarily by the actual content of the repertoire of skills. This is hardly controversial, one would suppose, though we have seen that it has to be spelled out because in practice arts come to be organized otherwise. Plato's more precise "to render something to something else" (*Rep.* 332 C), that is, to supply a specific sort of deficiency or introduce a specific sort of improvement in a specific sort of subject matter, is not taken up. The metaphysical analysis it invites, though vastly fruitful in its own sphere, is out of place in a practical context, for the end that defines an art could be clearly identified without anyone being sure how "subject matter" and "improvement" should be allocated within it.

Will any end serve to define an art? Any goal, however eccentric or depraved, can be skillfully and effectively pursued, provided only that it is clearly envisaged; and one might suppose that there would then be an art of attaining it. But neither our own concept of an art nor that of the ancients envisages this possibility, and both De Quincy on "Murder Considered as One of the Fine Arts" and Lucian on *The Parasite* have exploited this mild paradox. The end of an art must be a good end. Why is this? Plato's *Gorgias* suggested that it was because in the last resort only a really good end could be clearly enough known to establish an art. This seems reasonable in its way, since one supposes that otherwise the intensive study necessary to develop the art would inevitably reveal the fallacious character of the end; but it takes us too far in the opposite direction, since it excludes, as it was meant to exclude, many accepted arts. Perhaps we should rather say that the end of an art must be not a really good end but an accepted one, because an art is an *established* organization of knowledge and such establishment requires a steady pressure of demand from a sufficient public. This public acceptance need not be related to moral goodness. The shoemaker's art is a perfectly respectable art, but shoes do not make people more virtuous or even (in most situations) more healthy, merely more comfortable. Perhaps then we should say what Zeno said: "An art is a system of insights in a condition they have reached by being exercised together in the interests of some objective—*tōn euchrēstōn*, from among those that are of good use. . . ." Zeno does not make the adjective for "useful" agree with the noun for "end," as one might have expected; instead, he uses a partitive genitive, *"from among those that are* useful." The implication is that the need exists as one of the established needs of humanity, and then the art arises to fulfill it; the art does not create the objective it is to attain. The insight expressed here is essentially that articulated in Aristotle's account of the origin of art and the arts. It is also the precise opposite of the emphasis regularly given by Epicurus and his followers to their accounts of the origin of techniques, according to which a skill or a tool originates fortuitously (just as the cosmos itself does) and a use is then found for it (cf. Lucretius, *De Rerum Natura* 5. 1379 ff.).

The word Zeno uses for the sort of value the end of an art is to have, *euchrēstos*, is one whose precise flavor is a little hard to catch. One is inclined to render it "serviceable" or "useful," but it is not the plainest or commonest word for that, which would be *chrēsimos*. *Euchrēstos* has a word for "good" (*eu*) built into it. It is a word that can be applied to propitious days in astrology, or to men who have "done the state some service" and whom it would be subtly insulting to call "useful"—the services of an Othello are not really of the same order as the services of a Rosenkrantz. So "of good use" let it be.

Zeno adds a final phrase: *en tōi biōi*, "in life." This seems otiose, for where else could an end be serviceable? Perhaps the phrase is added to emphasize that the arts belong within the compass of human affairs, and are not to be judged within the economy of the rational process of the universe as a whole. That might be a point worth making as one more defense against the alienation of art implicit in Plato's way of referring all true arts to an ideal practice governed by an unknowable good. And, as a matter of logic, usefulness always implies a context: useful to whom, and for what? So Zeno supplies the answer: to that complex of ends whereby men take their place with other living things within that larger economy of the world.

That would be a possible explanation of the reference to "life," but the emphasis Zeno intended was probably rather different. The unity of "life" is less likely to be the system of living things, or the abstract unity of human concerns, than the specific unity of a person's lifetime from birth to death. This concept of life was certainly used by Chrysippus in contexts that are akin to ours. Virtue is an art, he said, that is concerned with life as a whole (SVF 3. 202); a natural life is one oriented towards virtue (SVF 3. 227); and arts in general are capable of cooperating in producing a natural life (SVF 3. 136). It may well be some such relationship to the supreme art of virtue as is here articulated by his successor that Zeno had in mind. An art, as a complex of intuitions interrelated in the service of a specific end, has its own integrity; but only respectable ends generate arts, and the ultimate ground of respectability is the possibility of integration into, or due subordination to, the art of arts which is virtue.

An art, then, is a system made up of "graspings" that are in a state they have reached by being exercised together in the interests of some objective or other from among those that are of good use within the compass of a human life. That is what Zeno said an art was, and what it seems he might have meant by it, and what would have been good reasons for him to say it, both in terms of what his predecessors had said and in terms of the perennial problems of human life.

NOTES

1. Cicero's text is explicit, and it does not seem to bear any other interpretation than the one given here. However, it does not correspond very closely with our general impressions of Stoic epistemology. This is partly because those impressions are mostly derived from the discussions of the criterion of knowledge that obsessed Hellenistic philosophers, and in that context the degrees of knowledge are correlated with types of phenomenon to which they are appropriate: bare ideation with the phenomena of dreams and such, assent with such sensa as are typical of sense perception, *katalēpsis* with "kataleptic appearances," such percepts as could not but be derived from a specific thing and which therefore almost compel our assent. There seems to be no way of working all the data into a consistent system: many of our reports are patently confused, evidently based on misunderstandings of a system with which the reporters were fundamentally out of sympathy.

2. The word Speusippus uses (*synaskēsis*) is one that specifically means training or practicing, whereas Zeno's word is one applicable to exercising generally. It is not part of the definition of an art that one should have gone through activities specifically designed to develop technique, as the musician does when he practices, but only that he should have acquired in practice an available and integrally functioning repertoire of skills.

Select Bibliography

I have listed works mentioned in the text, as well as a number of other works on Stoicism of particular interest to English-language readers.

Arnim, H. von. *Hierokles' Ethische Elementarlehre*. Berliner Klassikertepte 4, 1906.

Barth, P., and Goedeckemery, A. *Die Stoa⁶*. Stuttgart, 1948.

Barwick, K. *Remmius Palaemon und die romische Ars grammatica*. Leipzig, 1922. Repr. Hildesheim, 1967.

———. *Probleme der stoischen Sprachlehre und Rhetorik*. Berlin, 1957.

Becker, O. *Zwei Untersuchungen zur Antiken Logik*. Wiesbaden, 1957.

Bloos, L. *Probleme der Stoischen Physik*. Hamburg, 1973.

Bochenski, I. M. *La logique de Théophraste*. Fribourg, 1947.

———. *Ancient Formal Logic*. Amsterdam, 1951.

Bonhoeffer, A. *Epiktet und die Stoa*. Stuttgart, 1890.

———. *Die Ethik Epiktets*. Stuttgart, 1894.

Bréhier, E. *Chrysippe et l'ancien stoicisme²*. Paris, 1951.

Brochard, V. "La logique des Stoiciens," *Etudes de Philosophie ancienne et moderne*. Paris, 1912. 220-251.

Card, C. "Mercy," *PR* 81 (1972) 182-207.

Christensen, J. *An Essay on the Unity of Stoic Philosophy*. Copenhagen, 1962.

De Lacy, P. "The Stoic Categories as Methodological Principles," *TAPA* 76 (1946) 245-263.

Dihle, A. "Posidonius' System of Moral Philosophy," *JHS* 93 (1973) 50-57.

Döring, K. *Die Megariker*. Amsterdam, 1972.

Duhem, P. *The Aim and Structure of Physical Theory*. Trans. P. Wiener. New York, 1962.

291

Edelstein, L. "The Philosophical System of Posidonius," *AJP* 57 (1936) 283-325.
———. *The Meaning of Stoicism.* Cambridge, Mass., 1966.
Frede, M. "Stoic vs. Aristotelian Syllogistic," *AGP* 56 (1974) 1-32.
———. *Die Stoische Logik.* Göttingen, 1974.
———. "Some Remarks on the Origins of Traditional Grammar." In *Logic, Methodology and Philosophy of Science.* Ed. R. Butts, J. Hintikka. Dordrecht, 1976. 609-637.
Ganss, W. *Das Bild des Weisen bei Seneca.* Freiburg, Switzerland, 1948.
Gigante, M. *Diogene Laerzio².* Rome—Bari, 1976.
Goldschmidt, V. *Le système stoicien et l'idée de temps².* Paris, 1969.
Gould, J. B. "The Stoic Conception of Fate," *JHI* 35 (1974) 17-32.
———. *The Philosophy of Chrysippus.* Leiden, 1970.
Graeser, A. "Zur Begründung der Stoischen Ethik," *Kant-Studien* 63 (1972) 213-224.
———. "Zur Funktion des Begriffes 'gut' in der Stoischen Ethik," *Zeitschrift für Philosophische Forschung* 26 (1972) 417-425.
———. *Plotinus and the Stoics.* Leiden, 1972.
———. *Zenon von Kition: Positionen und Probleme.* Berlin/New York, 1975.
Hesse, M. *Forces and Fields.* London, 1961.
Hintikka, J. *Time and Necessity. Studies in Aristotle's Theory of Modality.* Oxford, 1973.
Hirzel, R. *Untersuchungen zu Ciceros philosophischen Schriften.* II. Leipzig, 1883.
Hunt, H. K. "Some Problems in the Interpretation of Stoicism," *AUMLA* 28 (1967) 165-177.
Jackson, B. D. *Augustine: De Dialectica.* Trans. with Introd. and Notes. Dordrecht and Boston, 1975.
Kahn, C. H. "Stoic Logic and Stoic LOGOS," *AGP* 51 (1969) 158-172.
———. "Language and Ontology in the *Cratylus.*" In *Exegesis and Argument.* Ed. E. N. Lee, A. P. D. Mourelatos, R. Rorty. Assen, 1974. 152-176.
Kerford, G. B. "The Search for Personal Identity in Stoic Thought," *Bulletin of the John Rylands Library of Manchester* 55 (1972) 177-196.
———. "Cicero and Stoic Ethics," in *Cicero and Virgil: Studies in Honor of Harold Hunt.* Amsterdam, 1972. 60-74.
Kidd, I. G. "Stoic Intermediates and the End for Man," *CQ* n.s. 5 (1955) 181-194. = *Problems in Stoicism.* Ed. A. A. Long. London, 1971. 150-172.
———. "Posidonius on Emotions," *Problems in Stoicism.* Ed. A. A. Long. London, 1971. 200-215.
Kneale, W. and M. *The Development of Logic.* Oxford, 1962.
Krämer, H.-J. *Platonismus und Hellenistische Philosophie.* Berlin/New York, 1972.
Kretzmann, N. "Aristotle on Spoken Sound." In *Ancient Logic and Its Modern Interpretation.* Ed. J. Corcoran. Dordrecht and Boston, 1974. 3-21.
———. "Medieval Logicians and the Meaning of *Propositio,*" *JP* 67 (1970) 767-787.

———. "Semantics, History of." In *Encyclopedia of Philosophy*. Ed. P. Edwards. 7 (1971) 358-406.

Lapidge, M. "Archai and Stoicheia: A Problem in Stoic Cosmology," *Phronesis* 18 (1973) 240-278.

Lloyd, A. C. "Activity and Description in Aristotle and the Stoa," *Proc. Brit. Acad.* 56 (1970) 227-240.

———. "Grammar and Metaphysics in the Stoa." In *Problems in Stoicism*. Ed. A. A. Long. London, 1971. 58-74.

Long, A. A. "Carneades and the Stoic Telos," *Phronesis* 12 (1967) 59-90.

———. "Aristotle's Legacy to Stoic Ethics," *BICS* 15 (1968) 72-85.

———. "The Stoic Concept of Evil," *PQ* 18 (1968) 329-343.

———. "Stoic Determinism and Alexander of Aphrodisias," *AGP* 52 (1970) 247-268.

———. "The Logical Basis of Stoic Ethics," *PAS* 1970-1971. 85-104.

———. "Language and Thought in Stoicism." In *Problems in Stoicism*. London, 1971. 75-113.

———. "Freedom and Determinism in the Stoic Theory of Human Action." In *Problems in Stoicism*. London, 1971. 173-199.

———. *Problems in Stoicism*. London, 1971.

———. *Hellenistic Philosophy*. London, 1975.

———. "The Early Stoic Concept of Moral Choice." In *Images of Man* (Studia Verbeke). Ed. F. Bossier et al. Louvain, 1976. 77-92.

Longrigg, J. "Elementary Physics in the Lyceum and Stoa," *Isis* 66 (1975) 211-229.

Łukasiewicz, J. "On the history of the logic of propositions." In *Selected Works*. Ed. L. Borkowski. Amsterdam, 1970.

———. *Aristotle's Syllogistic*². Oxford, 1957.

Mates, B. *Stoic Logic*². Berkeley and Los Angeles, 1961.

Moraux, P. "La joute dialectique d'après le huitième livre des *Topiques*." In *Aristotle on Dialectic. The Topics*. Ed. G. E. L. Owen. Oxford, 1968. 189-201.

Moravcsik, J. *Understanding Language*. The Hague, 1975.

Moreau, J. *Epictète ou le secret de la liberté*. Paris, 1964.

Mueller, I. "Stoic and Peripatetic Logic," *AGP* 51 (1969) 173-187.

———. "The Completeness of Stoic Logic," *Notre Dame Journal of Formal Logic* (1977).

Nebel, G. "Der Begriff des Kathekon in der alten Stoa," *Hermes* 70 (1935) 439-460.

Nuchelmans, G. *Theories of the Proposition. Ancient and medieval conceptions of the bearers of truth and falsity*. Amsterdam, 1973.

Owen, G. E. L. "Tithenai ta phainomena," *Aristote et les Problèmes de la méthode*. Louvain, 1961. 83-103.

———. "The Platonism of Aristotle," *Proc. Brit. Acad.* 51 (1965) 125-150.

Patzig, G. *Aristotle's Theory of the Syllogism*. Trans. J. Barnes. Dordrecht, 1968.

Pembroke, G. S. "Oikeiōsis." In *Problems in Stoicism*. Ed. A. A. Long. London, 1971. 115-159.

Pinborg, J. "Das Sprachdenken der Stoa und Augustins Dialektik," *Classica et*

Mediaevalia 23 (1962) 148-177.

——. "Historiography of Linguistics: Classical Antiquity: Greece." In *Current Trends in Linguistics* 13. The Hague, 1975. 69-126.

Pohlenz, M. "Zenon und Chrysipp," *Nachrichten der Gesellschaft der Wissenschaften zu Göttingen II* 9 (1938) 173-210.

——. *Die Stoa. Geschichte einer geistigen Entwicklung.* Göttingen, 1963.

Popper, K. R. *Objective Knowledge. An Evolutionary Approach.* Oxford, 1972.

Prantl, C. *Geschichte der Logik im Abendlande.* Leipzig, 1855.

Reesor, M. "The Stoic Concept of Quality," *AJP* 75 (1954) 40-58.

——. "The Stoic Categories," *AJP* 78 (1957) 63-82.

——. "Fate and Possibility in Early Stoic Philosophy," *Phoenix* 19 (1965) 285-297.

Reinhardt, K. *Poseidonios.* Munich, 1921.

Rieth, O. *Grundbegriffe der Stoischen Ethik.* Berlin, 1933.

Rist, J. *Stoic Philosophy.* Cambridge, 1969.

Sambursky, S. *Physics of the Stoics.* London, 1959.

Sandbach, F. H. "*Phantasia kataleptikē.*" In *Problems in Stoicism.* Ed. A. A. Long. London, 1971. 9-21.

——. "Ennoia and Prolēpsis," *CQ* 24 (1930) 44-51. = *Problems in Stoicism.* Ed. A. A. Long. London, 1971. 22-39.

——. *The Stoics.* London, 1975.

Schmidt, R. *Stoicorum grammatica.* Halle, 1839.

Sedley, D. "Epicurus, On Nature book xxviii," *Cronache Ercolanesi* 3 (1973) 71-77.

Sharples, R. W. "Aristotle and the Stoic conception of necessity in the *de fato* of Alexander of Aphrodisias," *Phronesis* 20 (1975) 247-274.

Smart, A. "Mercy," *Philosophy* 43 (1968) 348-359.

Solmsen, F. *Aristotle's System of the Physical World.* Ithaca, 1960.

——. *Cleanthes or Posidonius? The Basis of Stoic Physics, Med. der Kon. Ned. Akad. van Wet., Afd. Letterkunde* 24. Amsterdam, 1961. 265-289. = *Kleine Schriften.* Hildesheim, 1968. I, 436-460.

——. "Dialectic without the Forms." In *Aristotle on Dialectic. The Topics.* Ed. G. E. L. Owen. Oxford, 1968. 49-68.

Steinthal, H. *Geschichte der Sprachwissenschaft*². Berlin, 1890.

Straaten, M. van. *Panétius, sa vie et ses écrits.* Amsterdam, 1966.

Strawson, P. F. *Logico-Linguistic Papers.* London, 1971.

Taylor, R. "Aristotle's Doctrine of Future Contingents." In *Essays in Ancient Greek Philosophy.* Ed. J. Anton and G. Kustas. Albany, 1971.

Todd, R. B. "*Sunentasis* and the Stoic Theory of Perception," *Grazer Beiträge* 2 (1974) 251-261.

——. *Alexander of Aphrodisias on Stoic Physics.* Leiden, 1976.

Tsekourakis, D. *Studies in the Terminology of Early Stoic Ethics (Hermes Einzelschriften* 32). Wiesbaden, 1974.

Verbeke, G. *L'Evolution de la doctrine du pneuma du stoicisme à St. Augustin.* Paris, 1951.

Voelke, A.-J. *L'Idée de volonté dans le stoicisme.* Paris, 1973.

Vogel, C. J. de. "Personality in Greek and Christian Thought," *Studies in Philosophy and the History of Philosophy* 2. Washington, 1963. 20-60.

Watson, G. *The Stoic Theory of Knowledge.* Belfast, 1966.

————. "Natural Law and Stoicism." In *Problems in Stoicism.* Ed. A. A. Long. London, 1971. 216-238.

Weil, E. "Remarques sur le 'matérialisme' des Stoïciens," *Mélanges A. Koyré.* Paris, 1964. II, 556-572.

White, M. *Towards Reunion in Philosophy.* New York, 1963.

Zeller, E. *Die Philosophie der Griechen*⁵. 3. 1. Leipzig, 1923.